Effective Promotiona.
Planning for e-Business

The Chartered Institute of Marketing/Butterworth-Heinemann Marketing Series is the most comprehensive, widely used and important collection of books in marketing and sales currently available worldwide.

As the CIM's official publisher, Butterworth-Heinemann develops, produces and publishes the complete series in association with the CIM. We aim to provide definitive marketing books for students and practitioners that promote excellence in marketing education and practice.

The series titles are written by CIM senior examiners and leading marketing educators for professionals, students and those studying the CIM's Certificate, Advanced Certificate and Postgraduate Diploma courses. Now firmly established, these titles provide practical study support to CIM and other marketing students and to practitioners at all levels.

 The Chartered
Institute of Marketing

Formed in 1911, the Chartered Institute of Marketing is now the largest professional marketing management body in the world, with over 60000 members located worldwide. Its primary objectives are focused on the development of awareness and understanding of marketing throughout UK industry and commerce and in the raising of standards of professionalism in the education, training and practice of this key business discipline.

Books in the series

Creating Powerful Brands (second edition), Leslie de Chernatony and Malcolm McDonald
Cybermarketing (second edition), Pauline Bickerton, Matthew Bickerton and Upkar Pardesi
Cyberstrategy, Pauline Bickerton, Matthew Bickerton and Kate Simpson-Holley
Direct Marketing, Brian Thomas and Matthew Housden
Effective Promotional Practice for e-Business, Cathy Ace
e-Marketing Excellence, Paul Smith and Dave Chaffey
Excellence in Advertising (second edition), Leslie Butterfield
Fashion Marketing, Margaret Bruce and Tony Hines
From Brand Vision to Brand Evaluation, Leslie de Chernatony
Innovation in Marketing, Peter Doyle and Susan Bridgewater
International Marketing (third edition), Stanley J. Paliwoda and Michael J. Thomas
Integrated Marketing Communications, Tony Yeshin
Key Customers, Malcolm McDonald, Beth Rogers and Diana Woodburn
Market-Led Strategic Change (third edition), Nigel Piercy
Marketing Briefs, Sally Dibb and Lyndon Simkin
Marketing Logistics, Martin Christopher
Marketing Plans (fourth edition), Malcolm McDonald
Marketing Planning for Services, Malcolm McDonald and Adrian Payne
Marketing Professional Services, Michael Roe
Marketing Research for Managers (second edition), Sunny Crouch and Matthew Housden
Marketing Strategy (second edition), Paul Fifield
Relationship Marketing for Competitive Advantage, Adrian Payne, Martin Christopher, Moira Clark and Helen Peck
Relationship Marketing: Strategy and Implementation, Helen Peck, Adrian Payne, Martin Christopher and Moira Clark
Strategic Marketing Management (second edition), Richard M. S. Wilson and Colin Gilligan
Strategic Marketing: Planning and Control (second edition), Graeme Drummond and John Ensor
Successful Marketing Communications, Cathy Ace
Tales from the Marketplace, Nigel Piercy
The CIM Handbook of Export Marketing, Chris Noonan
The CIM Handbook of Strategic Marketing, Colin Egan and Michael J. Thomas
The Customer Service Planner, Martin Christopher
The Fundamentals of Corporate Communications, Richard Dolphin
The Marketing Book (fourth edition), Michael J. Baker
The Marketing Manual, Michael J. Baker
Total Relationship Marketing, Evert Gummesson

Forthcoming

Political Marketing, Phil Harris and Dominic Wring
Relationship Marketing (second edition), Martin Christopher, Adrian Payne and David Ballantyne

Effective Promotional Planning for e-Business

Cathy Ace

Published in association with
The Chartered Institute of Marketing

OXFORD   AUCKLAND   BOSTON   JOHANNESBURG   MELBOURNE   NEW DELHI

Butterworth-Heinemann
Linacre House, Jordan Hill, Oxford OX2 8DP
225 Wildwood Avenue, Woburn, MA 01801–2041
A division of Reed Educational and Professional Publishing Ltd

ℛ A member of the Reed Elsevier plc group

First published 2002

British Library Cataloguing in Publication Data
A catalogue record for this book is available from the British Library

Library of Congress Cataloguing in Publication Data
A catalogue record for this book is available from the Library of Congress

ISBN 0 7506 5268 3

For information on all Butterworth-Heinemann publications visit our website at
www.bh.com

Composition by Genesis Typesetting, Laser Quay, Rochester, Kent
Printed and bound in Great Britain by MPG Books Ltd, Bodmin, Cornwall

Contents

Chapter

1

An overview of marketing communications – the theory and the practice

The marketing context

UNDERSTANDING E-BUSINESS

There has been much discussion about what exactly constitutes an 'e-business'. That is because there has been an electronic aspect to many businesses for quite some time, with electronic transfer of funds, for example, having been standard business practice for many organizations for decades! What most people mean when they use the term 'e-business' is some sort of business that exists, at least in part, on the worldwide web, and which uses the web to do its business – be this in terms of selling products or services to customers, using it to manage the internal dimensions of operating the business or, in fact, being the total driving force behind the existence of the business.

Let's look at some of these categories in more detail, and let's begin by understanding how and why certain businesses use 'e' aspects within their business. Once we're all thinking along the same lines, it'll be a lot easier to work through how promotional planning can work most effectively for all types of e-businesses.

As Figure 1.1 shows, there are many ways in which a business can use 'e', and many reasons behind those choices. This book aims to cover the planning and implementation of effective promotional, or communication, programmes for *most* of these types of business: the only business not catered for within this book is the traditional bricks and mortar business that happens to use just e-mail and electronic funds transfer, etc. We will focus on the more 'e-d' business than that!

Throughout the text, references will be made to the accompanying website for this text and to web addresses of other organizations that might be of use and interest. Obviously, the web has a huge advantage over the printed word in that it can be constantly updated, and we aim to make use of this aspect of 'e-ing' our offering – so if you can't make a link from one of the addresses printed here, try checking the website, where you might find we have been able to give the amended information that you might need, or alternatives for your information and enjoyment (yes, learning can be fun!). You'll find that the website is easy to follow and should be enlightening in its own right.

Indeed, what we are doing is actually implementing one example of 'e-business' – where the new technologies available are being used to extend and make even better the offering of a respected publisher (no blowing of our own trumpet at all!).

So, without further ado, let's take a look at how general marketing planning issues need to be re-addressed for the e-business forum.

A. Organizations that use electronic communications only.	This means that an organization might use e-mail internally and externally, have an intranet, an extranet and an Internet website, but that there is no transactional activity taking place electronically – the 'e' is performing a purely communicative function.
B. Organizations that use electronic communications and transactional systems to fulfil non-e-business demands.	An organization might literally ship information and orders internally via electronic methods, might communicate internally and externally via the web, but not actually offer goods or services for sale via the web; rather it is using the system to pass information from one internal or partner source to another. There might be a pure fulfilment requirement, or just a 'back-end' application.
C. Organizations that use electronic communications methods, internal and external transactional systems and have a fully integrated on-line ordering, supply and customer relationship management system.	This would be a fully e-d organization, it might even have no physical presence at all, existing only in the electronic world, e.g. an on-line publication where the product exists virtually and maybe the team that operate it do not even sit in the same countries as each other.
	NB: It might be that the organization in question has one part of its business that uses 'e' in one way, and another part of its business that uses it in another; for example, a financial services organization might be operating at levels B and C in all probability, maybe with C having a totally different brand identity to B (e.g. Prudential and Egg).

Figure 1.1   The what and the why of e-business

UNDERSTANDING MARKETING PLANNING FOR GOOD BUSINESS – e OR NOT-e!

This book is not about marketing planning for e-business, but about marketing communications planning for e-business. But without understanding the classic role of marketing communications within the classic marketing mix, you will never be able to do the best you can in terms of marketing communications itself. This is because the job of marketing communications is, essentially, no different for an e-business than a non-e-business, in that its overall aim is to communicate what is attractive within the other elements of the marketing mix (see below) to those whose interest needs to be gained (buyers, specifiers, influencers, etc.).

Marketing communications can, itself, be used to differentiate a product, service or brand, building a unique personality for the offering in question that crystallizes the reason to purchase within the mind of the customer. With the thoughtful use of technology, the role can extend way beyond *finding* buyers through *promotional* activity and move into the area of Customer Relationship Management and making sure that the real Lifetime Value of a customer is obtained by *communicating* with customers, lapsed customers and prospective customers. But before we look at the detail of marketing communications planning, let's take a moment to look at the issues that surround marketing planning in the round – whether for e-business or non-e-business.

THE KEY QUESTIONS FOR ALL PLANNING

Marketing planning for e-business rests on the same pillars as all planning: six key questions that have to be addressed and answered to allow an organization, whatever its type, size or age, to move ahead effectively and efficiently. Those questions are:

Where are we now?

This means that you have to carry out an audit of all the internal and external aspects of your current position. In e-business, because we are often talking about newly formed organizations, the answer to this question is often 'We are nowhere so we can decide just where we want to be', but that is often too naive a response, since the track records of the individuals involved in a start-up almost automatically steer the start-up's launch positioning, as we will see in the next chapter.

How did we get here?

You have to ask this question to be able to determine all the factors that might have influenced your current position over time (e.g. are you market leaders because for two years you were the only players in the market?). Again, I often encounter e-businesses where I am reassured by the directors that they are market leaders – without their possessing a single research fact that would suggest this is the case.

Where do we want to be?

This gives the organization the chance to decide what its aims and goals are. When we look in more detail at objective setting, I hope that one aspect you will connect with is the need for objectives to be *achievable*. I am sorry to say that many young companies have foundered on spending against objectives they could never achieve.

How might we get there?

This is the process of assessing the alternative routes by which you might arrive at your goals. In other words, it is the stage when you assess alternative strategies that would deliver your agreed objectives. For e-business this is rather like trying to walk up a constantly shifting sand dune, given that many marketplaces are forming and reforming as I write, so strategic choices have to be based upon a whole set of unknowns – but at least there are some models that can be used to help in some of the minimizing of risk, which is what we are talking about here.

How is it best to get there?

This is where the organization decides on its strategic path and details that set of activities. Again, when it comes to moving forward there *must* be tactical flexibility built in – but it is important to not lose sight of the fact that constancy can aid effectiveness.

How will we monitor and manage our progress?

As with any journey, it is never wise to wait until the journey *should* be over to discover that you didn't make it to your destination: constant monitoring of progress against agreed milestones allows effective management along the way. This is particularly important in all fields of e-business, where there will be many parties who need reassurance that the journey is progressing well – you can lose good staff and much needed investment if you do not monitor and report on your progress with some level of authority and detail!

With this fairly standard planning outline, the marketer will be carrying out a marketing audit, assessing possible objectives and strategies, and deciding the direction in which to travel. 'Promotion' or 'marketing communications' will be the element of the so-called marketing mix that we will concentrate upon in this book. But what about the other elements, and the relationship of the marketing mix to them all?

GETTING BACK TO BASICS – MINDING YOUR Ps AND Cs

The Chartered Institute of Marketing defines Marketing as the management process which identifies, anticipates and supplies customer requirements efficiently and profitably.

This is our focus and our starting point. Frankly, it doesn't matter at all whether you are an e-business, a business with no 'e' in it or a business that's about to be 'e-d': the role of marketing, the marketing mix and promotion, which is an element within this mix, remain the same. We must consider marketing communications within this context. Thus, it is worth looking at the basics of the marketing mix to remind ourselves just where promotion fits into the overall picture.

The Marketing Mix consists of a various number of Ps – the Four Ps of the Marketing Mix have been around for a long time, the further development of the Seven Ps of the mix came along somewhat later. The Seven Ps are:

- Product
- Price
- Place
- Promotion
- People
- Processes
- Physical Evidence.

These seven key elements form what is often referred to as the Marketing Mix (the first four Ps) and the Service Mix (the last three Ps). My argument would be that all seven of the Ps need to be considered for all marketing decision making – all seven Ps contribute to the success of marketing and a marketing communications plan.

However, even all seven Ps have one major drawback – they look at marketing from the point of view of the producer of the goods (or the provider of the service). With this perspective then, yes, it is fair to think of successful marketing as offering the right product/service at the right price and in the right place to the right people through the right form of promotion, with the right people producing the products or providing the service, using effective management processes and delivering the right type of physical evidence of either service or product performance.

The problem with this approach is highlighted by the fact that as marketers we are supposed to believe that we are customer orientated, so we really should look at marketing from the customer's perspective too. This is where the Seven Cs come in – where each P is replaced by a customer orientated 'C' alternative, which deals with the same issues as its corresponding 'P', but from the customer's point of view, thus:

Product

Customers do not see products, they do not see product portfolio management techniques, matrices and product life cycles – they see that they have to make a *Choice*.

This Choice might be direct ('Which cinema shall I go to?') or it could be indirect ('Shall I go to the theatre or the cinema or the pub?') or it could even be very indirect ('I will stay at home tonight because I am saving up for a new car'). Marketers have to carry out research that will show them how customers make choices, what they choose between, and try to understand why they choose what they choose – only then will true customer understanding begin to be at the heart of marketing planning. This is particularly important for e-businesses where often the whole business proposition is that prospective customers have already made their choice about how to do something, and the e-business is offering a new choice.

E-APPLICATION POINT

I have been told too many times to enumerate by an enthusiastic CEO that 'Of course we'll succeed because nobody else offers this product/service'. What is forgotten is that the potential customer base is often already carrying out this business function/entertainment etc., but by another route. The challenge of the e-business is often to get a potential customer to meet their needs, that are already being satisfied, another way. This is where there **must** be research carried out into how many do it which way now, and why. Often, it is this **customer** focused view of choice that is almost avoided by some e-businesses. True, the rather colder investment climate of the twenty-first century has meant that some tougher questions are being asked about possible market sizes, and this is where the marketer needs real, hard information on how and why people make the choices they do from within the existing offering. If there is a basic misunderstanding of what the potential customers will believe they are being offered (rather than what you think you are offering them), then the whole message base for your promotional programme will be flawed.

Price

Customers do not see price, but perceive a *Cost* they have to bear, a part of which might well be something other than purely financial considerations. It might be that a contract can be fulfilled more cheaply, in purely financial terms, by one contractor than another, but only if the customer is happy to wait three extra weeks for delivery: sometimes the customer will see the wait as a Cost worth bearing to be able to pay the lower price, sometimes the Cost of waiting will be unacceptable – so they will go with the more expensive supplier who can deliver next week. Equally, if the government wants to encourage us to stop drinking and driving, we have to bear the Cost of not doing one or the other in order to comply and to benefit from our continued ability to legally drive on the roads because we haven't lost our licence, or our continued clear conscience because we haven't hurt anyone on the road, or our continued good health because we haven't hurt ourselves. Again, there are specific implications for any e-business here, because the customer expectation (whatever the sector) is for lower prices for an e-business proposition. This has sprung up because of the major cost savings to be made by shortening the supply chain and allowing customers' direct access to products and services via the web, and this psychological shift has progressed to such a point that it will be hard to turn back.

E-APPLICATION POINT

When planning e-business, you can easily get trapped in the 'Bargain Basement' if you don't clearly segment the market and build your proposition with a clear market position as your target. If you don't want to always offer your products or services on a 'Cheapest is Best' basis, you will have to build in value (beyond the access value that all your competitors who operate on an e-business basis offer too). This means that different levels of delivery, service and depth of access to site (e.g. a magazine on-line) will have to be used not only to allow you to be attractive to more segments, but also to be able to sustain cross-selling or up-selling strategies in the future. Another word of warning – getting the balance right between price and place (or Cost and Convenience) is one of the core issues for e-business: get it wrong and you will get clickthrough (people visiting your site), but no business!

Place

Customers don't see channel management decisions, or outlet selection or distribution strategy – they see *Convenience*, and they see convenience on their terms, not those of the producer or provider. Marketers must gain a real insight into what their customers, and potential customers, see as Convenience. A case in point is the recent rush to make almost everything available on the Internet, when, in fact, many customers do not have access to the Internet and feel disaffected by the move (UK high street banks moving to more Internet banking and closing bricks and mortar branches). This is e-business gone mad! It is terribly dangerous to assume that because e-business is more convenient for you it will be more convenient to your existing customers too! Consider the way that this could be addressed – you could keep the high street presence *and* offer an on-line option, thereby allowing your customer base to sub-segment itself and allowing you to attract not only new on-line customers, but maybe also those who have been disaffected by their own bank's attitude towards closing branches!

E-APPLICATION POINT

If you already exist as a bricks and mortar business, and you have decided to add clicks to bricks, be careful how you give this information to those who have been loyal to the bricks business! They are not only your existing customers, but they can turn into your loudest critics overnight and become a public relations disaster! Equally, if your e-offering will give you the chance to extend into new markets, don't assume you can talk to them with the same tone and proposition you have used in the past. When Prudential decided to move into e-business they launched an entirely separate brand – Egg – and used a very different tone of communication voice (upbeat, youthful, funky and positive) to that which they had been using throughout their many years of business to their existing customer base (traditional – the Man from the Pru; cautious – the very name of the organization coming from the word for cautiousness, Prudence and quite quiet and relaxed in tone and language). So, whilst what 'e' might offer is much more convenience, be sure you know who you are talking to about what type of convenience!

Promotion

The producer or provider might be seeking to promote their goods or services to an audience, but what the customer actually wants is *Communication* – in other words, they want the chance to listen to what the marketer has to say, but increasingly also want the chance to talk back! The word Communication implies this two-way process, whereas promotion smacks of just highlighting the good bits! Marketers stick to simplistic promotion at their peril.

E-APPLICATION POINT

The interactivity offered by the Internet is a fabulous addition to the armoury of the professional marketing communicator! The use of an established bricks and mortar brand to bring prospects to a clicks offering is not a tried and trusted method of growing at least the clickthrough rate – but it will only bring in real business if the visitor becomes a customer because your e-offering is what they want. With e-business you have to get prospects to the site, keep them coming back time and time again, and make sure that you take every chance to turn them into customers.

People

In face to face service delivery, it is easy to see how people provide *Care* – airlines emphasize the caring, smiling nature of their in-flight service, supermarkets make sure we all know how much the stackers, checkers and packers care about our shopping experience, but what about when it comes to product manufacturing, or non-frontline service staff in the service sector? Does the role of People as providing Care from the customer perspective still hold true? Well, yes, in that every worker on a production line can, and does, affect the delivery of the brand promise by how much they Care about what they are doing and how much Care they take in doing it: quality control systems are not infallible and every organization wants to produce as little waste, or below average product, as possible, so the amount of care with which people pack, wrap, check, fit or finish a part of a whole job, whether it is a television set or a packet of crisps, makes a big difference to the overall effectiveness of the organization, which has a direct knock-on effect to the customer.

E-APPLICATION POINT

One of the key issues that gets raised when setting up an e-business or when e-ing an existing one is the role of People. . .how will human customers cope with dealing only with a screen supplier? Should we give easy access to human helpers or should we put more effort into creating virtual helpers who **seem** human? Should we put the People behind the site up front, or hide them away? What will the role for People really be? Well, when it comes to the P for People and the C for Care with regard to e-business **never forget** that a website is only as good as the People who designed it, keep it updated and make sure that the products or services required are, in fact, being delivered in an appropriate and timely manner. Amazon.com prides itself on the way that orders are filled – it attracts the young and energetic to work in its vast warehouses and it realizes that costs will be incurred for every wrong order-fill that it sends out. . .a very good reason for making sure that the pickers and packers do a great job!

Call centre staff **are** the human voice of an e-business, so replace the 'frontline' staff of a face to face business, so of course their training and the role they play in delivering the brand promise is vital – but don't forget the backroom people: there will still be internal communications to be borne in mind (especially if you are talking about a virtual organization where even company staff never meet) and an impact upon customer experience of brand promise with every interaction they have with your e-business, so make sure that evey staff member understands their role in ultimately providing true, 360 degree customer care!

Processes

It is true to say that without business management processes in place, that allow best business practice to be connected and replicated throughout the organization, all organizations would offer a constantly varying level of quality or service to their customers across the range they offer, across the departments they house and over time. Thus, it is *Corporate Competence* that is being sought by the customer – they expect the whole organization to be able to deliver what is promised – from the sales person, to the service engineer, to the delivery driver, to the quality control manager. Many organizations suffer because the customer perception of them is that they are Corporately Incompetent, with expectations of service or reliability running at a very low level – this, in turn, affects the morale of the staff, who turn in lower levels of business performance, which serves to fulfil the low expectations of the customers – it is a vicious, downward spiral. Organizations need to understand the levels of competence expected of them, not just by industry standards, or even by legal requirements, but by those they serve – their customers and potential customers.

E-APPLICATION POINT

There can be few organizations who do not appreciate the role of processes that allow the meeting of user and customer expectations when it comes to website design. But just to clarify: your site should be designed to allow all interactions with browsers, potential customers and customers to **work**! This might sound as though I am stating the obvious, but one of the responses I have received when I have asked 'And how would a customer go back and change their order at this late stage?' has been 'Oh they wouldn't want to do that!'. When I pushed the issue the CEO's response was 'Well they must be stupid if they don't know what they want when they've just been through all these stages. . .' and other points of that type. But the issue is that the site, and your organization, **must** have business processes in place to allow the browser, potential customer and customer to do what **they** want, not force them to do what **you** want them to. Technological solutions must be sought to allow all interaction processes to flow easily – to make sure that selections, changes, enquiries, orders, alterations, etc. can be made.

One of the greatest problems faced by many start-ups has been the ability to deliver what they promised – they simply didn't have the business processes in place when they launched to be able to do what they said they could do. This led to orders going unfilled, tickets arriving late for events, customers being unable to download information they had paid for, and so on. Without adequate business processes an organization **cannot** deliver Corporate Competence – and this is particularly the case in the technological process-driven world of e-business.

Physical evidence

This is about the most difficult part of the mix to pin down in terms of specific meaning, as it can mean specifically different things depending upon specific circumstances, but if you think of it as meaning anything to do with the customers' expectations of *Consistency* being met, this might help. We all expect to be able to pick out a particular bank on the high street, because we know what logo to look out for, and this goes for, say, McDonald's on a global scale as well. But it's about more than just the logo above the door. To take the McDonald's example further, wherever you visit a McDonald's around the world you will find not only the same logo, but the same food (with some regional variations), the same quality and service, the same standards of cleanliness and facilities: in other words, McDonald's makes a real virtue of the fact that it is essentially the same all over the world, and attracts a lot of customers on this basis – because people like to know what they are going to get, and then, of course, like to get it, so Consistency isn't just about Consistency of the promise, but it also means Consistency of delivery too.

E-BUSINESS APPLICATION POINT

Millions of pounds have been spent, globally, by thousands of e-businesses who are trying to build a brand presence that is recognizable. Ask anyone who works in the UK poster industry and they will tell you about the boom-time they experienced in 1998–2000, with people clamouring for poster sites to promote their new brand identity and get their dotcom address recognized – availability plummeted and prices could be firmed up, if not raised considerably!

The main aim with many sites has been to get recognition, encourage traffic and try to convert browsers – quite rightly too! But what about the consistency of style, tone and language across a site? What about the consistency across the site and physical packaging upon arrival? Site and...offices, people, printed mail or brochures, on-line print offering, advertising, events, exhibitions, etc.? The list is almost endless, but it is a lack of attention to detail here that can undermine the millions of pounds of expenditure made on the TV commercials!

Thus, as summarized in Figure 1.2, we can view the Seven Ps as having a Producer focus, whilst the Seven Cs have a Customer focus.

It is only once the marketer utilizes true customer orientation that the customer, long hailed as king, will finally be crowned. It is the synergistic effect of the full marketing mix, with both its P and C elements, that makes a successful product or service.

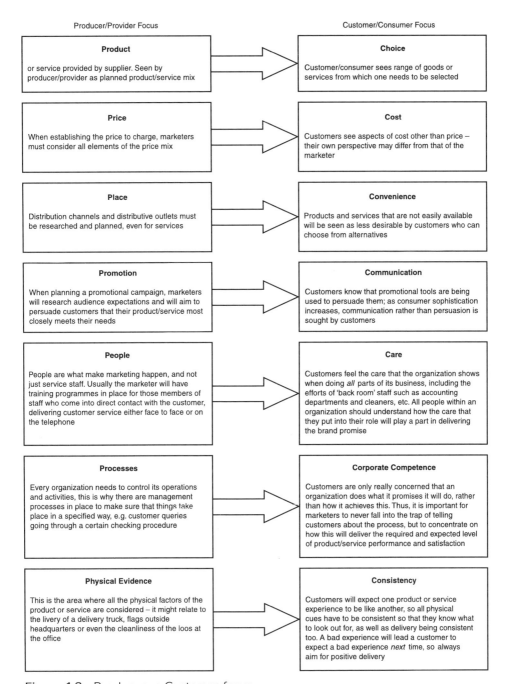

Figure 1.2   Producer → Customer focus

And what about the applicability of the marketing mix? Hopefully, it is quite easy to see from the examples above that the mix is easily applicable to fast-moving consumer goods (fmcg) marketing and on-line purchasing of commercial products and services. But what about the more subtle, complex types of marketing, such as social marketing, or health service marketing, for example? Well, if the mix didn't have an acceptable level of applicability across the board then it would have been replaced by something else by now – theories like the Marketing Mix only continue to be used because they are relevant and useful.

With every pound spent on marketing communications needing to produce a real effect in terms of an impact on profitable sales, it is important for both practitioners and students to weigh carefully the balance of the promotional mix. It is also important to approach marketing communications planning with both an under-standing of marketing planning and the actual business environment of the world of marketing communications itself, so this is where we will look now.

HOW COMMUNICATION MIGHT WORK – SOME THEORIES

If it weren't for all the work put in on building theories of how communication works, we would all flounder with each new programme that needed to be organized. If the basic truths at the heart of what is now recognized as standard promotional theory are, after all, myths, then they have been working their magic for a very long time and continue to do so today. Thus, it is by research, observation and practice that these concepts of how promotion works have become an accepted part of promotional planning and evaluation, and it is because campaigns that are running today are still bearing out the theories put forward many years ago that these theories still have credence. Even with the advent of e-business and interactive e-communication, the basics still hold true, because communication *is* still communication and, even when we rely upon machinery to do it, we are still human beings when we reach out to each other!

During the mid and latter parts of the last century, there were numerous theories of how promotion works. Most are based upon the common psychological concepts of perception, attitude formation and behavioural patterns. That sounds fairly straight-forward, until you dig deeper into each of those areas and begin to realize that each topic is inextricably linked to so many other areas within psychology, sociology and behavioural studies that, in order to follow the most simplistic arguments, you need to be a pretty well-versed student of the human mind and society in general!

Why address all these issues? Well, if promotion is to work at all it must:

● *be seen* – it must be physically placed where we will stand some chance of perceiving it;

- *be noticed* – seeing and noticing are different, noticing it means we actually give it our selective attention, selecting it from all the other stimuli around us at the time;

- *be interesting and relevant* – we must believe the message is for us, it must mean something to us at the time;

- *be appealing* – we must like the message in some way in order for us to feel positive about the object of the message;

- *make the target want to do something about it* – we need to know what we can do and how to do it, or what is the point of having sent the message in the first place.

When you receive a stimulus, a promotional message, you may not feel yourself passing noticeably through each of these stages, but we all do, all the time, with promotional work that is successful. Successful promotional work takes us through three stages of response: the cognitive, affective and conative stages, each of which needs to precede the others in order for promotion to work.

The cognitive stage refers to the knowledge stage – awareness, comprehension, attention to the message. If you don't even know about something, how can you formulate an opinion, or attitude? If you don't know that a website exists, how can you *begin* to make a decision about whether to visit it? Links on the web allow surfers to reach sites they might not otherwise have visited because they are *made aware* of their existence.

The affective stage refers to the liking stage – you are convinced that something will do what the message says, you desire it because it is relevant and interesting, you prefer it because it is most relevant. If you visit a website looking for information, you will want to get to that information quickly and without side-stepping the main issue – but if you are looking for fun you will want an engaging and entertaining experience – e-business *must* deliver what it promises, it must get a visitor to *like* it because otherwise they have a very simple way of not doing business with that business again – they just don't visit it!

The conative stage is that stage where the knowledge and the positive feelings now are likely to affect behaviour, so action will be taken, a purchase made, adoption of the product or service will result. Thus, by having the right level of interaction, the right processes and procedures in place, an e-business can actually get people to take action *because* it is marketing to them and not selling to them!

All the major theories of how promotion works are based upon these three key stages, and all are, thereafter, variations on a theme, whether it is a useful mnemonic like AIDA (Attention, Interest, Desire, Action) or a more complex proposition such as the Hierarchy of Effects (where we study the inter-relationship between the stages rather than the stages themselves).

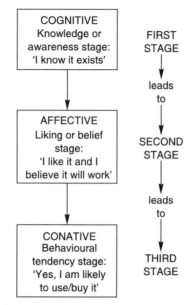

Figure 1.3   The psychological theory underlying how advertising might work

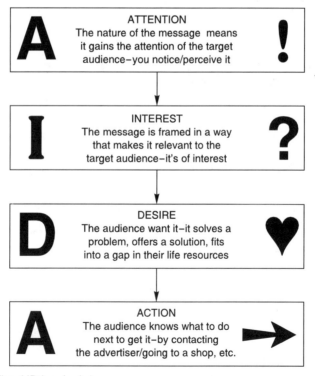

Figure 1.4   The AIDA principle

When it comes to the crunch, what marketers and promoters are really interested in, of course, is how behaviour is affected by promotion. If it is not affected at all, why bother? If we therefore agree that behaviour is affected by promotion, to what extent does it work? How can we tell ahead of time so that we can plan to spend exactly the right amount of money on just the right sort of promotional mix at just the right time? Well, it seems like a truism, but if anyone knew the answers to those questions for certain, all promotional campaigns would be perfect and achieve all their objectives on time and within budget. Unfortunately, or fortunately, human beings are not 100 per cent predictable: even the most ingrained habit can be broken once the reason for the habit is understood, so why shouldn't it be possible for a person to suddenly fancy trying out a new brand of washing powder, or order a book from amazon.com when they would never dream of pottering around a bookshop?

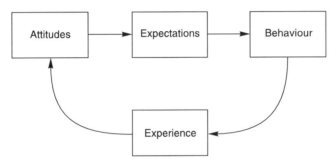

Figure 1.5 How attitudes and experience affect behaviour

Indeed, an understanding of why we do what we do is at the bottom of what the marketer wants to understand about all consumers. Figure 1.6 shows Maslow's hierarchy of needs, one of the most popular theories today that tries to address this terribly complex question.

Following from the idea that we all have needs (necessities – water), wants (preferences – beer) and desires (ideals – champagne), Maslow put forward the proposition that we have, in fact, a multi-layered approach to our requirements:

- physiological needs must be met first – unless we are alive all else is pointless;
- safety needs are next – once we are alive we want to be sure we will stay that way;
- next we want to belong – we are social animals and want to belong to some reference group;
- once we belong we want esteem within our chosen group – we all need to know our place, even if it isn't on top of the pile we like to know who to look up to and who to look down on;

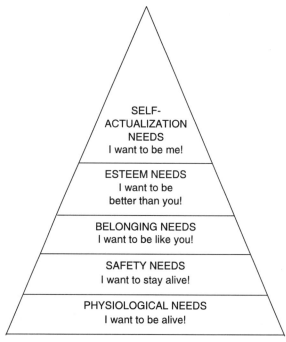

SELF-ACTUALIZATION NEEDS
I want to be me!

ESTEEM NEEDS
I want to be
better than you!

BELONGING NEEDS
I want to be like you!

SAFETY NEEDS
I want to stay alive!

PHYSIOLOGICAL NEEDS
I want to be alive!

Figure 1.6 Maslow's hierarchy of needs

- finally, and sometimes not even achievable by all, is the desire to be what we truly believe we can be – we seek to achieve self-actualization, a state where we are expressing as true a representation of the real 'us' as we can.

Many products are marketed using these concepts as a basis for not only their promotional messages, but their entire positioning strategy. And when it comes to applying old principles to new business, ignore what has been delivering the goods at your peril!

Maslow hasn't gone out of fashion just because business has become e-d. Let's take a look at how this fundamental theory finds itself having relevance in e-business terms. . .

Physiological needs

True, we all need to live, and many e-businesses are based upon delivering our daily bread – literally, for example, Sainsbury's and Tesco offer on-line grocery shopping, and literally allow us to keep living by bringing food to our door. But if you want to be truthful, the web and certain e-businesses have meant *real* life and death differences for some – health websites give information about symptoms and treatments; many medical schools use the web for learning, studying and teaching on a global stage, rather than working in isolation; people around the world now have access to an educational resource that would have been beyond their wildest dreams, allowing them to better their lives and build careers they could never have had; it could be argued that because certain businesses now operating on-line do so much more efficiently and therefore faster that lives have been saved – aircraft parts can be ordered on the web and can be shipped fast to wherever they are needed. I haven't even mentioned the pressure groups and charities who use the web to raise our awareness of conditions and occurrences that are life-threatening.

Safety needs

Other than e-businesses which offer products and services designed to keep us safe (smoke alarms, etc.), there is also the whole concept of having to address the issue of security on-line, and the prospect of fraud, theft and identity kidnapping. So safety is a real issue for many of those who currently refuse to shop on-line, and therefore a high priority for those marketers who want to sell to more people on-line. If you are a high street bank and you want to encourage more people to bank on-line, you will *have* to address safety issues to be able to build a viable customer base.

Belonging needs

E-business is not short of zealots! Often referred to as pointy-heads (no, I have no idea why, but all suggestions would be welcomed!), the technically minded see the web as a truly revolutionary development in the evolution of man. What has happened to the web recently is that is has begun to get beyond the stage where you had to understand a whole different language to be able to take part, where understanding the Internet was a bit like understanding the finer points of the rules of fantasy games with wizards, dragons and bowel-like caverns! But those who use the web are still encouraged to *belong* to certain groups – the most obvious belonging being your web address. Do you have your own website, or do you have a fun address for e-mail at hotmail? Do you AOL, or Compuserve? Rather like playing the ring tones of their mobile phones for fun, some people will recount how boring it is to have to check *six* e-mail addresses every day, whereas what they are implying is that they are important enough to *have* six e-mail addresses! Man almost automatically wants to belong, and chatrooms, mailing circles, closed lists and on-line clubs of all types utilize this desire.

Esteem needs

Technological devices have an almost unique ability to allow conspicuous consumption, with high prices being demanded, and paid, for innovative equipment that

allows access to the most up-to-date technology. It is almost a given that he or she who has the latest, most expensive 'toy' is the wealthiest and most cutting edge in the room! E-businesses are well placed to capitalize upon this phenomenon, with technically interested people having a much higher than average preponderance for using the web to gather information and buy goods and services. Allowing browsers to gather knowledge that they can use to gain leverage in a social or business situation can be valuable in building a relationship with a browser and a customer: the updateability of the web lends itself to such a method of building business links.

Self-actualization needs

The number of e-businesses that allow access to 'dreams' is almost endless: holistic spiritual advice, tarot readings, travel sites, holiday planning, last minute tickets for anything, books, on-line magazines and the virtual world of global chat amongst those whose passion is quilting, or building matchstick lighthouses, or carp fishing. . .it is a phenomenally powerful tool for allowing people to almost live a life beyond their own body. Now, you might think I have lost it a bit here, but follow me for a minute: allowing yourself to *be* your true self is what self-actualization is all about – and where better to be your true self than where you are faceless, and nameless if you choose. The web almost allows us to go beyond the physical and become what we most want to be – or if we can't become it, we can visit it! You want to be the perfect bread and butter pudding cook? Go and find a recipe site. You want to chat to someone about how you love your postage stamps? Go and visit a philately heaven! The web *is* heaven for some people – romances blossom over it, friendships are built through it, and many long-distance relationships survive because of it. E-mail and e-business can make a difference to people globally, allowing them access to information they could never have accessed before (educational information in China, communication ability from within a war zone) and can change lives on a small and large scale.

Like anything, the web is just a tool – how we use it to do business, to change lives, is up to us. Often, the two will coincide, which is a very happy marriage. But the web is about more than communicating, about more than making people aware or allowing them access to information that can change their attitudes – it is also about allowing them to take action they would not have had the chance to take before, so we must get beyond the *needs* of people in the passive sense and look to the active.

One way in which we can try to get a better understanding of why people choose what they do is by beginning to come to terms with the black box concept.

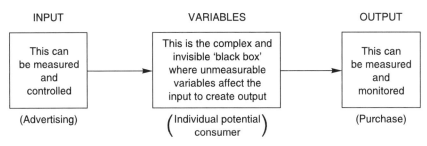

INPUT	VARIABLES	OUTPUT
This can be measured and controlled	This is the complex and invisible 'black box' where unmeasurable variables affect the input to create output	This can be measured and monitored
(Advertising)	(Individual potential consumer)	(Purchase)

Figure 1.7 The black box model

We can measure inputs, like advertisements seen, or number of visits to a site, and we can measure outputs, such as whether the person bought the product and after how many visits, but everything that makes one stimulus turn into the other response is hidden from us within the human mind – as though it were a black box, all the decision-making processes are hidden away (Figure 1.7).

Imagine that the black box contains not one process but many dozen; some happen because they are basic and physiological, others are psychological. We would get a much better idea of what was going on inside the black box if we could break down the inputs into small pieces, measure the smaller outputs and develop a series of black box inputs and outputs that make the size of what is going on in the box smaller and smaller. Models have been developed that do this. Research agencies have taken models and have built hybrids and exclusive models that are *predictive* (they predict what *will* happen, for example, if you spend three million pounds advertising a particular brand of beer you are likely to increase sales by x amount) and/or *projective* (they say how the results from a small sample would look if applied to a greater mass – they don't necessarily predict though; for example, the research that tells us that x million people watched a particular TV programme is a projective piece, taking the real data gathered from a small sample and projecting it onto the whole television-owning population).

The predictive models for e-business are still in their infancy, and there seems to be more than a little alchemy involved in many of them. Various figures float around the business, some saying that a 1 per cent purchasing to clickthrough rate is fabulous, some saying it's poor. Figures for sales and customer retention through lifetime value calculation are argued in the trade press regularly. Maybe there will never be any answers – the best way to keep abreast of this is to read, attend lots of courses, and keep up to date with both printed and on-line industry data. Of course, if you are using an agency of any sort to work with you on your e-business they should be able to offer opinion and advice – but if you are up to date too, you can at least keep them on their toes!

One factor that is undeniable, however, is the appearance of the 'viral marketing communications model' – which isn't as horrid as it sounds, although the name is a good description of what we are talking about.

Old-fashioned communication models all assumed one thing – that the message would come from a controlled point – the communicator, the marketer. Even when we consider the role of opinion leaders in communication, we still assume that their opinion will have been informed by the professional communicator, the marketer, at some point. The Internet has allowed the genie to get out of the bottle, it has allowed the concept of 'word of mouth' to run riot, globally, with huge e-mail lists being accessed with messages that do not come from the professional communicator, the marketer, but, rather, come from within the customer, or potential customer, community itself. We are all familiar with the frightening rapidity with which a computer bug or virus (like the LoveBug) can circumnavigate the world in a matter of hours, hitting at key systems with random abandon! Good opinions about a product, service, website or a great offer can travel just as quickly, with communications networks being used that actually belong to the recipients of messages, not to media owners or marketers. Rather than word of mouth, we are talking about word of e-mail. And it works. Person-to-Person (P2P) communication is not an airy-fairy concept, it is a reality in today's e-world – and it takes place in both the B2B and B2C environments we see operating. Because, after all, the Internet doesn't communicate from computer to computer, but from person to person – a factor that some so-called marketing communications experts seem to forget all too easily!

I therefore propose that we go beyond the concepts of the familiar One-Step and Two-Step communication models and consider a Three-Step model too. Its implications are still being considered by marketers – and the concept embraces both e- and non-e-business, because, of course, the fact that you don't have an e-business doesn't mean that people won't choose to communicate with each other about you via e-methods!

The business of communicating

> **THE DEVELOPMENT OF COMMUNICATION METHODS – THE OLD WAYS AND THE NEW**

The Industrial Revolution was the real catalyst for the emergence of mass markets, as we understand them today: the move to towns meant people could no longer subsist or rely upon simple barter, they had paid jobs so began to deal in cash rather than kind. Various providers of goods and services found themselves in competition with each other for the money in their potential customers' pockets, and so had to begin to differentiate their goods and services within the growing marketplace.

ONE-STEP COMMUNICATION

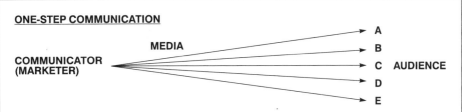

Here you can see that by the simple use of media the communicator reaches all the members of the target audience. A classic example of this would be any one-to-one form of communication, such as permission e-mail, telephone, direct mail, etc. Don't forget that we are still talking about the *opportunity to see* the message.

TWO-STEP COMMUNICATION

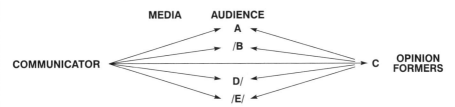

In this form of communication, audience members A, C and D are reached by the communicator's own, simple communication, but the communicator fails to reach audience members B and E. Luckily (or, hopefully, by design) C is an opinion former (maybe a pop star seen wearing a certain brand of wristwatch) and they communicate back to the audience, managing to reach members A and B, but not D or E.

Thus, A has reached the message in two versions, B from one, C from one, D from one and only E goes unreached.

The advantage of Two-Step Communication is that it gives the opportunity for extra ground to be covered by using those whose opinion will be seen as being more believable than 'just' advertising, or communication methods created by the communicator.

THREE-STEP COMMUNICATION

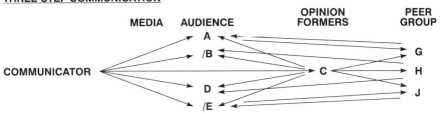

In this model we see that, following on from the diagram above, even though the opinion former C cannot reach audience members D or E, they go on to reach other peer group members, who in turn communicate back to A, B, C, D and E – just by sheer numbers of total individual interactions the chances of the message getting through to all members of our target audience are improved because of the huge numbers of cross-relationships within the Internet community. We all know (some of us to our cost) how quickly a virus can spread around the world – well, positive messages can move that way too – not quite as quickly, but in a more measured and targeted way – which is a good thing!

Figure 1.8   One-Step, Two-Step and Three-Step Communication models

By the twentieth century, the gradual rise in literacy amongst the working classes, together with the emergence of a merchant, or middle class, meant that producers could begin to develop brand identities and brand images that set them apart from their competitors and would remain at the front of the mind of the potential purchaser when they selected their goods or services.

With the development of mass appeal brands such as Persil, Pears' Soap, Sunlight Soapflakes, and so on, the use of the new mass media to communicate brand messages soon followed. Newspapers and magazines carried more advertisements, now with illustrations added; the cinema, the most popular mass medium of the early twentieth century, allowed brand identities to be shown to the majority of the population on a regular basis. Posters, one of the earliest and most effective forms of simple mass communication, continue to reach millions today, as they have done since the last century.

Commercial radio, Radio Luxembourg only until the 1960s, brought aural messages into the home, and eventually into the car, whilst the advent of commercial television in the latter part of the last century means that it is now possible to send a very detailed visual and aural message into almost every home in the country.

Perhaps the biggest change in mass communication has taken place, however, within the last five years: faster and cheaper computing facilities mean that mass communication can now be personalized communication at one and the same time. Huge amounts of information can be stored, manipulated and cross-referenced at a fraction of the cost of, say, ten years ago. The growth in both sales promotions that generate customer information and the methods of direct marketing that have been developed to capitalize upon this new information technology has been phenomenal. The Internet and all the possibilities it offers in terms of internal and external communication is another obvious addition to the communications toolbox.

The wheel has now turned full circle: in the early days it was often personal selling that captured customers. Then came the day when cost per thousand ruled, followed by the growth of non-contact personal communication with the customer.

Today, it is not unusual to see a television advertising campaign where the sole purpose is to generate website visits from the target audience. Who would have thought, even five years ago, that systems would be available to allow the generation of hundreds of thousands of on-line sales leads to be followed up almost immediately on an individual basis. Although many fight against the wealth of information held on databases about individuals, it is only through the proliferation of such systems that the marketer can truly move ahead to the, for some, ideal world of building a one-to-one relationship with each and every customer.

However, we should be aware that the rush towards personalized everything and Internet interactivity must be tempered with the need to communicate with groups of people who already have something in common – they form the segment of the market for whom the product or service in question is most relevant. As promoters, we lose sight of this simple point at our peril. Even personal communication needs to be planned within an overall framework of promotion.

THE BUSINESS OF COMMUNICATION TODAY

As described earlier, the twentieth century saw a rapid growth in the use of mass communication and, latterly, in personal or direct communication. This has not happened in a vacuum: service industries have provided the resources demanded by the manufacturers and providers of services.

With the main demand for promotional capabilities coming from the fast-moving consumer goods (fmcg) sector, most of these mass manufacturers initially had their own internal experts in communication – a type of in-house advertising and promotional function. However, as time passed, those working in the industry saw a business opportunity for setting up centres of excellence, staffed by those best at, say, coming up with creative ideas, copy for advertisements, etc., and for offering these services for sale to companies who might rather not carry the overhead of an in-house advertising department. Thus, the advertising agency was born.

The full service advertising agency, as it is known, offers the client company a range of services. Initially, these services mirrored those found in the client company, but over time they became more specialized, with the classic full service agency functions becoming well defined by the 1960s.

Over time, the special functions within the agency were seen by those who delivered the services in question as prime opportunities for setting up even more specialized

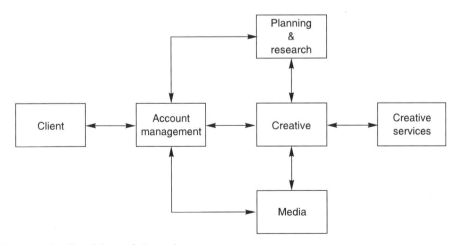

Figure 1.9 Traditional full service agency structure

centres of excellence. Thus, from about 1970 to 2000, we saw the emergence of creative hot-shops, media independents, sales promotion houses, direct marketing agencies, sponsorship agencies and web design agencies, as well as increased specialization from PR agencies, design houses and the emergence of e-communication agencies.

Now, in the twenty-first century, it is possible for the client to select a full service agency from the hundreds that exist, or to act as their own account handler and buy any and all promotional services 'à la carte'. The client must decide whether it is better to use a full service agency, and bear the costs that would be incurred, or to spend more time, and thus incur internal costs, coordinating their own promotional effort. The client's requirements might mean it makes good commercial sense to employ one main full service agency and split out only their media buying, for example.

If a marketer chooses to buy à la carte, then the range of services, and the number of people supplying them, is endless. Creative, production, packaging design, sponsorship, public relations, web design, sales promotion, media planning, media buying, point of sale display material construction – all these services, and many more, are available through specialist providers. Should the marketer choose to do so, then each can be planned, bought and controlled separately and directly. However, it is clear that the planning of such communications services purchasing must be a priority if synergy and integration are the desired outcomes.

Whether the marketer chooses to use a full service agency, with its affiliated specialized companies, or to buy such services à la carte, the marketer and the supplying agency are only two points in the triangle of reliance (see Figure 1.10). The third point is the media. Marketers need the mass media to allow them to reach their target audiences more effectively. Media might mean television or press, or even the postal system. And don't think for one minute that e-business doesn't need traditional media in much the same way as traditional businesses need it – they do, and they use it to great effect (we'll look at this in more detail in later chapters). By the way, an increasing number of traditional media owners are now offering web-based media; for example, on-line magazines, exhibitions and even telecasts are available on-line, and allow for a message about another location to be given to the visitor to the original location (in a superbly targeted way).

It is quite clear that marketers need the media to reach their customers, and that marketers need the services provided by the range of agencies available. It is also clear that the agency needs the marketer to provide them with business and needs the media to allow them to communicate with their client's customers. It is also clear that the media need the clients to provide them with advertising revenue. But why do the media need agencies? Why could they not just deal direct with the clients? Well, in reality, many media owners' sales forces do actually communicate a great deal with

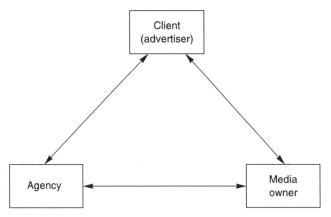

Figure 1.10 The promotional triangle of reliance

client companies direct, but usually only those who spend a great deal of money on the particular medium. It makes sense for the media to deal with agencies, or media houses, because these act as bulk purchasing centres and allow the media to concentrate their sales effort, keeping sales forces to a manageable size, rather than having to deal direct with all potential advertisers.

The balance within the triangle of reliance is key to its continued success. With the current pressures upon all parties to ensure value for money, it is in the interests of all parties that the balance is maintained. One area where there might be a future imbalance is in the fact that the more business that is done through the marketers' own websites, the more worried the media owners become that their role will be undermined. In fact, 'traditional media' are still used by e-businesses largely to direct people to websites, etc. and to ensure that big messages get delivered into the homes and lives of the marketplace at a point in time that is controlled.

BUSINESS RELATIONSHIPS TODAY

In 1992, the Incorporated Society of British Advertisers (ISBA) published its Best Practice guidelines on managing the advertiser/agency relationship (see next section for an explanation of the ISBA's role in the communication business). This document addresses the key issues of how the marketer should set about dealing with their agency and what they should expect from their agency. Whilst some controversy arose at the time of its publication, it is true to say that the document is based upon the concepts of fair dealing and on clarity of purpose on the part of all parties concerned. The guidelines make it clear that, in the advertiser/agency relationship, as in all business relationships, there should be trust on both sides, and suggest that trust is best based upon discussion and written agreements.

The document contains sections on selecting and appointing an agency, the agreement that should be drawn up and signed between a client and its agency, agency remuneration procedures, the day-to-day relationship between agency and client, briefing procedures, creative and media issues. It has been written to help both advertisers and agencies to be clearer and more informed about some of the key areas in which problems and disagreements can arise. The user-friendly approach of a question and answer format has proved popular. (NB: at the time of writing the ISBA is planning to publish an updated version of this document; see ISBA web information below.)

The relationship between agencies and media owners is also under scrutiny at all times. Media owners need to be certain that those who buy advertising space from them can actually afford to pay the bills, whilst the agency needs to be sure that the audience coverage they believe they are buying for their clients is achieved by the media selected.

In all dealings within the business, and the triangle of reliance, there must be both understanding of the other parties' interests and a clarity of purpose. The industry has recognized this for many years, and the bodies it has set up for itself play a leading role in ensuring that all parties benefit as they should.

As mentioned earlier in this unit, all the functions offered by a full service agency, namely account handling, account planning, media planning and buying, creative conceptual work and production facilities, can all be bought direct by the client from independent companies or even freelance individuals.

From the client's perspective, the advantage of using a full service agency is that you have immediate access to a whole range of experts who are able to bring a fresh and unjaundiced point of view to bear on your problems. However, it is a very expensive way of operating if you do not intend using all the services on offer: your fees are having to service the overheads, so you might as well use the facilities!

This has to be balanced with the huge amount of extra time that the client who chooses to buy each element of service individually must dedicate to the task. Sometimes it is easy to lose sight of the fact that the internal costs of staff who coordinate matters in-house is as real a cost to your company as the fees paid to an agency. The client should weigh up the objective pros and cons of using a full service agency as opposed to buying à la carte, as circumstances change and alter with time.

When it comes to an e-business, there can be a temptation to underestimate the range of services you might need to use in order to promote your business efficiently and effectively. Hopefully, at least, this book will help you better understand the way that the various promotional and communication disciplines fit together, so that your decision making about whether to use a full service agency or a selection of specialist service providers is better informed.

THE BUSINESS THAT LOOKS AFTER ITSELF

Let us take a look at the various industry bodies that are greatly involved in providing the business framework for the industry itself. All these bodies work together – they need to in order for the client, the person who finally pays the bill, to get what they need. Also, of course, all these bodies have at the back of their organizational 'mind' the fact that, unless the business as a whole runs smoothly, the process of communication with the potential customer will break down, an end they will all seek to avoid at all costs. Whether you are an e-business start-up or an existing business that is going to be e-d, you still need the insider information that these bodies can offer.

Statutory bodies

These bodies are given their powers by Parliament. They have responsibilities laid down in law, or statute, and are funded by public monies. Both bodies were created as a result of the 1990 Broadcasting Act. 2001 will see a re-vamping of the Authorites, though at the time of writing the final arrangement has not been made clear.

Independent Television Commission (ITC)

This body licenses and regulates the independent television industry in the UK. It is responsible for drawing up and enforcing a code governing standards and practice in television advertising and the sponsoring of programmes, as well as ensuring all statutes affecting television advertising are adhered to. Under its powers, derived from the Broadcasting Acts of 1990 and 1996, the ITC:

- Issues licences that allow commercial television companies to broadcast in and from the UK – whether the services are received by conventional aerials, cable or satellite, and whether delivered by analogue or digital means. These licences vary according to the type of service, but they all set out conditions on matters such as standards of programmes and advertising.

- Regulates these services by monitoring broadcasters' performance against the requirements of the ITC's published licences and codes and guidelines on programme content, advertising and sponsorship, and technical performance. There is a range of penalties for failure to comply with them.

- Has a duty to ensure that a wide range of television services is available throughout the UK and that, taken as a whole, these are of a high quality and appeal to a range of tastes and interests.

- Has a duty to ensure fair and effective competition in the provision of these services.

- Investigates complaints and regularly publishes its findings.

Radio Authority (RA)

The Authority licenses and regulates all commercial radio services. These comprise national, local, cable, national FM subcarrier, satellite and restricted services. The latter includes all short-term, freely radiating services (for example, 'special event' radio) and highly localized permanent services such as hospital and student radio. The Authority will also be licensing digital radio services, both national and local, over the next few years. The Authority is responsible for monitoring the obligations on its licensees required by the Broadcasting Acts 1990 and 1996. The Authority has three main tasks: to plan frequencies; to appoint licensees with a view to broadening listener choice; and to regulate programming and advertising. It is required, after consultation, to publish Codes to which licensees must adhere. These cover programmes, advertising and sponsorship, and engineering. There are also rules on ownership. The Authority can apply sanctions to licensees who break the rules. Sanctions include broadcast apologies and/or corrections, fines and the shortening or revocation of licences. Licensees pay annual fees to the Authority and application fees are charged to applicants applying for licences. These fees are the Authority's only source of income and cover all its operating costs.

Trade associations and bodies

Trade associations exist in all business fields with a common purpose – to represent the interest of their members as appropriate to the prevailing circumstances. This is certainly the case in the field of communication and promotion. There are literally dozens of trade associations and voluntary bodies. What follows is not an exhaustive list, but a résumé of the ones you are most likely to encounter, read about, and need to know about.

Cinema Advertising Association (CAA)

The CAA is a trade association of cinema advertising contractors operating in the UK and Eire. Its primary functions are to promote, monitor and maintain standards of cinema advertising, including pre-vetting all cinema commercials to ensure conformity with the British Codes of Advertising and Sales Promotion and the Advertising Standards Authority for Ireland, and to commission and conduct research into the cinema as an advertising medium. This includes the UK cinema admissions monitor, publishing master lists of cinemas taking advertising and providing an industry umbrella for the annual CAVIAR (Cinema and Video Industry Audience Research) studies. The CAA has also commissioned a series of cinema advertising recall studies (for further details please contact the CAA).

Commercial Radio Companies Association (CRCA)

The Commercial Radio Companies Association is the trade body for commercial radio companies in the United Kingdom. It is a voluntary, non-profit-making body, incorporated as a company limited by guarantee, and was formed by the first radio companies when Independent Radio began in 1973. It has always enjoyed the overwhelming support of the radio industry – all but a handful of stations are in membership – and has been an influential force in British broadcasting throughout its existence. It is funded by the subscriptions of its member radio companies, who share the cost of the CRCA in proportion to their shares of the industry's broadcasting revenue. CRCA affairs are managed by a board of nine non-executive directors who are elected annually and one executive director, the Chief Executive of the CRCA, who manages the seven-person directorate.

 @ http://www.crca.org.uk

The ITV Network (ITV)

The ITV Network commissions and schedules the network programmes transmitted to all fifteen ITV regions. It also carries out other functions, including network programming promotions and marketing. The Network provides a platform on which policies common to all the ITV companies can be discussed and determined and an organization through which these can be communicated. Although the companies preserve their independence and formulate their own policies, the Network acts on common cause issues, including public affairs (domestic and European), the maintenance of TV advertising standards, engineering and the formulation of digital policy.

 @ http://www.itv.co.uk

Newspaper Publishers' Association (NPA)

The NPA is the trade association for Britain's national daily and Sunday newspapers and the *Evening Standard*. Founded in 1906, its aims are to promote and protect national press interests.
Activities include:

- promotion of the national press;
- monitoring and lobbying activities on UK and European legislation affecting the newspaper industry, especially on advertising, copyright, environment and social areas;
- promotion of good practice in advertising, including vetting and monitoring of agencies and advertisers for creditworthiness;
- provision of accreditation and other services, including issuing press cards and administering press rotas for major royal, political and sporting events.

Outdoor Advertising Association (OAA)

The OAA is the trade association representing the UK poster contractors (both Outdoor and Transport). It is the central reference point for the outdoor or poster industry, with the objective of advancing and protecting the general trade interests of its members. It is also charged with maintaining the OAA Code of Practice. The primary function is to contribute to the provision of an environment which encourages growth of business.

 @ http://www.oaa.org.uk

Periodical Publishers' Association (PPA)

The PPA, established in 1913, has member publishers covering the full spectrum of magazine publishing, from mass circulation consumer magazines to highly technical business and professional journals. Approximately 80 per cent of the revenue from magazine publishing is represented by the association.

The main aims of the PPA are to promote and protect the interests and freedom of the periodical press. It maintains a system of agency recognition, oversees the mail order protection schemes operated by members, and plays a crucial part in determining the policy and monitoring the daily application of advertising standards. The PPA maintains close contacts with magazine distribution organizations, print and paper associations, the Post Office and government departments. Current activity includes the promotion of magazines as an effective advertising medium, the enhancement of editorial standards, the protection of publisher copyright and the provision of accurate data on the magazine industry.

 @ http://www.ppa.co.uk

All these bodies have as their members the companies that are involved as media owners in the relevant field. For example, the OAA has as its members the contractors that erect poster hoardings and who have the right to sell the advertising space, whilst the NPA has as its members the companies that publish national daily newspapers, with the PPA being the body that deals with magazine publishers. Other bodies also exist, and will continue to be developed, within this field, as interest groups see it as being in their interests to have a trade association that can speak on their behalf, whether to the general public, to government or to the European legislature.

Most media owner trade associations have a small secretariat financed by the subscription of their members, but carry out a great deal of work by committee, with committee members being drawn from member companies. Committees might deal with anything from research to setting the standards against which agency recognition is granted.

Other trade associations

Most of the names of the following associations describe exactly the nature of their membership. Where there might be some ambiguity a brief explanation has been given.

Direct Marketing Association (DMA; formerly BDMA)

The DMA is the only industry association dedicated to promoting and protecting the direct marketing industry as a whole, in all its forms, including both advertisers and suppliers of services. The mission of the DMA is to represent the best interests of its members by raising the stature of the direct marketing industry and gaining consumer trust and confidence in direct marketing.

The DMA fulfils many roles, including presenting a unified voice for the industry in discussions with the British government and the institutions of the EU, and with statutory and other bodies. It promotes the use and understanding of direct marketing to members and consumers alike through seminars, conferences, public relations and market development activity.

The members of the Association adhere to a Code of Practice, derived from the codes of the four founding associations, which is administered by the Direct Marketing Authority – chaired by Lord Borrie QC. The Code includes a requirement that all members abide by the British Codes of Advertising and Sales Promotion.

 @ http://www.dma.org.uk

Institute of Practitioners in Advertising (IPA)

The IPA is the industry body and professional institute for UK advertising agencies. It has been servicing the needs of advertising agencies since 1917.

The IPA serves two purposes:

- It acts as spokesperson for agencies, representing them on issues of common concern and speaking on their behalf in negotiations with media bodies, government departments, trade unions, and industry and consumer organizations.

- It makes an important contribution to the effective operation of advertising agencies through its advisory, training and information services.

Its objective is to represent all those companies concerned primarily with providing strategic advice on marketing communications, creating and/or placing advertising. There are 210 member companies who collectively handle over 80 per cent of all advertising placed by UK agencies.

 @ http://www.ipa.co.uk

Incorporated Society of British Advertisers (ISBA)

The ISBA is the only body representing the interests of British advertisers in all areas of commercial communications, including TV advertising, radio, press, outdoor, new media, direct marketing, sponsorship, sales promotion, PR and exhibitions. Founded in 1900, the ISBA has around 300 member companies, whose total communications spend is over £8 billion.

The ISBA's membership includes most of the UK's largest advertisers. These include companies operating in all areas of business, including financial services, technology, packaged food and goods, telecoms, automotive, entertainment and leisure. The single factor which binds ISBA members together is that they each rely on advertising to promote their goods and services to the public.

The ISBA works together with government, media owners and advertising agencies to promote the importance of advertising in driving competition in our economy, to promote the argument for self-regulation of commercial communications, especially in light of the changing media environment, and – always – to defend the freedom of businesses to advertise responsibly.

The ISBA exists to voice the interests and opinions of its members both to the public at large and to the key decision makers. It is through expression and discussion of members' concerns, interests and ambitions within the ISBA's Council, Executive Committees and Action Groups that the organization's direction is set and the policies of British advertisers are formalized.

The ISBA's key strategic aims are to:

1 Achieve recognition from government and business of the fundamental importance of marketing communications to the nation's economy and consumer choice, and the key role of advertisers in funding the media.

2 Resist unwarranted media cost inflation and strive for a more competitive TV airtime marketplace.

3 Encourage a constructive and workable legislative and regulatory framework within which to advertise legally marketable products.

4 Build member involvement and ISBA profile, especially at senior management level, and create a sense of ownership in the ISBA through a more effective internal marketing programme.

5 Encourage excellence of marketing communications practice among members.

6 Stimulate maximum effectiveness and commercial transparency from communication agencies/consultancies.

7 Assist in the effective utilization of new media channels to the benefit of advertisers.

Institute of Sales Promotion (ISP)

The ISP is the pre-eminent professional association for everyone in the UK promotional marketing industry. From its inception in 1979, the ISP has aimed to ensure the highest professional standards in all issues relating to promotional marketing, and is firmly committed to providing all members with the essential services and professional advice they need.

The ISP has a vital function to fulfil as the 'neutral ground' on which promoters, consultancies and marketing service companies can meet to the mutual advantage of all industry practitioners.

The Institute provides the following services and activities for members: Legal Advice and Guidance, Education, European Lobbying, Industry Task Forces, Research and Marketing Intelligence, Publications Service, Social Events.

 @ http://www.isp.org.uk

Public Relations Consultants' Association (PRCA)

The PRCA Mission Statement states that the organization exists to encourage and promote the advancement of companies and firms engaged in public relations consultancy. Its stated objectives are to:

1 Raise and maintain professional and ethical standards in consultancy practice, including the encouragement of Quality ISO 9000, Investors in People, Best Practice and the use of Evaluation.

2 Provide facilities for government, public bodies, associations representing industry, trade and others to confer with public relations consultants as a body and to ascertain their collective views.

3 Promote confidence in public relations consultancy and, consequently, in public relations as a whole, and to act as spokesperson for consultancy practice.

4 Educate potential clients, establishing the reputation of professionalism of members who conform to its Professional Charter.

5 Promote that members are registered and that there is a Professional Practices Committee to oversee standards and arbitrate on complaints.

6 Offer practical industry-wide training and management development services.

7 Monitor and react to perceptions of the sector amongst key opinion-leaders.

8 Provide a forum for discussion on key PR industry issues.

9 Demonstrate the effectiveness of good PR in consultancy work.

10 Increase opportunities for members to develop new business.

11 Improve cooperation/relationships with fellow professional bodies in the UK and internationally.

12 Help members improve their efficiency, understanding, skills, professionalism and ethics.

 @ http://www.prca.org.uk

Advertising Association

Most of the aforementioned bodies are its members, even if their primary motivation is not pure above the line advertising. The Advertising Association acts as a collective forum within the communications industry and often acts on behalf of several member associations when there is a common good to be gained, for example in representing the interests of the UK advertising industry in all its parts to the European legislature or the UK government. The Advertising Association is a federation of twenty-six trade associations and professional bodies representing advertisers, agencies, the media and support services. It is the only body which speaks for all sides of an industry currently worth over £15 billion per annum.

Its remit concerns the mutual interests of the business as a whole. It operates in a complementary way with the vested interests of its members who have specific roles for their individual sectors.

The Advertising Association speaks as 'the common voice' for all on:

● Promoting public understanding of, and respect for, commercial communication and its role in promoting competition, innovation, and economic and social progress in society.

● Upholding standards and the principle of self-regulation.

● Providing information, research and statistics about the advertising business.

● Combating unjustified restrictions and outright bans on commercial communication for freely and legally available products or services.

The Advertising Association exists to provide a coordinated service in the interests of its wider membership, i.e. the individual companies that make up this large, diverse and competitive business.

Its remit is 'to promote and protect the rights, responsibilities and role of advertising' in the UK. This is in line with Article 10 of the European Convention on Human Rights, which recognizes commercial freedom of speech as a right, alongside political and artistic freedoms of speech. The Advertising Association is a non-profit-making company, limited by guarantee, and funded by a combination of subscriptions, donations and revenue-raising activities such as seminars and publications.

 @ http://www.adassoc.org.uk

Membership associations

These bodies have individuals as members, with the gaining of a qualification approved by the body concerned usually being the only way to obtain membership. Professional status for those who hold qualifications is enhanced by the work carried out by each of these bodies.

Communication, Advertising and Marketing Education Foundation (CAM)

Membership relies upon passing the CAM Diploma.

The CAM is the examinations board for vocational qualifications in the disciplines that make up marketing communication. Its Advisory Council is made up of principal trade associations and professional institutes which, between them, represent all parts of the marketing communication business. It is from that industry-wide representation that the CAM syllabuses (on which the examinations are based) are multi-disciplinary in their scope, and the qualifications awarded reflect a breadth of knowledge and competence in all the key activities.

 @ http://www.camfoundation.com

Chartered Institute of Marketing (CIM)

Membership relies upon passing the CIM Diploma.

The CIM is the professional body for marketing, representing 60 000 marketers worldwide. Their branch and special interest group networks aim to provide members with the opportunity to make contact with other professionals in all industry sectors and on every continent. They offer access to a wide range of professional services aimed at developing careers and aiding professional development.

Only members of the CIM can work towards Individual Chartered status and call themselves Chartered Marketers. Just like Chartered Accountants, Chartered Marketers keep their skills and knowledge up to date. To help, the CIM provides a Continuing Professional Development (CPD) structure to keep marketers qualified, experienced, innovative and competitive. The CIM is the only marketing body able to award the Individual Chartered status. CIM was given authority by The Queen's Privy Council Office in the UK. The first awards were made in October 1998. In 1999–2000, the number of Chartered Marketers increased by more than half to over 3000.

 @ http://www.cim.co.uk

Institute of Public Relations (IPR)

Membership relies upon passing the CAM Diploma in Public Relations, the IPR Diploma, a PR Degree or holding another recognized qualification in public relations.

With over 6000 members, the IPR is the largest professional body for PR practitioners in Europe. It represents the interests of people working in public relations, offering access to information, advice and support, and providing networking opportunities through a wide variety of events, seminars and training workshops.

The aims of the IPR are:

- To provide a professional structure for the practice of public relations.
- To enhance the ability and status of members as professional practitioners.
- To represent and serve the professional interests of members.
- To provide opportunities for members to meet and exchange views and ideas.
- To raise standards within the profession through the promotion of best practice – including the production of best practice guides, training events and seminars, and a continuous professional development scheme.

 @ http://www.ipr.org.uk

Market Research Society (MRS)

Membership relies upon holding the MRS Diploma or another recognized qualification.

The MRS is the Society representing the professional interests of 7000 market research practitioners. The Society sets qualification criteria for admission to its various grades of membership. It issues a Code of Conduct and oversees compliance with the Code. Supplementary Guidelines are also issued on specialist dimensions of research practice. In addition to professional accreditation, MRS members receive access to publications and information services, career development via training and CPD, and a wide range of conferences, seminars and meetings geared to special interests. As the Society has members on both the agency and client sides of market research, as well as in the academic community, it is neutral and independent of each of these 'constituencies'. It is the lead body in coordination of the Market Research Industry Liaison Group, with the British Market Research Association (BMRA) and the Association of Users of Research Agencies (AURA). It also leads the Marketing Market Research Initiative, which aims to foster conditions which enable market research to flourish, and to promote the identity and value of market research to business, government and the general public.

 @ http://www.marketresearch.org.uk

Most of these bodies have a great deal of involvement with the development of qualification syllabi and the monitoring of standards of practice and ethics within their respective fields. Once again, a great deal of the work carried out by them is actually administering decisions made by committees made up of members.

Summary of chapter one

Within this chapter, we have covered the following:

The marketing context

In this section, the aim is to gain a real overview of how and where marketing communications fit into the overall picture of marketing and marketing planning, and why this basic information is relevant to the e-business person. The three main sections are:

Understanding marketing planning

This is an overview of the key steps in planning – whether it be marketing planning or, indeed, marketing communications planning, for e- or non-e-business.

The role and importance of auditing as a part of the planning process, as well as setting objectives, selecting strategies, building implementation plans and the importance of monitoring activity are also dealt with.

Getting back to basics – minding your Ps and Cs

This section looks at the traditional Seven Ps of the Marketing Mix through fresh eyes, as this is where the author proposes the adoption of the Seven Cs when addressing marketing and marketing communications planning and their application to e-business.

This is an important insight into the basis for planning truly customer orientated marketing and marketing communications programmes.

How communication might work – some theories

This section looks at some of the respected theories of how the process of communication works, from an academic and even psychological viewpoint, and a suggestion of how we might need to consider them for the e-future.

The business of communicating

In this section, the focus is on how the business of marketing communication works within the UK today. With a historical perspective, and by referring to many of today's leading trade association websites, this section should clarify the working relationships found in the modern business.

The development of communication methods

This section contains an overview of the historical development of today's communication methods.

The business of communication today

This section addresses how clients, service suppliers and the media inter-relate in today's business environment. It introduces the concept of the triangle of reliance.

Business relationships today

This section introduces a later part of the text, which will deal in detail with how to find, brief and manage service suppliers.

The business that looks after itself

This is the section of the book that gives readers an insight into how the business is run: by an explanation of the roles of many of the leading trade and member associations, the reader should now better understand how the industry oversees its own people.

 ## Self test questions and opinion development

These are not exam questions, nor are they meant to represent the sort of question you might expect to face anywhere else. They are designed to help you check whether you have understood the content of this chapter. All you have to do is read the questions, give them some thought and maybe jot down some notes on what your response might be. Not all the questions will have factual answers – rather, they might encourage you to think about a topic or an issue and formulate an opinion based upon what is now, hopefully, a better understanding of the topic.

What are the key questions that have to be asked and answered in any planning process?

What are the seven Ps of the marketing mix?

What are the seven Cs of the marketing mix?

What is the relationship between the Ps and the Cs?

What does AIDA stand for, and in what way is it relevant to understanding how communication might work?

Who do you think understands better how communication works: a psychologist, a sociologist, an advertising agency account executive, a market researcher, a marketer?

Why do you think mass communication developed at all, and why is there now such an emphasis on one-to-one or one-to-few marketing communications?

What is the triangle of reliance, and how do you think it might change in the future?

Name three media trade associations and explain what they do and why they do it.

 ## Extending knowledge and understanding

You are encouraged to undertake the following activities to further your knowledge and understanding of the topics covered in this chapter in the following ways:

1 Visit at least five of the websites listed. In order to be able to assess how well the websites communicate with their target audiences, do the following:

- draw up a list of potential target audiences;
- assess how easy it is to navigate the site;
- assess how well both visual and verbal communication techniques are used;
- give comparative scores to the sites;
- track the sites over at least three months to see how live they are kept.

2 Make sure you hunt out copies of the following trade press from *now on*! You might be able to get them free if you are a student, or may have to beg them or borrow them from someone else's desk – however you get them, get them! Usually, you have a choice between the paper version and an on-line version – which may give you just a very little without subscribing, or which might give you really rather a lot without a subscription! Check out both the printed *and* on-line versions if you really want to get up to date with and keep up to date with issues that really matter in the world of marketing communications!

As you work through the book, you will find that different chapters refer to different areas, but all of these areas will have their own trade press and it's not worth waiting until you get to the chapter to sort out what can be a lengthy ordering process, so here goes with a list of at least the major titles you should look for and their website starting points so you can begin the process:

Marketing @: http://www.marketing.haynet.com

Marketing Week @: http://www.mad.co.uk

Campaign @: http://www.campaignlive.com (advertising magazine)

Media Week @: http://www.mediaweek.co.uk

PR Week @: http://www.prweek.net

Precision Marketing @: http://www.mad.co.uk

Revolution @: http://www.revolution.haynet.com

Chapter

2

Planning your marketing communications

An overview of planning

It is worth starting here with an overview of the whole picture. Marketing communications planning and implementation will be most effectively carried out if it is planned with a clear set of objectives, over a timescale using the right tools for the job and with cost-efficiency at its core. That means you need to understand how to organize promotion, the nature of the tools available and how to use the tools of planning in this field. This is the point we have now reached: you should have a better idea of how the business of promotion works, how the minds of consumers work, how promotion aims to reach the psyche of the customer generally, and how specific tools aim to do that individually and as a planned whole.

Let's begin by taking a look at where marketing communications planning fits into the overall picture.

The specifics of marketing communications planning must fit into an overall corporate planning framework, which allows all those involved to see how their functional

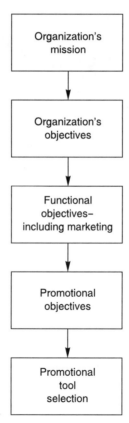

Figure 2.1 The stages that lead to the selection of promotional tools

responsibilities work with those of others. As you read more and more widely, you will realize that many authors develop their own visual and mnemonic aids to describe the planning process. What follows is my own memory jogger, which I drew up after looking at a whole range of texts and study notes.

Figure 2.1 shows that it is an appreciation of the inter-relationship of the elements that is essential. However, in order to be able to decide upon where we want to go, we have to establish where we are, what opportunities exist for us, how the rest of the marketplace is operating and how the overall environment might allow us to exploit the chances that are available for us to take.

The key questions that have to be answered by the process of planning are listed below, and can be summarized as SOSTCA (MMMMM). This model can be applied to any level of planning – business, divisional, marketing or marketing communications. The same questions always have to be asked and answered, and these headings could usefully become the headings with, say, a marketing plan, or, indeed, a marketing communications plan, whether for an e-business or a non-e-business.

Situation	Where are we now and how did we get there?
Objectives	Where do we want to be?
Strategy	How will we get there?
Tactics	Our detailed explanation and justification of activities
Control	What will be measured, when and how will it all be managed?
Action	A calendar of specific events
(MMMMM)	What should be shown on the calendar of activities: i.e.
	Men/women – exactly who will be responsible for the activity
	Money – the cost
	Minutes – exactly when the activity will take place
	Measurement – what information will be gathered to measure what, when
	Management – shows when management meetings will take place

Where are we now and how did we get there? The marketing framework. . .

There are many paths that can be followed. The process of auditing to discover the full truth of present circumstances must be carried out throughout the range of functions, but our focus needs to carry us towards marketing communications (marcomms) planning and implementation via an understanding of marketing planning, so we must look at what is often called the *Marketing Audit*. I have developed my own system, which proves useful both in practical terms as well as in being relatively simple to visualize and memorize for examination purposes. My process for establishing a true

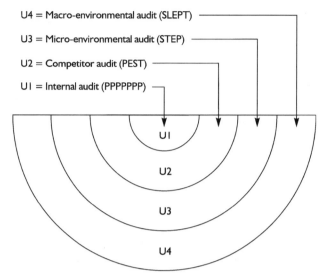

Figure 2.2 The 4U Audit

picture of where you are now is called the 4U Audit – which will, I hope, always work '4U'!

Figure 2.2 illustrates how the corporate environment nestles within the outside world 'Us' of your direct and indirect competitors, the micro-environment and the macro-environment. What do I mean by each of these terms?

Note that you need to use terminology in an acceptable way, so here are some commonly used terms that might help you with this process:

● *Direct competitor* – this is an organization that offers a direct alternative to your product/service in a way that is very close to your own, e.g. Cannon Cinemas and Odeon Cinemas; McDonald's and Burger King; Lycos and Alta Vista. Customers can choose between two different cinemas or two different fast food burger bars or two different search engines. This is direct competition.

● *Indirect competitor* – this is an organization that offers an indirect alternative to your product/service in a way that is different from your own, but serves the same essential purpose on the part of the customer, e.g. Blockbuster Home Video and Odeon Cinemas; Pizza Hut Home Delivery and McDonald's; a branded portal that specializes in entertainment sites rather than a general search engine. As you can see, in each example the customer will still be either entertained or fed, but has chosen a very different way of getting his or her entertainment or food. Taking the cinema example, be aware that other indirect competitors would include a huge range of other leisure and entertainment pastimes.

- *Micro-environment* – all those external factors not directly related to your competitors, but which form a part of the environment within which the whole market operates. An example would be the general change in eating habits towards more healthy options: this is happening and you must note it. It is measurable from existing data or research that you might wish to commission, and it will affect not just your marketplace as, say, Pizza Hut, but the whole social attitude towards fast food versus salad bars, for instance. Many micro-environmental changes come about because of pressures brought to bear by direct and indirect competitors or by interest groups, e.g. the activities of various groups against McDonald's farming methods or the fat content of their burgers. With care, you can 'deal with' the problems and opportunities thrown up by a study of the micro-environment. It might be that the increasing level of boredom with, and blanking out of, banner ads on websites might mean that you have to be very careful about the extent to which you rely on banner ads in future.

- *Macro-environment* – this is not just encountered when looking at other countries with an eye to entering their marketplace, although it does have a specific significance in such cases. If you are a fruit juice bottler, a cold winter in Florida can raise the price of orange juice concentrate on the world market to such an extent that you have to develop new recipes that use less of the expensive orange concentrate and more of other ingredients such as mango juice, passion fruit, etc. Politics here means the widest political climate of a country or region, whilst in the micro-environment it could mean more localized political issues. It might be that the development of a new software technology or hardware development might be just around the corner and there is nothing you can do about it, even though it might change the way you, and all the marketplace, will do business in the future: you need your antennae on full alert at all times to make sure you don't miss the boat!

Let us look more closely at how the 4U Audit works in practice (see Figure 2.3).

U1 – INTERNAL AUDIT (PPPPPPP)

This means that you carry out a full assessment of your internal abilities. The focus on a marketing audit means that it is useful for us to look at the marketing mix in great detail, so, once again, the Seven Ps have their uses. By assessing against each of the Seven Ps (Product, Price, Place, Promotion, People, Processes, Physical Evidence), you will have a framework that will force you to address all the key issues relating to either the single product or service involved or the whole range of products/services under consideration.

Your e-business might be a start-up, or you might be looking at building an e-extension to your existing business – so there is only a plan at this stage about how

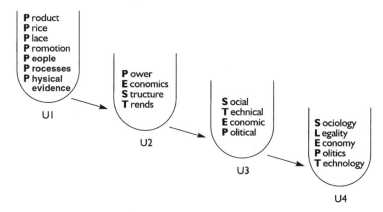

Figure 2.3 Using the 4U Audit – the factors to assess when auditing

the Seven Ps and Seven Cs will be implemented. That does not mean that you do not need an Internal Audit! Even if you are just vetting your plans for internal development, this is a vital part of your business planning process, so, just because you 'don't exist yet' don't think you can ignore the internal dimension of the business you are proposing.

One of the most disconcerting factors I have encountered with start-ups (in particular, though not exclusively) is the mentality that just because something *can* be done, technically speaking, that it *should* be done – and all the emphasis within the marketing mix then falls on to the P for Promotion, without any background work having gone into the *true* marketing issues, which are concerned with bringing something to the market that is actually wanted. A thorough analysis of the Internal Mix should yield useful results when it comes to ensuring that there is balance within the offering and that the organization actually has something to offer that the market will want – so the emphasis will be shifted from selling to buying, and re-buying!

U2 – COMPETITOR AUDIT (PEST)

Look at all your competitors, both direct and indirect. Once again, I have been told by so many e-businesses, especially start-ups, that 'We have no competitors – we'll be the only ones offering this', that it is clear that those proposing the business idea haven't thought through the concept of indirect competition in sufficient detail.

It might well be that you will have no direct competitor, offering exactly what you offer, or even something similar, in a similar manner. It might even be that you will be offering a process that is truly unique, is patented or protected to keep it unique and that the only competition you might face both now and for the next five years, let's say, will be indirect competition or competition from those who mimic your offering but can never match it. Well, that's a great business position to be in – but customers and potential customers can still see your offering as being one of a number of things they can choose to do with their money/time/effort, so beware of assuming you'll have no competition.

Let's say that your business proposal is a B2B portal – well, if all you are offering is a refined search engine (which is what most portals are), don't forget that those searches and discoveries are being made *now*, some other way, and that what you are offering is just another way of doing the same old thing. True, what you are offering might be as far advanced from current searches as a tumble dryer is from a mangle, but not only do you have to get people to be aware of what you are offering, and to understand why they should want to use a tumble dryer instead of a mangle, but then you will have to deal with all those other mangle manufacturers who see their market threatened and suddenly switch to offering tumble dryers too!

If you audit on the basis that you have no competitors, you are being very short-sighted in business terms – so look up, look ahead and *think* like a customer.

The focus here is on seeing all your competitors as pests, or as throwing up challenges which you will need to meet. Thus, the mnemonic PEST really does become memorable. Just go one step further and remember what each letter stands for in *these* circumstances, and you'll be well on your way to showing that you understand what needs to be investigated to build up a full picture.

In this instance, P stands for *Power*, which means assessing and quantifying the power held by each player in the marketplace (maybe market share, number of passengers carried, etc.).

E is for *Economics*, not in the huge, textbook sense, but in terms of which competitor has what type of financial standing within the marketplace; it might even mean an assessment of what players *might* enter the market, even if you are first.

S is for *Structure*, which means that you must analyse the structure of the marketplace via the products/services offered by both your direct and indirect competitors, looking at how the position has arisen and assessing what lessons can be learned from this. Once you have a structural picture of the market, develop a similar picture of the customers within the market. Now, if all this is predictive, because the marketplace doesn't exist in its predicted form until some time after you launch your offering, then that's fine: your aim is to predict as accurately as possible, and that is never easy. Better predictions rely upon greater amounts of more valid data, so the responsibility lies with the researchers to make sure that the information they are gathering is not just relevant, but that it is up to date too. In life, death and taxes might be the only certainties, in e-business the only certainty is change – so be on the lookout for it all the time!

T is for *Trends*, which need to be analysed historically if they are to help in the future – you need a sound basis for prediction here. Certain trends will be well established and therefore easy to track, e.g. more leisure time, higher levels of disposable income, baby-rearing fashions, etc., others will be more difficult because they are just beginning and might not, therefore, yet be seen as trends! If you are heading up a record company, the trend for Britney Spears sound-alikes and look-alikes might grow or die, so you need to be able to predict the next trend – will it be Irish rock, acoustic playing, heavy rock? Will portals cease to be sexy and be replaced by hubs and broadband? Change is all around us – research will help.

U3 – MICRO-ENVIRONMENTAL AUDIT (STEP)

Look at the micro-environment as offering the opportunity to STEP all over your competitors and really succeed by becoming top of the pile! STEP as a mnemonic will allow you to focus on the correct areas to ensure that you are taking on board all points that really matter.

S is for *Social* factors, which must be studied in depth. With a micro-environmental audit for, say, young girls shopping on the web, the micro-S would focus on the social tendencies of the target audience, i.e. the girls themselves, looking at how they often spend time surfing the shopping sites on the web either as members of groups or as individuals, how their fashion sense is heightened by what their pop idols wear or don't wear, etc., whereas the macro-S (see below for more details) would focus on how many female children of what ages lived where and how they differ in general from their predecessors and try to stand out from the crowd. Thus, the micro-S and the macro-S are slightly different. Interestingly, you might want to visit the Barbie website to find out how such research helps with business decisions: the site designers talked to six- to twelve-year-old girls to find out what interested them, and what would keep them coming back to the site. A real interactive world has been built at the http://www.barbie.com site. You can build your own Barbie, tell stories, have a secret backpack full of 'stuff'. Interestingly, it is reported that 98 per cent of the tailor-made Barbies are never purchased (presumably because six- to twelve-year-olds don't have access to credit cards), but the researchers can keep a finger on the pulse of what the target market *wants* from Barbie, and her friends, and have the chance to be on top of social change rather than following a long way behind.

T is for *Technical*, which, if we follow through the above example, would allow us to look at what machinery/equipment/fabrics are available for doll manufacture now, and how they can be made relevant. Can we make clothes more quickly, from lighter weight/cheaper fabrics, if they are only intended to have a short lifespan? Can we make more bendy, athletic Barbies, and better, more lifelike Asian or Afro-Carribean friends for Barbie? Can we have tattoos that disappear, or hair that grows? Or can we just use the website to create such a high level of interaction that the Barbie site becomes a real world for the target market, thereby building a huge level of loyalty? So in this section we look at the technical features that we can control.

E is for *Economic* factors. How much can six- to twelve-year-old girls afford to spend on Barbie and her friends in an average month? Or do they all have access to parental budgets beyond their allowances? Has this profile changed? What about pocket money or allowances themselves – are they going up or down? Do more children now get paid for doing chores, or do parents still pay for toys and thus retain responsibility for selecting them? These economic factors are specific to the micro-environment. And don't forget, although we are still following the Barbie example at this point, the e-factor in 'Barbie World' is very high, and there is a significant e-business profile here.

P is for *Political*, which does not necessarily mean party political, although some politicians specifically court popularity with children who are still not old enough to vote, because they want to be sure they will be the choice of the next generation of voters. If we stick with the Barbie theme, then it can be said that children can be politically aware and have opinions, but that they might see politics in a different way, not in the party structure of the day. You would need to assess this and be aware, for example, of the impact of 'green' politics on today's youth, of the access to Barbie's friends from ethnic minorities, of the feelings against Barbie and all she represents within certain communities. It might be that the children of families who follow a certain faith will have a parental block on visiting the Barbie site, for example. It might sound strange, but even Barbie has become a political football in her time! At this level it might well be the case that 'political' means different things for different classes or groups.

U4 – MACRO-ENVIRONMENTAL AUDIT (SLEPT)

This refers to those factors which will, frankly, happen whilst you have SLEPT. They are the factors about which you can do nothing, but of which you need to be as aware as possible, and which you need to watch like a hawk to try to predict how they might affect the future success of your product/service.

S is for *Sociology*, in the *big* sense! The sociology of a locale, region, country or continent will be studied by the sociologists, not the market researchers, in the first instance. Often linked to historical factors, you must study the sociology of your target audience's geographic and demographic location. If you look at Eire versus Northern Ireland, although two very small populations share the same small land mass and a great deal of common history, you will find that some products choose to show themselves as having the same market position, relative to competitors, in both the north and the south, but that Southern Irish actors and actresses are used in the Eirean TV commercials, whereas the commercials shown in the north are exactly the

same as those shown in England, Wales and Scotland. This is to make the products seem more 'Irish', and thus more socially acceptable, in the south. Some might say that this is a political point, but in reality it has become sociological. See the notes on politics below.

When it comes to great sociological shifts and their impact on e-business in general, one of the key issues here is the fact that most children have more of a relationship with the Internet and the basic concepts of e-anything than their parents. Now, this is not to say that e-business will not come of age until this generation of schoolchildren forms the adulthood of society, but certainly their propensity to accept change and to expect swiftness of communication and a global range of potential suppliers of *anything* is likely to have an enormous impact on the way the e-business develops in the future, and is accepted now.

L is for *Legality*, which must be checked but cannot be changed, unless you change whatever is illegal about your product/service or advertisement. It might be that you are facing new food labelling legislation, or that the law on who you can and cannot mail has altered. It might well be that you are trying to adopt best practice on-line, in an area where there is no law: it is no secret that e-business is posing tremendous problems for the law givers and law enforcers of the world! Laws can affect marketers and promoters in many ways, and as the person planning a promotional programme your audit will focus mainly on laws relating to all types of promotional activities. Up-and-coming changes in legislation that might adversely affect your business can be planned for and even lobbied against.

You should be checking the laws, and potential laws, that affect, and could affect, every aspect of your business, from the products or services you are intending to offer, through the ways in which you select to make them available for sale to the ways in which you promote them. Maybe e-business, more than most forms of business, leaves itself open to some allegations that it is being run like a business in the Wild West – where you get away with what you can until you are caught and prosecuted. Now, this isn't true of all businesses, but, unfortunately, the Gold Rush mentality has infected enough people to give this impression, so that we are now in a situation where the laws and rules governing doing business electronically, and especially on the worldwide web, are being looked at very carefully by legislators the world over – and it is likely that laws will be set, enforced and updated in this field – so auditing needs to be ongoing!

E is for *Economy* in the *big sense*. We are not just looking at single markets here, we need to look at the bigger picture: in times when money is very tight, promoting money off standard product lines can win customers, when an emphasis on continuing high levels of quality might keep some loyal customers but is unlikely to attract new business. Similarly, when levels of disposable income are higher than usual in certain demographic sub-groups, they attract the attention of the marketer. Currently we are seeing an enormous growth in the number of over-fifty-year-olds with a reasonable level of pension income – the 'wrinkly' pound is attracting the efforts of many marketers, such as tour operators for example, who are tailor-making products and services for this affluent age group. And this is compounded by the Silver Surfer phenomenon – not for them the world of Barbie and her chums (though their grandchildren might be entranced), but if you visit http://www.saga.co.uk you'll see one site that shows how the over-fifties target market is being offered its own world on-line – with health, holidays and financial services being available through this site, which itself capitalizes on a well-known brand name in the market.

P is for *Politics*, but, again, in the major sense rather than just the domestic party political sense. The politics of any country totally colours the outlook of its people, even if this is covertly rather than overtly. In terms of international marketing and promotion, it is quite obvious that the political 'climate' of a country or region is a vital factor to be investigated, but it is no less important in terms of domestic marketing and marcomms planning. Following on from the example above, the way that a country treats its elderly will often be mirrored in grey politics in that country – do you have a vocal grey lobby, calling for good later life care, or are the elderly not spoken of as anything other than a drain on resources – or is the elderly person so revered by the family that the thought of residential homes for the aged is ridiculous! Politics, and political decisions, can affect the readiness with which people save or spend, move home or invest in DIY. All businesses are affected by politics, not just e-businesses, but e-businesses have the potential to be even more affected by politics because they are often cross-border businesses and can therefore be affected by the local and national politics of many regions.

T is for *Technology* in the broadest sense, in terms of looking at the capabilities of a region (e.g. Minitel in France affecting the uptake of the Internet) or the lack of them (e.g. reliable telephone connections in Albania). The availability of constant power systems is necessary for so many applications that just a simple break can create chaos. The technological climate of an area must be investigated, as must all the others. Will you take technology forward, or will you rely upon what exists? Will you need to build a technical infrastructure, or will you use what is there? Of course, when it comes to e-business, we aren't just talking about the ability to get an electronic message to someone – they might be able to order goods off the Internet, but is there the delivery infrastructure that will allow you to get those goods delivered? And within the time window you promised?

A country doesn't have to be backward to make delivery difficult – just big! Canada Post, for example, now has a delivery service available for those companies and small businesses that use its website to sell goods on-line – Canada Post did not want to miss out on the delivery potential associated with e-business, so it works in partnership with those companies that would otherwise maybe bypass its services.

The web works wonderfully well in Canada, with most homes being linked to either cable or satellite already for television. The majority of homes have 24-hour 'free' Internet access (i.e. it costs no more when the package includes TV and telephone plus Internet), so using the Internet does not incur a cost. This proves liberating in the extreme for Internet use, allowing free browsing to lead to more sites and therefore open the door to greater familiarity, greater confidence and higher levels of purchasing. Transportation, as well as digital cabling, for example, is a type of technology – so should be considered when auditing!

Where are we now and how did we get there? The specific marketing communications issues

Once you have agreed your marketing position, your marketing objectives will follow, as will an agreement about your marketing strategy.

We are interested in the P for Promotion, or the C for Communication. So we will now turn to the planning process for marketing communications within the marketing planning process. It might be that a part of your overall marketing auditing will involve your marketing communications activities, and their results – it certainly *should* be covered. But you actually need to consider the very specialized nature of marketing communications auditing as a separate entity.

COMMUNICATIONS AUDITS – WHAT THEY ARE

A Communications Audit is an investigation that will allow you to discover the answers to the following questions:

- What are you already doing in terms of your communications effort?
- How, exactly, are you doing it?
- How long have you been doing it for?
- What have the effects of having done it been?

These might seem to be perfectly obvious questions, but you might be surprised that some organizations not only rarely ask these questions, but that even more never bother to dig beneath the glib, simplistic answers to the questions that it might be possible to produce at an instant's notice. There is no point making assumptions about the effect of marketing communications activity – this is dangerous and will always work against you.

The other warning point is that it is *not* enough to ask those who are doing it about what they are doing – you must get out there and ask the recipients of your marketing communications about how they feel about it.

You might be sending your customers what you think is a great series of informative letters, individually addressed, carefully tailored and sent at key moments in the purchasing calendar – your customers might think you are wasting money sending them letters they don't want, don't read and could well do without because they find them irritating. You would only discover this if you actually asked them – so do! This would be an example of the sort of thing you would do as part of a Communications Audit, but, as you can imagine, a real Audit, that is to form the basis for important future planning and decision making, needs to be a formalized, professionally planned business exercise, rather than just a piecemeal investigation into effectiveness.

Communications Audits present an objective report on the communications of an organization. An audit can be widely focused, covering all stakeholder groups, or more narrowly focused on one or more groups, such as customers, employees, investors, the community, etc. It can also be limited to one or more specific communication programmes.

In today's rapidly changing technology-driven environment, organizational communicators are challenged to be more flexible, responsive and innovative in meeting both the immediate communication needs of the organization and anticipating future needs. An audit today must address this dual challenge.

A Communications Audit is akin to a medical check-up or financial audit. It is a thorough and systematic examination to determine what is functioning well and what is not. It will often provide guidance and direction on how communications can be improved.

Its primary purpose is to determine the degree to which communications with specific groups are effective, useful and valuable in supporting and advancing the organization's strategic objectives. Findings of an audit may result in minor or major changes in communications strategies and the ways in which communications are planned and implemented in the future.

You might ask why you should do a Communications Audit if you are moving from Bricks to Clicks. Well, the key, of course, is that if you already exist in the marketplace, you must understand the mindspace you inhabit in your target groups, before you decide to build on that or if you have to shift it!

An excellent example here is the Prudential's launch of Egg. By conducting research into existing attitudes towards the Pru's offering, it was quickly established that there wasn't the brand equity needed in the name and the image to allow an on-line offering to appeal to the agreed target market. Egg was launched as a totally separate entity, because it might not have succeeded as a clear offshoot of the old-fashioned, reliable Pru!

If you do not exist at all, and are starting with a totally clean slate, then research your competitors! Find out where they are in the communications map so you can work out how to position yourself against them.

There is no situation in which it is unnecessary to carry out a Communications Audit!

SO HOW DO YOU DO A COMMUNICATIONS AUDIT?

Audit methods, completion time and costs vary depending upon the audit's scope and the organization. Each organization has its own communications needs, goals and climate. It has a unique culture, history, dynamics, and competitive and financial environments. An audit for one organization will be quite different than that for another. That said, there are some commonalities.

The audit process unfolds in several stages:

I. Planning and design

This involves getting samples of *all* your marketing communications from every part of the organization – a mammoth task, and one which might be made easier by the marketing communications department keeping at least two file copies of everything it creates, or knows is being created, within the organization.

You might think it makes sense to gather all of your external communications, and it does, but don't omit your internal and partner communications too.

Thus, you might be putting out the call for literature from Istanbul and staff letters from Iver, making sure you have staff newsletters from the plant in Cologne as well as from the plant in Coventry. Whatever it takes, you must gather a total pool of what you have been doing. Whilst a big job, this is pretty straightforward when it comes to advertising, photos of exhibits, literature and even websites – but what about the results of your press relations efforts? Well, you can gather the clippings, get the feedback from the assessment services you might be using, etc. And as for internal letters, etc. – well, you might have to be content with a cross-section, plus a list of times/dates when such documents were sent, and to whom.

It could take months to do this, so don't leave it until the last minute, and don't let it stand alone as an activity: by always planning ahead you can make sure you have a sample gathering system in place all the time so you are continuously gathering materials, thereby making this a process, not a one-off huge job! You could then be getting on with your 'Effect Research' at the same time, although again this should be a part of an ongoing process.

The planning and design stage defines the audit's scope and goals, population involved, communications to be audited, audit methods to be used, timeframe and budget. The audit plan is often developed through interviews, discussions and collaboration with a variety of senior managers within the organization and the auditor or audit team.

If much of your communication is virtual then gather this too! Just because it disappeared from the website three months ago doesn't mean it didn't have an impact when it was there – so this word of warning might serve you well – keep back-up copies of everything, of every version of everything, so you can look at it again in the cold light of a new day and be able to discuss and analyse content as well as effect.

II. Research and measurement

Many organizations spend a great deal of time and money finding out what their external marketing communications budget has achieved for them, but never carry out research into the effectiveness of their internal communications, so never discover that they are having to spend millions of pounds telling customers that they will deliver better service when all they really need to do is communicate more effectively with internal audiences about what they expect from them in terms of service delivery! It might be that it's your intranet that needs upgrading, not your Internet site! But a lack of the right sort of research can be your undoing!

The lessons here are clear – if you do it, you must evaluate the effect of it! It really is that simple. Whatever it is – whether it is on-line, off-line, in-line, printed, broadcast or face to face. And it applies to issues like print, where it might seem that this one print job is too small to research, as is the next one, as is the next one – then you get to the end of the year and find you have spent £500 000 on print in total, without any evaluation at all!

Of course, auditing and evaluation cost money, so don't expect to get them done for free. But even if you put aside a small percentage of your total budget at the start of the year for this purpose, you will find you have a much better idea of what is working and what isn't – so you can spend your money more efficiently next time, even if it didn't work well for you this time.

Research and measurement begins with informal, exploratory research and often moves to formal, scientific methods of gathering information. The two informal, exploratory research methods used most often are in-depth interviews and focus groups. The formal, scientific measurement method used most often for primary source research is a survey. Analysis of existing databases of information (prior surveys and other databases) are sometimes used to add a further dimension to the audit findings. This is known as secondary source research.

Depending on the goals and design of the audit, research and measurement of some or all of the following may be involved: face-to-face communications and the grapevine; flow patterns among individuals, departments, divisions and leadership; publications in print, video and audio plus other audiovisuals; large group meetings and events; memos and written communications; leadership and manager-based communications; electronic communications such as e-mail, voice-mail, intranets; and feedback systems.

In addition to communications media, patterns, flow, channels, and technologies, a Communications Audit examines: content clarity and effectiveness; information needs of individuals, work groups, departments and divisions; non-verbal communications and corporate culture issues; and communication impacts on motivation and performance.

You need to be sure you are auditing those areas upon which people can be most affected by communications: people's knowledge, understanding and perceptions; opinions, attitudes and beliefs; issues, concerns and feelings; needs and preferences; abilities; intentions; and behaviours.

III. Analysis and reporting

The final phase is analysis and reporting. After examining all the information gathered in the research and measurement phase, an analysis is conducted to determine how well the communications satisfy the needs of the organization and the stakeholder groups today and how well these communications will serve changing needs in the operational future (one to two years).

Conduct of a Communications Audit is usually performed by outside consultants because of their professional experience, expertise and objectivity. I have been commissioned to carry out quite a few audits, and have found that the fact that I am an external consultant has helped me to gather information that might not have been made available to someone from within the organization itself – this has particularly been the case when gathering information and feedback on internal communications programmes!

In addition, an independent third party's guarantee of confidentiality often produces a higher level of trust from employees and other stakeholders in in-depth interviews, focus groups and surveys. This often produces more open, candid, real-world information than that which can be acquired by in-house research efforts. This is especially true when an organization is in the process of transformation. I have been told several times by a communications team head that the intranet and internal communication are top of the agenda for an organization, only to discover that the employees feel that the intranet is unappealing, dull, full of data they don't want to access and of facts they don't want to know, whilst senior management seem to view it as an extension of the company newsletter that was always full of the Chairman's smiling face or of cheque presentations and the obligatory retirement photographs! An outsider can get to the truth very effectively, and will sometimes be believed more readily than an insider would. Sad, but true!

WHEN WOULD YOU PERFORM AN AUDIT?

Though it is always advisable to audit an individual communication's effectiveness on an ongoing basis as an integral part of the communications cycle, broader communications audits are essential when an organization is undergoing change. For example: major expansion, merger or acquisition; reduction of personnel; new functions or business lines are undertaken; external circumstances are forcing changes; and when there is an acquisition of new technology – especially if it is information or communications technology. It might be that you conduct an audit as an integral part of your ongoing business auditing cycle, and my best advice would be to both audit individual projects as they occur and keep building into a moving overall communications profile and picture over time, so you get early warnings when they appear and can do you most good, helping you to decide on tactical responses!

Benefits of an audit

A well done Communications Audit will produce a clear understanding of how communications are really working and the degree to which they are satisfying needs. From this flows a number of possibilities: improved productivity and competitive advantage, better use of existing and future communications and information technology, more efficient use of time, discovery of hidden information resources, improved morale and a more vibrant corporate culture, among others.

In the fast moving world of e-business, constant auditing of the total business, with a particular emphasis on communications, should be the norm. But I'm afraid to say that often it is far from the norm. Why? Because in a fast moving business it is very tempting to be always looking forward – and that can leave little time for looking backwards. The importance of (a) understanding where you are and (b) learning from what you have done cannot be overemphasized. Sure, plan ahead, but for heaven's sake, don't forget to keep checking on where you are moving ahead *from*!

 ## Where do we want to be?

So, once you have found out where you are, and have analysed how you got there, you can decide where you want to go. You will set your objectives. In a marketing plan these will be marketing objectives, such as capturing 21 per cent market share, or increasing volume sales by £2 million, for example. But we are considering marketing communications, so we have to consider a different type of objective.

What is your communications objective? Unless you can answer this question you cannot begin to plan or implement a communications programme. It doesn't matter whether it's an e-business or not, the fundamentals remain the same. So let's start at a logical point: What could your objectives be?

There is no such thing as a definitive list, but here are some reasonable objectives for marcomms:

- Sell direct to consumers.
- Create direct sales leads for your sales force.
- Support your sales force in the field.
- Create product awareness.

Specific	All objectives must be drawn up precisely – this means they relate to specific, detailed end results and are not merely vague statements of intent.	
Measurable	If an objective is not quantified it cannot be measured – if it cannot be measured, how will you know whether or when it has been achieved?	
Achievable	What is the point of setting sights so high that goals are unlikely to be achieved? It is demotivating and reflects poorly on the whole organization.	
Relevant	This means ensuring that objectives are relevant to the overall thrust of the business – don't undermine all your other efforts, use the right tool for the job.	
Timed	Objectives must be achieved within agreed timescales – be it by the end of day three or within the next 48 months.	
Targeted	You will target different sectors of the market with different objectives – don't just set 'blanket' objectives.	

Figure 2.4   Defining objectives

- Inform/educate about product uses.
- Stimulate product trial.
- Remind existing users.
- Reassure existing users.
- Encourage extra sales within a timeframe (short term).
- Retaliate against competitor presence.

The specific reason why any of these might be your objective must be considered, and will depend on the circumstances you find yourself to be in. Care should be taken when setting any objectives, including promotional objectives, with the very useful mnemonic SMARTT coming into play, which is explained in Figure 2.4.

Once you have decided your objectives, your aims, then you can decide your strategy. This means selecting from your toolbox the right promotional tools to allow you to get the job done. By weighing the advantages and disadvantages of each of the promotional tools that this text deals with, you will develop an overall pattern for your promotional programme. Then you can decide on tactics: the weight to be given to each tool; how, over time, each will be deployed to balance your promotional achievements. Look at the ways that certain tools are good at certain jobs, reassess in your mind how timescales can affect effectiveness. Of course, all of this activity has to be paid for somehow – so let's look at getting the money sorted out!

 ## Budget setting

Marketing budgets may be broken down into an operating costs section, a product development and research section, and a promotional expenditure section (sometimes referred to as the promotional appropriation). Organizations vary in their budget-setting framework, and there is no right or wrong way for overall budgeting to be calculated in this broad sense – it will depend on the business and, often, historical methods.

When it comes to the promotional budgeting, budgets may be set against a product, a product range, a brand, a brand group, a business unit, a division or an entire business. Once again, you will probably find that, until you reach board level, there is little you can do to influence this framework. That said, when it comes to a specific budget there are many ways to decide the amount to be spent upon promotion, and many of them are considered below.

In e-business, the setting of promotional budgets has been one of the biggest reasons for the lack of credibility in terms of business plan acceptance that I am aware of. So many business plans have been written that contain either multi-million pound/dollar communications budgets, that it is often clear that the person writing the business

plan truly believes that if you spend enough money on marketing communications (or just advertising as many seem to think) then the product/service/dotcom will succeed. Well, it's just not true, but it seems that it has to be seen to not be true time and time again before business proposers, and even some investors, will believe it.

Not even a big name will save you (HM Queen Elizabeth, Joanna Lumley and William Shatner have all been associated with dotcom flops) if the business proposition isn't right. So throwing money at advertising can, literally, be just a waste of money. Thus, how you have set your budget comes to the fore.

THE ARBITRARY METHOD

This means you pick a figure by hunch and work within it! Yes, you're right, it sounds odd and is largely based on the experience of the person picking the figure. This method has little in its favour, but should be mentioned if only because so many organizations still seem to rely on it. An alternative is simply to work within the budget handed down from on high, without putting any work into arguing for a different figure based on another budget-setting method. To be fair, many promotional campaign managers, whatever their title might be, find themselves having to work within this sort of framework. It at least has the advantage that you know an amount of money is being made available for promotion, but it has little else to recommend it.

PERCENTAGE-OF-SALES METHODS

These look either at the past performance of a product/brand, etc., or at its predicted future performance. There are some problems here. First, what percentage do you spend? Despite the fact that some people throw around 'guestimates' of 3 per cent for B2B and 20 per cent for B2C, there is no real or right answer here – remember that! Second, if you are working on historical performance you are not recognizing changing market forces, and if you are looking ahead your estimate is dependent on the accuracy of your forecasting. What percentage to use can be addressed by examining industry averages. But then, are you an average performer within the industry, or do you want to rise above this?

When looking backwards in time at past performance you are at least setting a figure in line with sales levels you know were achieved last year, but can you achieve them this year? Are you aiming to maintain market share or increase it? If you had a poor year last year, should this year's promotional budget suffer because of it? Will your competitors be spending the same? All in all, although this is a very popular method of setting a budget, it can hold you back and can be misleading.

When looking forwards you need to be pretty sure that you are going to meet your sales targets, or you will be overspending wildly. Indeed, overspending early in the period due to poor forecasting can lead to one of the worst possible positions – results coming in show you will not hit targets, so promotional budgets are slashed and you end up not only with little or no promotional presence towards the end of the period, but an incomplete effect achieved by what you spent to start with.

THE UNIT PERCENTAGE METHOD

This means you carry out detailed costing analyses on each unit produced and add in a percentage to the selling price that is to be allocated directly to promotion. This has a built-in problem in that you still have to decide what percentage to add, as well as being directly tied into sales levels, which might be highly seasonal. It is used a lot in the automotive industry and in fields where the unit costs of a product, or service, are quite high.

THE COMPETITIVE PARITY METHOD

This has merit – it means that you look at what your competitors spend (or the expenditure of those whose offerings currently satisfy the needs of the marketplace to which you are aiming to bring a new, alternative way of achieveing the same satisfaction levels – or higher) and match or exceed this, depending on your position in the market. This method can be very useful if you are entering a new market, when what others spend can at least guide you. But no two marketing mixes are the same, and who is to say that the promotional mix chosen by competitors will be the one that is best for you? Also, if you miscalculate your competitors' expenditure you can totally miscalculate your own budget! It is worth remembering that most media monitoring services can only monitor the ratecard value of the media presence that your competitor has out there – they don't actually know what they paid for it!

THE OBJECTIVE-AND-TASK METHOD

Sometimes also called the target-sum method, this method at least does not get bogged down in the questions that all the previous methods ask, i.e. how much should we spend. Rather, this method approaches budget setting from the other direction by asking how much it will cost to achieve given objectives. Here you begin by deciding what you want to achieve, design the best promotional plan to achieve those objectives, cost the whole programme and use that figure as your budget. This sounds as though it is the perfect way to set a budget, but even this is not perfect, as you might well exceed what the product/brand can, in reality, afford. Not only this, but, because all markets are so dynamic, whilst it is fine to set overall promotional strategies in place ahead of time, you really do need to retain flexibility of both implementation and budget spending over time. This is particularly the case with e-business, where the dynamism of the marketplace might mean that guerrilla tactics,

and low budgets, might work for a short period, but then the entry of a giant competitor might mean you have to react, match spending or lose share of media voice and mindspace rapidly!

THE COMPOSITE METHOD

This means using several budgeting techniques all at the same time and is, in truth, the approach most often adopted. A mixture of the arbitrary method with a nod in the direction of a percentage of sales, usually under the auspices of a set figure, but with some recognition of the task in hand, is often used by organizations who operate in the real world, rather than in the academic textbook!

There really is no such thing as a perfect, single method of setting a budget. Look at the situation in hand and discuss the alternatives, deciding which is the best, given the circumstances. What you should be able to do is at least have an idea of the comparative merits and demerits of each method, and be able to apply them to any situation the examiner gives you.

 ## Summary of chapter two

In this chapter we have given an in-depth insight into how all planning works.

An overview of planning

The introduction of the SOSTCA (MMMMM) planning framework, which leads into the rest of the chapter.

Where are we now and how did we get there? The marketing framework. . .

This section allows a detailed insight into the whole auditing process. The author introduces her unique 4U Audit for the total marketing auditing process and discusses what communications audits are, and how to do them.

Where do we want to be?

This section addresses the issue of what types of objectives can be set as marketing communications objectives.

Budget setting

This section takes a look at the key ways in which budgets can be set, as well as their strengths and weaknesses.

Self test questions and opinion development

These are not exam questions, nor are they meant to represent the sort of question you might expect to face anywhere else. They are designed to help you check whether you have understood the content of this chapter. All you have to do is read the questions, give them some thought and maybe jot down some notes on what your response might be. Not all the questions will have factual answers – rather, they might encourage you to think about a topic or an issue and formulate an opinion based upon what is now, hopefully, a better understanding of the topic.

What does SOSTCA (MMMMM) stand for?

What is the SLEPT of the 4U Audit? What does it mean to marketers?

What is more important – auditing or setting objectives?

What stages are there in carrying out a Communications Audit?

Who do you think should be involved in a Communications Audit either for the organization you work for, or for one that you know?

Name three different types of communications objectives, with three examples from current communications campaigns for e-businesses for each.

Write notes on all the possible ways that a well-known manufacturer of a leading brand of motor car who is planning on adding a website to sell cars globally, through assigned distributors, could set a marketing communications budget, with the most likely method first and the least likely method last. Why are they in that order?

If just spending a lot of money on marketing communications always worked, then all the dotcoms that ever launched with multi-million pound budgets would now be famous and doing well. So what do you have to do within your communication planning to make sure it's successful, other than just spend a lot?

 ## Extending knowledge and understanding

You are encouraged to undertake the following activities to further your knowledge and understanding of the topics covered in this chapter in the following ways:

1 For an organization of your choice (preferably your own or that of a relative/friend), try to find out what their stated marketing communications objectives are, or have been in the past. Are they good? Are they useful? Or are they 'woolly'? How does the quality of marketing communications objectives affect life in the real world?

2 If you want to see how things work in the real world, try some surfing – often a good guess at a product's name, plus '.com' or '.co.uk' within a search engine will get you to your favourite brands.

For example, just by entering 'coca-cola.com' into the Lycos search engine I found myself able to go to a fascinating site – the Coca-Cola Enterprises Inc. website – just take a look for yourself: this is a great website that takes you through the whole production process for Coke, that shows you an insight into the whole marketing process and tells you about their ethics.

Find this site @: http://www.cokecce.com

When you have visited this site, then go to the Consumer-facing Coke site.

Find this site @: http://coca-cola.com

In what ways are the sites different? What do you think are the reasons for the differences? Does it make sense for Coke to have two sites like this? What do you think are the communications objectives behind each? What will Coca-Cola be measuring for each site to judge whether it is a success or not?

What insights have you gained about the different ways in which the web can be used to enhance a non-web-based business?

Chapter

3

Above the line
communication methods

What exactly are above the line media?

Above the line refers to all media upon which a commission is paid. It refers to television, press, posters, cinema, radio, and certain applications of electronic media and direct mail. The term 'above the line' is a traditional term that goes back to the times when advertising agencies would send their bill to their client with a list of media upon which they had already received commission at the top of the page, and then, below a line drawn across the page, a list of all the other activities they had carried out on behalf of their client for which they were yet to receive payment. Thus, 'above the line' and 'below the line' were born as terms referring to the different media.

HOW THE COMMISSION SYSTEM WORKS

The commission system is another tradition in the media that grew through practice. It actually refers to a discount on advertising space given by the media owner to a recognized agency or media-buying shop. It works like this. Media owners find it beneficial to deal with the 'bulk buying' centres represented by agencies and media shops. This means they are able to have smaller sales forces and a concentrated sales effort, rather than having to keep in touch with all potential advertisers direct. Media owners are therefore prepared to offer a discount to these bulk purchasers, the percentage of which will vary from medium to medium, but which is generally about 15 per cent.

Whilst the media owner will grant this discount to an agency, they will not do so to a client direct, although normal sales-driven discounting does of course occur in all situations when necessary. Thus, whilst the client is charged for 100 per cent of the media space cost by the agency, the agency pays the media owner 100 per cent less their discount. The agency pockets the difference – this is their 'commission' (see Figure 3.1).

Some clients prefer to deal with their agency on a commission-only basis, where the agency keeps all the commission on media purchasing, and finances all other work carried out on the account from this commission. Other clients prefer the agency to pass the discount on to them, paying the agency only the exact amount that they have paid for the space, with all the work carried out on the account being charged for separately on an itemized basis. Many client companies have developed a system where they use a mixture of both methods, with a portion of the discount being passed on to them and with a variety of methods of charging for services rendered by the agency being employed.

Indeed, with the introduction of media shops, and the splitting of the media planning and buying functions away from many full service agency accounts, together with the pressure of the recession meaning that clients have increasingly wanted every pound

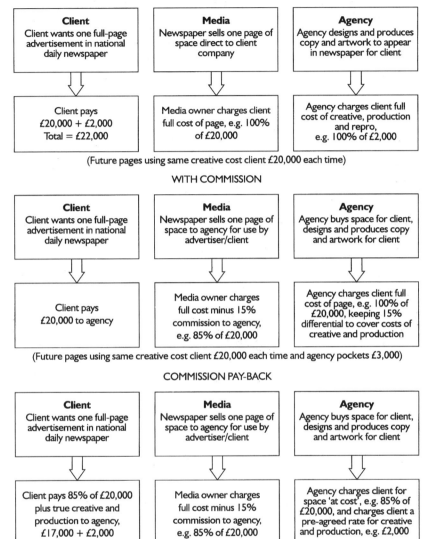

Figure 3.1 The commission system

they spend to be producing a tangible and measurable result, the use of commission-only payment systems has all but disappeared, with either a straight fee basis, or a mixture of fee and commission becoming the norm in the client–agency relationship. Indeed, figures from the Advertising Association show that more than 50 per cent of accounts are now handled on a split commission/fee basis in the UK.

GENERAL ASPECTS RELATING TO ABOVE THE LINE MEDIA PLANNING FOR E-BUSINESS

The above the line media are television, press, radio, posters and cinema. The growth in the availability of 'other electronic' media is still in its infancy, but it will be dealt with under each of the 'traditional media' headings. Each section will also look specifically at how the medium in question is best used for e-businesses of different types – but the key here is to gain a full understanding of a medium and how it works.

- *Inter-media decisions*: decisions to be made between media, e.g. should you use television or press?
- *Intra-media decisions*: decisions to be made within a medium, e.g. should you use the *Daily Telegraph* or *The Times*, having decided to use press instead of television?

All media decisions must be made in the light of the actual situation. Factors to consider are:

- Target audience.
- Budget.
- Timing.
- Nature of product/service.
- Nature of task (e.g. launch, build loyalty).
- Historical activity.
- Competitor activity.

Because there are so many variables, it is impossible to say something like: 'If you are launching a new B2C website that target teenagers you must use television advertising'. If anyone ever says to you, '*Of course* we will use *x* medium', you must be the one who stops them and asks 'Why?'.

The word *why* can be the most useful in advertising campaign planning, as in all promotional planning. There are also some other definitions that you could do with understanding, so here's some jargon explained:

- *Target audience*: the audience you aim to reach with your advertisement. The number of members of the audience may be thousands or millions, and you will develop your cost per thousand (CPT) for reaching them by dividing the media costs by the number you reach.
- *Reach*: the percentage of the potential audience you reach, or cover, with your advertising. The same as *cover*.

- *Frequency*: the number of times this audience sees your advertisement. Equates with OTS (opportunities to see) and OTH (opportunities to hear). It is an average, not a specific.
- *Ratecard*: the rates published by media owners for the medium they are offering for sale.
- *Burst advertising*: the term used to describe a short, sharp, heavy burst of advertisements, where a large 'share of voice' within the chosen medium is the aim. This type of high-density advertising usually occurs at the start of a campaign and at intermittent periods thereafter. The aim is to gain maximum awareness and impact in a short space of time.
- *Drip advertising*: the term used to describe an ongoing low level of advertising activity. Used to keep the product/service in the audience's mind.

Each medium has two types of characteristic: its media characteristics and its creative characteristics.

Think of it this way. The media characteristics refer to those aspects of the medium relating to how it reaches what type of audience, i.e. the factors that influence the choice of, quite simply, a blank space.

The creative characteristics refer to those aspects that involve what you then do, creatively, with that blank space, or empty airtime.

Of course, each set of factors will affect the other and, in turn, influence the choice of medium.

In an advertising agency, because all members of the account team are well versed in their own specialism, say the creative aspects, that does not mean that they know nothing about the other aspects, such as the media characteristics. Through discussion and teamwork a media selection will be made, with the account handler steering the discussion by introducing useful little pointers such as the budget available!

When looking at above the line media selection, it is tempting to ask which comes first – the creative considerations or the media considerations, or, indeed, the budget, historical performance, etc. Just like the chicken and egg question, there is no right answer. Team discussions leading from briefing sessions mean that the balance of influence will be different every time. Try not to get bogged down in 'what is more important' at this stage, therefore; rather, concern yourself with gaining an overall understanding of the points for each medium that would need to be considered – all around.

Now let's take a look at each of the above the line media in turn – we'll consider the 'pure' media issues initially, then consider the application possibilities for e-businesses.

 **Television**

This is a powerful medium with which we are all familiar. Different time segments have different viewer profiles. Certainly, each television programme will have a different viewer profile to all others, with groups of similar types of programme having similar types of profiles. Indeed, the companies that have won the franchise to broadcast are in the business of buying and making programmes to broadcast that will attract a certain type of audience – an audience they believe will be a saleable commodity to advertisers. That said, all those who currently hold franchises did have to put forward proposals in their franchise bids that showed the Independent Television Commission (ITC) that they would not simply run programmes designed to attract 'lowest common denominator' audiences, or just the very lucrative B, C1 or C2 housewife to whom most fast-moving consumer goods (fmcg) marketers wish to speak.

Thus, with careful planning and the purchasing of specific timed spots on television, it is possible to reach almost any type of viewer in the UK. Bearing in mind that about 98 per cent of the UK population own at least one television set, you have an almost unique opportunity to enter the sitting rooms of almost everyone in the country. However, because television can be an expensive medium to buy and produce advertisements for, it might not be the most cost-effective method of reaching your target audience. And cost-effectiveness is one of the key factors in planning media selection. It just is not good enough to say 'We want to reach lots of people so let's advertise on the telly', though you might be surprised at how often that conversation can be heard around a board table, where television is seen as the panacea for all advertising problems.

CREATIVE CHARACTERISTICS

Television is a very flexible medium creatively, offering:

- Sound, vision, movement.
- The ability to demonstrate.
- Slice of life opportunities.
- 'Serialization' opportunities, e.g. Nescafé Gold Blend advertisements.
- Lots of entertainment opportunities.

But even television has its problems:

- You cannot smell a television commercial.
- Unless you respond, there is no sampling opportunity.
- Commercials are transient and can easily be missed.

- Zipping (fast-forwarding commercials on video-recorded programmes) and zapping (changing channels during the commercial break) are also problems, but unquantifiable ones!

Using the framework of the medium itself is possible, so many television commercials are treated almost like mini television programmes, with the expectations we have as viewers of anything we see on television being met: some commercials are mock news programmes, some are mock chat shows, and so on. So the conventions of the medium as a whole are capitalized upon by the creative teams developing advertisements for the medium itself. Why is this? Well, a viewer will feel comfortable when viewing a commercial that meets their expectations, but, equally, this means that many creative teams specifically aim to fight against the conventions in question. Some commercials are designed to challenge our expectations of what a television commercial should be – a commercial for a bank that is all text in black and white with no sound track might actually catch our attention more than one with a more 'conventional' approach, purely because it is so out of the ordinary. Of course, that sort of creative treatment would need to match with the bank's overall proposition to the marketplace, or else there would be a problem.

This is a key point: whatever the creative characteristics of any medium, they should only be used insofar as they meet with the overall campaign aims and objectives and live with the integrated promotional programme.

Thus, with television, whilst so many creative possibilities exist, the creative treatment should be a part of a synergistic approach to campaign planning.

MEDIA CHARACTERISTICS

This is a field full of terminology that needs to be explained, so here are some essential television media terms:

- *Impacts* – an impact is the actual exposure of an advertisement to a member of the target audience, i.e. one person seeing an advert once. They are a vital measurement as they are used to calculate cost per thousand and, in turn, station average price. They might also be referred to as impressions, or messages.
- *Station average price (SAP)* – the currency against which the majority of business on ITV is negotiated; the same as cost per thousand. SAP is the average CPT that a particular station has sold its airtime at over a particular month, as follows:
  - Gross Revenue divided by Station Impacts = Station Cost.
  - Station average price can be further calculated to give SAPs for particular demographics, e.g. men, ABC1 adults, etc.

- *Dayparts* – There is an agreement between the agency and broadcaster which will stipulate when adverts are shown. The day is divided into segments and each segment is allocated a percentage of rating delivery, e.g.:
  - 0930–1715   25 per cent
  - 1716–1930   35 per cent
  - 1931–2300   30 per cent
  - 2301–2630   10 per cent.
  - (NB: a 'day' lasts from 0600 to what is termed 2959, i.e. six o'clock the following morning; therefore, 0300 on Monday = 2700 Sunday.)

- *TVR (television rating)* – each TVR represents 1 per cent of a specified audience, e.g. 40 housewife TVRs; 1000 TVRs, all adults. Whilst you cannot reach 100 per cent of an audience, you can reach less than 100 per cent more than once, so TVRs are actually an expression of both cover and frequency. The TVR is used by the broadcasting industry to measure the audience for a programme or a commercial break. It is done by comparing the audience to the population as a whole. If, for example, a soap opera achieves a 'Housewife TVR of 30 in Yorkshire', this means that 30 per cent of all housewives in the Yorkshire region watched an average minute of that episode, while the other 70 per cent watched another channel or were not watching television at all. TVRs are calculated for each minute of all channels measured. Programmes and commercial breaks take their TVRs from the average TVR for the relevant minutes. TVRs are not to be confused with 'channel share'.

- *Channel share or Share* – the percentage of the viewing audience watching one channel rather than any of the others, over a given period of time, e.g. a channel share of 37 per cent for ITV in September means that, of all the individuals watching television in an average minute in September, 37 per cent were watching ITV and the others were watching other channels or their VCR. The calculation is made minute by minute, and an average taken. Channel share is sometimes referred to as 'audience share', 'share of viewing', 'percentage share' or just 'share'. It should not be confused with TVR.

- *Overlap* – used to describe that point of an ITV region able to receive the signal of more than one terrestrial commercial channel.

- *Gross homes* – all those homes able to receive an ITV region's programmes. Overlap homes are counted two or three times.

- *Net homes* – overlap homes are allocated to one region only.

- *Revenue share* – the percentage of all ITV advertising revenue that one regional contractor commands.

- *Flow* – an analysis of the audience for the five terrestrial channels, 'other' and VCR playback. It shows how many viewers, at each minute, were watching the same channel as in the previous minute, those who were watching another channel or their VCR the previous minute (i.e. they have joined the programme) and how many who were watching the channel the previous minute have changed to another channel or their VCR (i.e. have switched out). It also shows who had their set on the previous minute and have now switched off, or vice versa. Used by broadcasters to construct competitive schedules.

The ownership of television broadcasting companies is changing as this book is being written – the ITV Network website is a great place to visit to find out what is going on and being planned for ITV (http://www.itv.co.uk).

Currently, it is possible to buy television airtime from a mixture of sales forces that work specifically for a television company, or sales houses which represent a number of companies – but even that is a constantly changing situation.

BUYING AND SELLING AIRTIME

Airtime is usually sold on a spot-by-spot basis with three commercial breaks per hour. Only seven minutes of advertising per hour is allowed, rising to eight minutes at peak times (6.00 p.m. to 10.30 p.m.). Airtime is sold in metric lengths, with 30 seconds being the most common. The laws of supply and demand apply in this market, and television companies operate on a pre-empt, auction system. This means that the highest bidder wins the spot in question, unless the original purchaser pays what is called a 'non-pre-empt premium', which safeguards their right to the spot. The actual rate will depend on the buyer's judgement of the size and nature of the audience, with the ratecard being the starting point for negotiation. Television airtime buying is not for the amateur! The following gives you some idea of the current comparative cost indices for television airtime, with 100 for 30 seconds being the norm:

60 seconds: 200
50 seconds: 167
40 seconds: 133
30 seconds: 100
20 seconds: 80–85
10 seconds: 50

As can be seen, there is a 'penalty' for buying short periods of time – bear this in mind if you are putting forward plans for 'top-and-tail' 10-second spots that appear at the beginning and end of a commercial break. They are a good idea creatively and can add real impact to a campaign, but they cost a lot!

The actual cost of airtime and the specific structure of ratecards varies from contractor to contractor, so it is impossible to generalize.

The other factor which means that a ratecard can only ever be used as a starting point is the way in which either discounts are offered or surcharges are added. Television companies like to get new advertisers on to their channel, or encourage test marketing in their area, and thus they offer discounts other than the usual commission arrangement. Alternatively, they levy surcharges in order to allow the media buyer to ensure the position in the break they want, etc.

When planning television campaigns it is not just the spot cost that must be considered, but also the overall aim of the campaign. Burst advertising, as a general rule of thumb, would employ 400 TVRs over four weeks, utilizing a cross-section of airtime. A ball-park figure for this level of activity would be £1.2 million which, over the course of the month in question, would allow the advertiser to reach their audience as follows:

- 82 per cent of the adult population (i.e. 35 725 000 adults) would see the advert at least once. This is known as one-plus cover.

- 40 per cent of the adult population (i.e. 17 427 000 adults) would see the advert four times or more. This is known as four-plus cover.

- Coverage of the population would grow very quickly initially, with frequency, rather than cover, building more the further through the month (and the accrued TVRs) you move.

Drip advertising is sometimes used by well-established brands, or brands that have been launched recently. Again, as a rule of thumb, about 50 TVRs per week would be bought. The cover and frequency of TVR packages have been calculated for you, so all you have to do is refer to the appropriate table (see Figure 3.2). Do remember that the length of a television spot (60 seconds or 10 seconds) does not affect its TVRs.

No. of TVRs	1 + coverage	Average frequency/OTS
100	50	2.0
200	67	3.0
300	75	4.0
400	80	5.0
500	83	6.0
600	86	7.0
700	88	8.0
800	89	9.0
900	90	10.0
1000	91	11.0

Figure 3.2 Approximate coverage and frequency guide (assumes ITV/C4 80:20 split)

RESEARCH

So what are you buying? One of the oft-quoted concerns with television advertising is that it is expensive, with anything less than a £500 000 expenditure on airtime really not making much of a dent in terms of TVRs. Thus, the research that shows planners and buyers what they are planning and buying is vitally important.

The Broadcasters' Audience Research Board (BARB) is the main television industry source of audience data. It is owned jointly by the BBC, ITV, Channel 4, Channel 5, BSkyB, Flextech and the IPA. It commissions professional research suppliers to measure how many people are watching television (audience measurement) and their enjoyment of programmes (audience reaction). The ITC subscribes to both services.

BARB's Audience Measurement Service provides estimates of television viewing on a minute-to-minute basis of all channels received in the UK. The sample of 4485 households is constructed to be representative of 17 ITV regions and 12 BBC regions. An Establishment Survey of some 40 000 interviews per year is conducted on a rolling basis to provide the profiles of the television households for panel control purposes and to provide a pool from which new households may be recruited to the panel. The activity of television sets, VCRs, and cable and satellite decoders is monitored electronically, and all permanent residents in panel households and visitors declare their presence in a room while a television is on by pressing an allocated button on a special handset. Throughout each day, the meter system collects viewing information and holds it in a memory store. Each night, the data from all the panel households is automatically transferred to the data processing centre via phone lines, and results are available daily. Under contract from BARB, RSMB Television Research Limited is responsible for the Establishment Survey, panel control, panel maintenance and quality control, while Taylor Nelson Sofres is responsible for supplying and installing meter systems, data collection and results processing.

Other facts recorded are the individual age, sex, social class, marital status and ethnic origin of the viewer, plus the number of television sets in the household, whether a video recorder is owned, the work status of the housewife, the work status of the adults and the adult terminal education age. The sample is disproportionate and weighted results are produced in both electronic and printed forms.

The main panel for the BARB was set up in the early 1990s to fulfil a number of objectives, namely:

- *To measure guest viewing more accurately.* Guests in or out of home viewing accounts for some 10 per cent of television viewing. Until recently, guest characteristics were taken as those of the average audience at the time of viewing. The new system allows true guest viewing to be measured at the time of viewing.

- *To measure video usage, recording and playback, using a system called 'fingerprinting'.* When a transmission is recorded the videotape is marked, when it is played back it can be recognized. This is referred to as 'time-shift' viewing, and the ability to measure this means there are now two television currencies: 'live viewing', i.e. the viewing that took place when the programme was broadcast; and 'consolidated viewing', i.e. live viewing with all time-shift viewing added.

- *A larger sample allowing more accurate measures of smaller audiences.* As the number of UK television channels grows, so television audiences are likely to become more fragmented. In theory, advertisers will want to target more discrete audiences rather than merely mass markets. Thus, the new panel samples disproportionately large numbers of 'desirable' audiences.

- *Boundaries of taste.* In summer 1997, the ITC began to place a series of questions in the BARB's special questionnaire booklet (see above) each week. Respondents were asked to identify anything they had seen on television in the preceding week which they judged to be 'outstandingly good', and what it was. They are also asked if they had seen anything, including advertisements, of which they personally strongly disapproved, to identify the item and note reason for disapproval. The final question was 'do you think it was wrong for it to have been shown?'. Since 1998, the BBC and BSkyB have shared the results of these questions and propose to publish the findings quarterly, starting in 1999.

OTHER TELEVISION OPTIONS IN THE UK

Satellite and cable

These forms of viewing have been widely available since 1989. Subscribers must buy or rent a dish or box to be able to receive any programmes, and then must also buy a de-scrambling device in order to be able to watch certain specific channels. Once the satellite is set up viewing can begin – many mainstream hours of viewing are free, but movie channels, for example, usually have to be paid for on a monthly subscription basis.

Both forms of getting broadcasts into the home offer the advertiser more opportunities to talk to potential customers. Although research is available on these media, and therefore there is knowledge about who an advertiser would be addressing, ratecards are even harder to stick to in this field, as, since it is a comparatively new medium, there is still an enormous amount of negotiation going on! Discounted rates, special deals and packages are the norm, so it is difficult to give any price guidance.

Digital television

Digital television is now rolling out across the UK too. The trade press is full of stories about the difference that digital TV will make to the UK, the main thrust of digital being that fact that very high resolution programming can be delivered to a household by request or as the result of the household having elected to purchase a channel. This gives viewers a huge choice (thousands of channels can enter the home) and the channel owners the chance to know exactly who is viewing what.

What is digital television? Digital television is a new, more efficient method of transmission which can squeeze several television channels into the space currently used to carry a single analogue channel. This will create opportunities for many more new channels and programme services. Eventually, all television services in the UK will be transmitted digitally.

What does it mean for viewers? By using digital technology, around 200 channels, perhaps more, are being made possible. Digital also offers other advantages to the viewer, such as widescreen pictures, CD-quality sound, and near video-on-demand (where a film is shown with different start times on several different channels so that the viewer can choose a convenient time to start watching). Interactive services such as home banking, home shopping and connection to the Internet are being made available digitally through the television set.

How does it work exactly? Digital television has two main building blocks: picture production and transmission to the home.

- *Picture production.* Television pictures comprise a successive series of picture fields changing at 50 times a second which, if directly converted to a digital signal, would require 216 million bits of information a second. From frame to frame, much of this information is repetitive and therefore redundant. A more sophisticated approach uses computer analysis to predict changes in motion between frames and keep, as information, only the unpredictable portions. A further process, DCT, is able to reassemble all the remaining information, making it easier to identify only the wanted detail. All other parts are discarded.

- At the receiving end, the essential information is decoded while the previously discarded detail is reproduced. When these two elements are brought together again a picture is formed that has virtually no loss in quality. A typical picture now occupies only about 3–6 Mbit/s, a reduction of about 1/50th from the original 216 Mbit/s. This form of compression, known as MPEG-2, has become a world standard.

- *Digital terrestrial transmission.* Current analogue signals using the PAL System I standard reach about 99 per cent of the UK population via a network of some 1200 transmitter sites. Each site uses four frequency channels to transmit the BBC, ITV and Channel 4 services. Channel 5 has a smaller network of transmitters. Only a limited number of frequency channels are available for the transmission of UK television services.

- Analogue transmissions use these 8 MHz wide frequency channels to provide a single service, but the ITC has found a way of inserting up to six services in the same space. Known as multiplexes, six of these channels can, using digital techniques, be interleaved between the analogue channels. They are to be broadcast from 81 transmission sites where the first four multiplexes will reach about 90 per cent of the population and the remaining two some 75 per cent. Digital transmissions are much less liable to interference such as ghosting and electrical noise. Although at a much lower power than analogue transmission, the service can be received on existing aerials and portable reception is possible.

Overall, the big question is whether more and more TV channels will increase the size of the TV viewing audience, or will it merely allow for keener targeting of much smaller audiences? If we look at North America, we can see that the more channels that exist the thinner the audience is spread, with advertisers who want to talk to mass audiences having to buy space on a wide range of channels – so this proliferation of channels might be bad for an advertiser who wants to reach 'the housewife', for example. On the other hand, with smaller, much more carefully targeted audiences being available, some channels can sell keenly targeted space for a relatively low total cost, so it might be possible for a single insurance broker to afford to advertise on a Female Money Management programme on a Family Money Matters channel, for example.

E-APPLICATION POINTS

Television advertising is sexy – of that there is no doubt. There is a great buzz to be had from sitting at home, with your family and loved ones and seeing your company's TV commercial – your baby – on the screen in front of you. Then there is the possible lure of location shooting and filming schedules – which sound great even though they can be a phenomenal bore! Why do I mention all this? Because it is so easy to be swayed, when you are launching a start-up and an unscrupulous agency 'guru' (yes, I'm afraid they do exist) talks to you about how advertising on TV will build immense awareness across the nation for your new brand name, and will turn it into an almost overnight success. Yes, it is possible to advertise on TV in such a way that in one evening a large proportion of a target group of residents of the UK will have had the opportunity to see your brand name on their TV screens. But (and it's a big but) one evening of a name appearing, fleetingly, does **not** make a successful business.

Television advertising can be very effective – if you have a specific campaign objective, if you need to build some trade credibility, or if you need to build awareness and familiarity with a distinct target group over time. But it is not a panacea! It can be a very effective directional medium – bringing your business proposition to the attention of millions of people either fast, or many times over time, but it is a medium that should be used with care. Fragmentation might mean that there is a greater ability to target discrete audiences, but it might also lead to big brands with big budgets dominating the schedules in order to reach their ever more difficult to communicate with target groups. Either way, the likelihood is that television advertising rates will remain high. In the chapter that looks at below the line communication methods, we will consider other ways in which marketers might be able to reach the TV audience without paying for advertising space.

In the meantime, let's take an example of a start-up dotcom that is basically an on-line temping agency. They need two commodities in order to survive – temporary staff and employers who need temporary staff – and they need those two resources in a pretty good balance, or else they will end up with disappointed employers, for whom they have no staff, or temps who cannot get a position through their books. Television advertising might work well to build brand awareness so that all other marketing communications begin with the background thought 'Oh yes, I've heard of them', thereby beginning to build a feeling of confidence which is needed by both the temps and the employers, and it might work well to actually elicit enquiries from both types of person. But the question remains, is it the **best** way to spend marcomms money to achieve objectives? In this case I would suggest that the answer is no – the targeting of TV is too diffuse, the cost too high for the possible returns. But if money were plentiful it could easily be argued that TV was vital to success – and there have been some very persuasive arguments put forward in business plans that have produced multi-million pound and dollar budgets to launch such businesses through TV advertising. If pushed I would have to say that the financiers who have lost billions by backing businesses in this way have only themselves to blame: the TV stations have done very nicely, thank you, as have the advertising agencies – all of whom have demanded payment up front just in case things didn't go too well.

But the truth of it is that small businesses with big bankrolls are still small businesses, and they are made up of some people who are not greedy and some who are – unfortunately the not-greedy ones can get dragged down by the greedy ones, and nothing will do that faster than a big TV advertising budget that doesn't produce a sustained business result. Never be attracted by the lure of great riches, or great results, unless someone can give you some real, hard evidence that this sort of result has been achieved before. Even in a world where every start-up seems to think it is the first in any field, there are always examples of businesses **like** the new ones, so it should be possible to look at the results that TV has achieved for them. Or, if they haven't advertised on TV, ask yourself 'Why not?', and if the answer seems to be merely because they didn't have enough money, then ask yourself 'Do we?' and if you think the answer to that is in the affirmative, then stop again and work out the other ways in which the same amount of money could be spent. I am not anti-TV advertising, but I am pro-good planning.

Also, even if TV does do a phenomenally good job for you – ask yourself if you are in a business position to be able to capitalize upon that? Can you fill the potential orders? Can you deliver the customer satisfaction to that number of customers? TV can let you down, if it's not the right medium for you, or bring in so much business that you can't cope – maybe it is something you should work up to? Working with an advertising advisor who is trustworthy, who takes the time to explain the alternatives to you and makes sure that you are aware of the possible results of all your marcomms activities can make a tremendous difference!

The prospect of interactive television and infomercial channels opens up whole new vistas for the e-business entrepreneur. But once again, the warnings are out there – be sure that the targeting is right, so that you get value for money, and be sure you can cope with the predicted response. It might well be that, as the penetration of digital TV grows, so the market for Internet access grows exponentially. This might mean that your customer relationship management programme **can** be run through the Internet alone sooner than you might have thought, because you get access to your customer base through the TV set, not the computer.

Radio

OVERVIEW

The first commercial stations went on air in London in October 1973; London Broadcasting Company (LBC) and Capital Radio were the first stations. Nineteen stations were on air across the UK by 1980. For the first twenty years of its life it is probably true to say that commercial radio was undervalued as an advertising medium by client companies and advertising agencies alike, unlike the USA, where commercial radio was around long before commercial television.

However, the late twentieth and early twenty-first centuries have seen radio come of age as a UK medium. This has been helped by three key changes in the radio industry:

- national commercial stations have made national radio advertising campaigns easier to buy;

- advances in planning and buying via RAJAR (see the following research section for full explanation) and IMS (one of several computerized campaign planning systems) make it easier for advertisers to get what they want;
- the birth of the Radio Advertising Bureau (RAB) with its mission to 'improve the climate of familiarity and favourability towards commercial radio amongst advertisers and their agencies' has led to an increased level of promotion for radio as a medium.

Commercial radio has developed dramatically during the 1990s and is now attracting more advertising revenue than ever before. Commercial radio recorded its highest ever quarterly revenue figure at £145 million across October–December 2000. This was up 10.9 per cent year-on-year, boosted by a 17.1 per cent increase in revenue from national advertisers; airtime revenue from national advertisers took a 73.8 per cent share of the total for this period.

The full year 2000 saw commercial radio firmly establish itself as a £500 million medium – total revenue grew 15.4 per cent year-on-year to reach £536 million. Again, demand amongst national advertisers was particularly high, with revenues growing at the faster rate of 25.7 per cent.

Finance (+20.8 per cent) and Government Institutions (+51.4 per cent) were the fastest growing product sectors, although Retail was, unsurprisingly, the highest spending category across the October–December 2000 quarter.

The majority of money comes into radio stations via the straightforward sales of airtime, or 'spots'. Licensees (the companies with the franchise rights to broadcast) set their own levels of 'minutage' (the amount of advertising minutes within an hour), which is usually about nine minutes per hour.

The radio medium is controlled by the Radio Authority and its trade body is the Commercial Radio Companies' Association (CRCA). There is a layered set-up for the various stations, comprising national, regional and local stations:

National stations

The four national stations on air at present are:

- *Classic FM*: the first official national station in the UK began broadcasting between 100 and 102 FM in September 1992. Its popular classic format targets ABC1 adults aged between 25 and 40.
- *Virgin 1215*: an AM frequency which was Richard Branson's first foothold in the radio market. Launched in April 1993, the station has an adult orientated rock format. The signal, like all AM broadcasts, is particularly weak during the hours of darkness in most areas, and in some built-up areas during the day. London was a

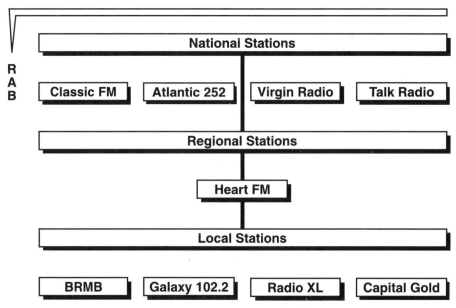

Figure 3.3   Typical radio station layered structure (e.g. Birmingham)

particular problem, which is why the Radio Authority awarded Virgin a London-wide FM licence which allows them to broadcast the same output as the national station, with split commercial breaks (thus, advertisers can target London, or the rest of the UK, or both).

- *Talk UK*: the last national licence awarded, again broadcast on AM, however not as successful as the two previously mentioned national stations. Talk tried to attract different audiences to different programmes, in the same way television does. However, radio listeners tend to tune in to the station, not the individual programmes.

- *Atlantic 252*: transmitted from the Irish Republic on long wave, Atlantic was launched on 1 September 1989 and reaches most of the UK. Pressure from advertisers and agencies forced the station to be included in the RAJAR research (see later notes on RAJAR). It is an all music station aiming at 15- to 34-year-olds.

CREATIVE ASPECTS

Radio can take your potential customer to a desert island with the sea lapping gently against the shore for a fraction of the cost of sending a filming team on location to shoot the scene, because radio takes the listener's imagination to places, rather than their eyes. There is an increasing amount of research evidence that the way people consume radio (and radio advertising) is very different from the way they consume other media.

For a start, the vast majority of people listen because they are doing something else. Radio is merely an accompaniment, and acts as a 'personal climate controller' for the listener. Unlike traditional TV viewing, there are few expectations of positive entertainment.

Also, radio has no pictures.

They call it 'the intimate medium', and this makes sense – people listen on their own, in their personal spaces, and they are loyal to the stations they choose (this already sounds more like magazines than TV). The texture of radio also seems to be different. People don't see radio as aspirational, they see it as human and genuine in nature. It speaks with a very human voice. In a recent research study, people projected the nature of Radio-Land as being *warm, caring, earthy, jolly* and *real*. They projected TV-Land by contrast as being *glamorous, callous, shallow, sunny* and *false*. Immediately, this calls for a different approach: how can you impress the consumer when your orthodox advertising techniques – glamour, polish, aspiration – simply don't apply?
Radio can:

- Create sound pictures in the audience's mind.
- Take listeners anywhere, cheaply.
- Grab the attention with music.
- Remind listeners of your TV advertising by using the same music/voices.

It is the responsibility of the creative team within the agency to ensure that these advantages are exploited, but one must bear in mind the following disadvantages:

- Radio cannot show a product.
- Radio needs high levels of repetition to ensure memorability.
- Radio has to rely totally upon sound.

The Radio Advertising Bureau has a vested interest, on behalf of the Commercial Radio Companies, in ensuring that it is the creative benefits of the medium which are focused on rather than the disadvantages. The RAB is funded by a levy on all commercial radio advertising, and has the promotion, through better understanding, of the radio medium as its task. Its stated aim is 'to guide national advertisers and their agencies towards effective advertising on commercial radio'. Its messages do, therefore, focus on both the media characteristics and the creative characteristics of the radio medium and they have an excellent website full of facts and insightful Case Studies.

Find them at http://rab.co.uk

They have made an enormous difference in the way in which advertising creativity on radio has been viewed, and their promotion of the concept of Sonic Brand Triggers (SBTs) is one example of this work.

Sonic

SBTs use sound, but there are brands triggered by other senses:

- Visual: e.g. company logos, little red telephone (Direct Line), jar for Nescafé; most contemporary brand triggers are visual.
- Taste: e.g. the taste of the Burger King Whopper.
- Smell: all identifiable perfumes do this.
- Some brands work in more than one sense – in the cases of Intel and Direct Line, their brand identity evokes in both vision and sound (which each evoke each other – you hear the tune, you see the visual).

Brand

There are many familiar sounds out in the real world which consumers do not relate to any particular brand – many TV advertising theme tunes seem very familiar but what was the brand? Sonic Triggers can become linked to brands over time through repetition; they can also lose their brand linkage over time, through lack of repetition (e.g. the Haddaway track 'It's my life', which used to be tightly linked to Tampax advertising).

Importantly, SBTs elicit a response of some kind, rather than just existing for their own sake; the responses vary – making the consumer feel something, think something, know something, be reminded of something, feel closer to something, associate with something (or associate something with something else). . .an SBT which doesn't trigger a response clearly needs development.

SBTs vary in the way they evoke the brand. While some, like the British Airways theme, are very 'soft sell' and evocative, others are much more urgent and persuasive. Some are linked to the brand by association (Papa and Nicole), where others are explicitly linked to the brandname (PC World) – the latter style is typically less subtle, but offers a very short route to an effective SBT. So an SBT is something which works in sound (words, music, noises) to trigger a response in the consumer relating to a given brand and is widely used in radio advertising. Why are they so important?

SBTs are important for four reasons:

- *They allow unmistakable branding.* Consumers famously don't care which brand an advertisement is for – a Sonic Brand Trigger implicitly confirms the identity of the brand (ads where the brand is not recalled are of questionable value).

- *They go in 'under the radar'.* They allow an advertiser to deliver a branded 30-second message without requiring the attention of the listener; SBTs are recalled easily, even by those listening who felt they were paying little or no attention.
- *They can operate continually at the emotional level.* Most SBTs are musical and evocative rather than verbal and hard sell; this allows them to be repeated continually, gradually adapting the consumer's brand perceptions.
- *They can create 'virtual TV'.* Many SBTs are created initially on TV (example: Diet Coke's '11.30 Diet Coke break') and these can often be successfully adapted for radio, with consequent benefits in terms of increasing frequency and campaign longevity.

There is also always a big question about how effectively telephone numbers work within radio commercials. There appear to be three principal roles for telephone numbers in radio ads:

Short-term direct response only

It is common for exclusive music compilations, e.g. 'Call now – this album is not available in the shops', to major on the memorability of the telephone number, as there is no other way for the listener to access the product. These ad campaigns live or die by the number of people who actually call up and order the product – they have no longer-term goal.

Brand response advertising

This type of advertiser – the biggest category on radio – includes a telephone number to offer access to those listeners who wish to respond directly, but recognizes the fact that most listeners, most of the time, are not (or not yet) in the market for the product or service advertised.

Examples would include Direct Line Insurance and The Carphone Warehouse: both advertisers receive measurable direct response as a result of the radio advertising, but both know that this is only a fraction of the true effect of the advertising. They are building up awareness amongst the listeners who will be coming into the market at various points over the coming weeks, months and years.

Advertisers like these rely on the fact that radio is *not* the only link to the brand – they also have directory entries, websites, outbound call centres, brochures, salespeople, ambient media, stores, ads in the print media, etc. (in fact Direct Line have often left out a specific phone number and guided listeners towards their directory entry). Typically, the telephone number of advertisers like these is not the main hinge of their radio commercials, but it's there, clearly spelt out, for anyone who is motivated enough to want to ring straight away.

Other/emotional

A third category of advertisers is apparent on radio – these brands include the telephone number mainly for emotional reasons. For example, one of the regional electricity companies includes its customer care number mainly to reinforce the impression that they are committed to this service ethic. One of the major financial institutions uses a similar tactic – they appear highly accessible to the customer, though in fact they expect very few calls in response.

It is probably true to say that this 'accessibility' impression also applies to the brand response advertisers referred to above.

MEDIA CHARACTERISTICS

Once again this is an area full of terminology that needs to be explained and understood – here are just some of the terms used in the radio business, together with some brief explanations of their meanings:

- *RAJAR*: Radio Joint Audience Research.
- *TSA*: total survey area. The marketing area of a service, used as a basis for audience measurements.
- *Listening*: recorded in terms of 15-minute segments and defined as at least five minutes' listening within a particular segment. (Between midnight and 6.00 a.m., listening is recorded in 30-minute segments.)
- *Average audience*: the average number of people listening in any time segment.
- *Total hours*: the total length of time listened to radio, or to a station, by the population group being measured. Calculated by summing every 15 minutes listened.
- *Average hours*: the average length of time spent listening to radio, or to a particular station.
- *Share of audience*: the percentage of the total audience to radio that is listening to a particular station.
- *Share of listening*: the percentage of total hours listened to radio that are accounted for by a particular station or demographic group.
- *Cumulative audience (reach)*: the number of different people listening during a specified period of time. The cumulative audience is the potential group that can be exposed to advertising on a radio station, and is usually expressed both in actual numbers and as a percentage of the population.
- *Reach*: the number of different people who are exposed to a schedule of advertisements.

- *Impacts (gross impressions)*: the total number of exposures to a schedule of advertisements; *not* a measure of the number of different people exposed to a commercial.
- *Radio ratings*: impacts expressed as a percentage of the population group being measured.
  - Impacts × 100 divided by Population = Rating.
- *Frequency*: (opportunities to hear – OTH) the average number of times the audience reached by an advertising schedule is exposed to a commercial.
  - Gross impressions divided by Reach = Frequency.
- *Gross rating points*: impacts expressed as a percentage of the population being measured. 1 rating point equals 1 per cent of the population.
- *Cost per thousand*: the basic term used to express radio's unit costs. Most frequently used to compare the cost of 1000 impacts on different stations; it is also used to compare the cost of reaching 1000 people via different media.
  - Schedule cost divided by Impact (in 000s) = Cost per thousand.

PLANNING AND BUYING RADIO AIRTIME

Basically you can buy exactly what you want! One spot, run once on one local station, or very heavyweight campaigns on national stations and bought on national networks too!

Computer-aided planning

Computer-aided planning such as the IMS planning system means that campaigns can be planned very fast and very simply. Commercials can be input into the system manually by studying the RAJAR diaries, or by the computer by way of 'optimization': a schedule can be 'optimized' by inputting certain criteria, such as the reach required, the level of frequency which you want to achieve, the cost per thousand desired or the budget. The computer mouse is then clicked on the 'optimize' window or button, which results in the computer scheduling slots to give the best performing campaign within the budget.

National stations

Campaigns will be planned using RAJAR data to reach the right number and type of people at the right time, and for the right cost. A computerized planning system like IMS might be used, or the station itself might put together a proposal for the client that includes a mixture of traditional spots plus sponsorships or promotions.

Commercial radio packages

Local commercial radio stations have collaborated in the setting up of ease-of-purchase packages. The packages are branded under the name National Network Radio (NNR) and aim to simplify the buying of airtime targeting specific target markets. In addition to NNR, there are several opportunities for advertisers to buy into programmes or features that are broadcast across a large number of local radio stations. The environments that advertisers can buy into include the chart show, news, sports programmes and traffic reports.

These packages provide the benefits of being associated with local programming and the convenience of a single point of purchase, as they are available from all the big sales houses.

RESEARCH

Background

To sell airtime against competing media, such as press and TV, the media owner will want to know how many people listen to the service(s), not only so that the agencies and advertisers know how many people their campaign will reach, but also to decide the rates for certain commercial spots at certain times of the day or week.

Radio audience research underwent a big change in 1992, when the system used since 1977 called JICRAR was replaced by a new service, RAJAR, which stands for Radio Joint Audience Research.

RAJAR

RAJAR is the audience research system used by the UK radio industry. Since its launch in 1992, there have been many developments in the radio broadcasting industry and, in 1996, it became clear that a new methodology would soon be needed to cater for the increasing number of stations that listeners could choose from. The new methodology was launched at the beginning of 1999 and the first results were reported in June 1999.

RAJAR is jointly owned by the British Broadcasting Corporation (BBC) and the Commercial Radio Companies Association (CRCA). RAJAR was established in 1992 to provide a single source of radio audience data for all radio services in the UK, both BBC and commercial radio stations. It replaced two separate services – the BBC Daily Survey (which was conducted for BBC Radio) and JICRAR (the Joint Industry Committee for Radio Audience Research, which was conducted for commercial radio stations).

There is no doubt that the creation of RAJAR has greatly improved overall confidence in radio as a medium over the years since 1992, principally because it provides a single accepted measure of radio listening. Much has changed since 1992 and the radio market has become, and will continue to become, increasingly complex. The number of national services has grown from seven to nine stations, and regional and local services have increased from 130 to over 250 stations. The period has also seen rapid growth in many more specialist services – ethnic, specialist music, speech based and so on. Stations and advertisers are demanding more timely information and in ever greater detail. And the arrival of digital radio and the plethora of possibilities it offers are soon to take effect.

Currently, there are over 250 national, regional and local BBC and commercial radio stations in the UK. These stations, in turn, create over 500 unique areas because of the way in which stations' transmission areas overlap. Each of these 500 unique station areas must be surveyed. Every week, more than 200 trained interviewers place radio listening diaries with more than 3000 different and carefully selected respondents. Respondents can be anyone aged 4+ living in private households. Each respondent (or guardian) is interviewed and shown how to record and complete a seven-day diary of his/her listening habits. At the end of the week, the diaries are collected by the interviewer and returned to the research company, where they are electronically scanned and checked. The data are then ready for processing and analysis. Once processed, the radio audience data are published and are available, in print or electronically via the Internet, every three months.

E-APPLICATION POINTS

Whatever the RAB might say, and I do believe that radio has a great creative ability and potential, when it comes to special applications for e-business, as opposed to non-e-business, it is difficult to see how radio surpasses other media. The advent of digital radio and radio available globally via the web means that, yes, the radio industry is able to benefit from e-ing itself. Indeed, many changes in technology have made it possible for radio stations to set up and exist profitably because they are taking advantage of e-business-based cost savings. But, other than the radio using the web and wireless communication possibilities, there are few avenues for e-business to embrace the radio medium.

The main way in which e-business can 'use' radio, and make it its own, is to capitalize upon the wireless nature of the medium, make sure that all the potential advantages of digital radio are used (e.g. excellent sound quality, possibly sidetracking the need for CDs) and use the targeting it offers to best advantage. Imagine if you will a mobile telephone that is not just a telephone, fax, Internet access point and gatherer of instant messaging, but is a total entertainment centre too. Now, the attraction of watching DVD quality movies on a hand-held screen is plain, especially for the busy executive with long periods of time spent in cabs or at airports, but we cannot always give visual attention, whereas we can usually give aural attention – thus, radio via WAP has a great chance of succeeding, and the targeting would make it a prime medium for communicating with the groups who use WAP, namely high disposable income businessmen, who are notoriously difficult to reach through other media.

The potential for interactivity exists too – with advertisements maybe being able to give out a telephone number that acts rather like a web link – with a click of the pad at the right moment taking the user direct to the offer being mentioned either via telephone or screen. Where exactly the radio medium will go is just a guess at present, but the fact that it is flexible, can be mobile, is wireless and can be programmmed either ahead of time or live mean that it will always be a useful reminder medium – though not necessarily the best way to get a web address to be remembered, it can talk about what will be found there, and might even provide a link to take you there.

One issue here is to realize that what radio has been might not be what radio will become: the strengths of radio are its intimacy and the way it can create a real relationship with the listener. If radio stations rely on music they might find that they are squeezed out by total music stations on digital TV in the home, or MP3 on the move with the teenage audience, but the use of people, voices, interactive programming and being the source of truly local information could make radio a very successful medium for the digital, mobile age.

Press

OVERVIEW

You need to be aware that the UK press scene is so busy that there is no such thing as 'press' other than in the very broadest inter-media decision-making sense.

We can break up press into a couple of broad categories, with some subdivisions:

- *Newspapers* – including daily nationals (e.g. *The Daily Telegraph*), weekly nationals (e.g. *The Observer*), daily regionals (e.g. *London Evening Standard*) and weekly regionals (e.g. *Western Mail*), daily locals (e.g. *Swansea Evening Post*) and weekly locals (e.g. *Bromley News Shopper*), plus daily (e.g. *International Herald Tribune*) and weekly internationals (e.g. *The Economist*).

- *Magazines* – consumer magazines: weekly (e.g. *Woman's Weekly*) and monthly (e.g. *Tatler*); interest magazines (e.g. *Biking Times*) that are often monthly, bi-monthly or even quarterly; business magazines that might be trade press that are available on the news-stand or for a subscription (e.g. *Marketing Week*) and might be weekly, monthly or quarterly; and professional journals, that again might be weekly, monthly or periodic, but which are only available to what is know as a 'controlled circulation' – very often you have to be a member of a specific institution to receive the publication in question (e.g. *Marketing Business*, which is the magazine received by Members of the Chartered Institute of Marketing).

Each publication will have its own specific reader profile etc., but there are some general creative and media characteristics that we can look at here.

The press always was, of course, a printed medium, but has recently begun to become an Internet medium too, with many publications becoming available on-line. This development has great implications for e-communication, but before we look at 'Virtual Press', let's look at the traditional form of the medium, because this too has its uses for the e-communicator.

CREATIVE CHARACTERISTICS

Print has the advantages not only of allowing for advertisements to appear as a part of the print itself, but also the additional option of including an insert.

Let's consider the creative characteristics of the printed medium:

- Long copy is possible, with the possible retention factor for lists of stockists, telephone numbers, etc.
- Colour is available in most publications – if you want it and are prepared to pay for it.
- Couponing is possible.
- Creatively inspired 'runs' can be taken, e.g. a series of advertisements in one issue building a story.
- Samples can be attached, e.g. perfume, face cream.
- Specially designed advertisements that are of specific relevance to the reader who has chosen *this* publication can be highly impactful.

However:

- Reproduction is out of the advertiser's control (except for inserts).
- The editorial environment might prove less than suitable, depending on the news that day.

- Demonstration, other than by sample, is impossible.
- There is no sound or movement available.

Technological developments mean that now it is more cost-effective than ever to use CD-ROMs as cover mounts or inserts, that new ways of inserting different types of materials into magazines are being developed all the time, and that this is an area where short-run printing methods and the massive reduction in set-up costs for print publications means that we are likely to see the continued proliferation of new titles for ever more specific and focused target groups.

MEDIA CHARACTERISTICS

In the UK there is a huge variety of press available, offering the advertiser and the media planner many opportunities for reaching specific groups of customers, or audience segments. A good publication has a personality which attracts certain readers, whilst repelling others, and advertisers select publications which reach their desired group. Let's look at the various sections of the press available to us.

Newspapers

About 65 per cent of the UK population read a daily national newspaper, 28 per cent an evening paper, 72 per cent a national Sunday newspaper, and 72 per cent a free local weekly paper. Newspapers have a short lifespan and aim to have general appeal based on their news stories, editorial stance, and the other forms of information and entertainment carried within their pages.

We are fortunate in the UK to have one of the most diverse ranges of newspapers in the world, with the 'Wapping revolution' making newspaper production much cheaper than in the past and allowing publishers to reach more reader segments. That said, the investment required to set up a newspaper, even with editorial and print separated and the advance of technology, is huge. That means that publishers have to work hard to attract a readership that is appealing to advertisers.

National daily publications break down, generally, into:

- Quality: *Daily Telegraph, The Times, Guardian, Independent, Financial Times.*
- Midmarket: *Daily Mail, Daily Express.*
- Popular: *Sun, Daily Mirror, Daily Star, Daily Sport.*
- Special interest: *Morning Star, Sporting Life, Racing Post, Lloyd's List.*

Be aware that the capacity for offering regional advertising within the national dailies is growing, and it will be interesting to see to what extent the regional press will be affected, and how their owners will fight back.

Consumer magazines

The key characteristic of consumer magazines is their flexibility in reaching keenly defined audiences. They range from high-circulation general titles (including colour supplements to national newspapers) to small-circulation special interest titles. Three out of four magazines sold are weekly titles, with the largest sectors (in terms of circulation) being television listings and female interest magazines. Rapid growth in the male interest sector has taken place over the last couple of years, and might be set to continue.

There is a huge number of titles. The best way to get a feeling for the range and circulations available at any one time is to check *BRAD (British Rate and Data)*. Usually, rates are set annually; however, the firmness with which the ratecard is adhered to by sales people will be determined by the prevailing business climate. Experienced media buyers, with a lot of business to place either in one publication or with one publishing house, can still get huge reductions on the published ratecard prices, sometimes up to 50 or 60 per cent.

Euromagazines

A good example here would be *Hello!* magazine, with the emphasis on converging lifestyles across Europe. Bear in mind that pan-European advertisers seek pan-European advertising opportunities, and they want to reach the same market segment in each country. The German publishing houses have been particularly successful in 'exporting' titles to other European countries. On today's news-stand, *Elle, Marie Claire, TV Quick* and *Hello!* are all examples of how the Euromagazine has really begun to come of age.

Business magazines

These are trade, technical and professional journals. Generally speaking, trade publications (e.g. *Marketing Week*) are available in most large newsagents, technical publications (e.g. *Plastics and Rubber Weekly*) need to be ordered, subscribed to or are received on a controlled-circulation list basis depending upon job title, whilst professional journals are usually received free of charge as a membership right for those who belong to a given professional body, or can, again, be bought by subscription (e.g. *Marketing Business*, the journal of the CIM).

The number and range of business publications serving any one sector will tend to be determined not by the number of people buying the magazine, but by the value of the advertising market. For example, solicitors have one major weekly publication, the *Law Society Gazette*, with a circulation of about 60 000, but dentists, who number about 17 500 in the UK, have six major titles. Why? Well, there are more advertisers wanting to talk to dentists who buy supplies, equipment and services than want to talk to solicitors, whose purchasing needs are very much smaller. This is what rules the market in terms of titles available, and the rates charged for advertising.

Usually, business magazines pay a 10 per cent commission to agencies, rather than the usual 15 per cent. Once again, ratecard prices are the starting point for negotiation, and good seasonal discounts can often be negotiated. Sometimes monthly titles only publish eleven issues per year due to seasonal dips in business, often during the summer.

Some general press media terminology

- *SCC (single column centimetre)* – the basic unit of advertising space in newspapers, with the usual minimum size in display being three column centimetres.
- *Classified* – advertising only in sections, usually sold by the word and set by the publication.
- *Display* – any advertisement that is not sold as lineage (as it is in classified). (NB: display advertisements can appear in classified sections.)
- *Semi-display* – paper-set advertisement given a rule around the edge to make it stand out from the rest of the classified advertisements with which it appears; sold by size of space, not by the word.
- *Spot colour* – single colour added as a solid colour; helps advertisements stand out in all sections.
- *Horizontal* – refers to a broad-appeal publication, usually weekly, where high circulation is the aim; e.g. in the building trade *Building* magazine carries a weekly editorial of interest and relevance to builders' merchants, architects, local authority specifiers, construction engineers, etc.
- *Vertical* – refers to a narrow-appeal publication where the aim is coverage of a given interest group, however low that might make the circulation; e.g. in the building trade there are titles of interest specifically for builders' merchants, architects, local authority specifiers, construction engineers, etc.

RESEARCH AND INFORMATION

The Audit Bureau of Circulation (ABC) is a key body in terms of establishing press circulation figures. It is a non-profit-making company with a membership of advertisers, agencies and publishers. Its purpose is to verify and certify circulation figures on an independent and audited basis. It provides the circulations which are used as currency within the marketplace by publishers and planners, and it is now estimated that well over 90 per cent of press advertising expenditure is placed in publications that have ABC audited circulations.

ABC provides audits for every class of publication: national newspapers (monthly); paid-for newspapers and magazines (twice yearly); specialist consumer and business titles (generally annually). ABC also offers other services:

- *VFD (verified free distribution)* – an equivalent certification for free circulation publications.
- *EDF (exhibition data forms)* – a verified system of monitoring exhibition attendance.
- *MDF (media data form)* – can be appended to an ABC certificate by a business publication to contain a statement on quality of recipients.
- *ABC Profile Audit* – ABC's own analysis of a business magazine's readership profile.

The NRS

The National Readership Survey (NRS) is a non-profit-making but commercial organization, which sets out to provide estimates of the number and nature of the people who read UK newspapers and consumer magazines. Currently, the Survey publishes data covering some 245 different publications.

- It provides editorial and other interested parties with an up-to-date description of the readers reached by individual publications.
- It provides the publishers of newspapers and magazines with the data they need to sell advertising space.
- It provides advertisers and their agencies and media specialists with the (same) data they need to plan and buy advertising space.

Thus, the NRS provides a common currency of readership research data for newspapers and magazines, using a methodology acceptable to publishers, advertisers and their agents. It operates at all times to the highest professional standards, in a manner that is cost-effective, and sufficiently flexible to take account of change and the needs of its users.

The data produced by the survey are published in a number of formats. Hard-copy volumes are published twice a year: in August Volume 1 is issued, covering the previous twelve months July to June, and in February Volume 2, covering the previous twelve months January to December.

These volumes contain some 220 tables each, and primarily give the Average Issue Readership figures for all of the publications covered. Readership is reported by All Adults, with subgroups covering sex, age, class, region, a large number of other demographics, and exposure to other media. Volume 3, also published in February, gives data on the duplication of readership between publications.

In addition to these volumes, subscribers also receive monthly bulletins of basic data which update the data in the volumes. The data in these bulletins cover the most recent twelve, six or three months for different publications, depending on the size of their readership and the frequency of their appearance.

However, this hard-copy publication of the data, though substantial, is limited in the amount of detail it can deliver. NRS Ltd has therefore authorized a number of computer bureaux to offer subscribers special analyses of the NRS data, via which subscribers can specify whatever cross-tabulations of the basic data they wish. The NRS supplies these bureaux with quarterly updates of the entire database on tape, and receives from the bureaux a royalty on each analysis that is conducted.

Heavy users of NRS data who commission frequent special analyses through these bureaux may find it advantageous to take out a Special Analysis Licence, which would enable them to load the quarterly data tapes on to their own PC systems. Licence holders are able to conduct any number of their own analyses without payment of further royalty fees.

More information about the NRS can be found on their website:

 http://www.nrs.co.uk

JICREG (Joint Industry Committee for Regional Press Research)

The purpose of the JICREG is to allow media planners to deal with regional press as they do with other media. Launched in 1990, it has greatly changed the way in which regional and local press advertising is planned, bought and sold. It has become the main currency used by advertisers, agencies, regional press publishers and their sales houses.

JICREG readership data are generated by applying readers per copy (RPC) figures to circulation breakdowns at postcode sector level. The RPC figures are generated either from market research, undertaken to strict JICREG guidelines, or by using JICREG models. These models have been developed following detailed analysis of all available research and are regularly updated to ensure that they continue to reflect current research findings. The amount of research being undertaken by regional and local newspapers is on the increase and currently accounts for 62 per cent of total readership. Five years ago, the proportion of titles with RPC figures based on actual research was barely a third. Today, the figure is nearly half and still rising.

JICREG data are incredibly complex, with hundreds of data fields on over 1000 titles. A major recent development – jointly funded by JICREG and the Newspaper Society – was a sophisticated electronic system for checking data that publishers supply for inclusion on the Newspaper Society database.

JICREG software, JIC-IN-A-BOX, is a Windows PC system which enables the entire JICREG database to be stored on a local PC or network and provides quick and easy access to the entire JICREG database for any area. Subscribers may now also access the full JIC-IN-A-BOX system on the web via JIC-IN-A-BOX Online.

Non-subscribers may also access JICREG newspaper readership data at location level *totally free of charge* on JIC-IN-A-BOX Online. This service now includes the facility to export readership data to spreadsheet applications, such as Microsoft Excel, for off-line viewing and analysis.

More can be discovered about the JICREG offering at their website:

 http://www.jicreg.co.uk

E-APPLICATION POINTS FOR PRINTED PRESS

Bearing in mind the targeting potential of all press, this medium, generally speaking, provides a superb environment to deliver complex messages to keenly targeted audiences about e-offerings. This can be done either with printed advertisements or inserts. Of course, because of its format, the press lends itself to providing a printed reference point, sometimes with advertisement features focusing on, say, local summer entertainment for teenagers, with all the relevant website addresses appearing in the supporting advertisements. As a directional medium, it is excellent, as an informative medium it is second to none and the ability for press to carry cover mounts and inserts means that it has rightly grown in popularity for offering free trials of, for example, games in the form of CD-ROMs that are cover mounted, inserted or tipped in.

So, whatever type of e-business offering you might have, the printed press is bound to have at least one title that will reach your target audience, thereby offering you that chance to give information, give a free sample, a trial offer, sell off the page or just direct people to a website.

VIRTUAL PRESS

Many of the publications listed above are now available on-line.

Here are some sites to visit – it's interesting to compare the on-line version of a publication with an off-line one.

| *The Daily Telegraph* | @ http://www.telegraph.co.uk |
| *The Daily Mail* | @ http://www.dailymail.co.uk |

The Sunday Times	@ http://www.sunday-times.co.uk
The Economist	@ http://www.economist.com
Revolution	@ http://www.revolution.haynet.com
Good Housekeeping	@ http://www.goodhousekeeping.com
GQ Magazine	@ http://www.gq.com

Titles like those above, and the thousands of others that now exist, have many of the same advantages as printed press: they are well targeted, they offer high quality content that is of real interest to readers and they offer advertising opportunities with a ratecard price range available and commission payments on offer. This means that most on-line publications do, in fact, operate as above the line (or commissionable) media. They also offer below the line communication opportunities too, but more of those later. What this chapter deals with is the traditional advertising space that is paid for and appears just as you want it – it includes banner advertisements (that give a direct link to your website from the on-line magazine page itself) to other shapes of advertising space that lend themselves to being more informative. Real-time animation, sounds and eye-catching effects are all available within these publications, and your targeting can be even more refined – depending upon your exact position within the publication (on the motoring pages, or specifically next to the female money matters section, for example).

Thus, on-line publications offer the normal ability to direct readers to your site, but they make it so much easier by actually containing the link within the advertisement. Yes, you can buy a big space and put lots of information in it, but what's the point when a small ad, with a smaller amount of information, can take a reader directly to *your* site, where you can give the reader as much information and access as they want? There's very little point in trying to invent a parallell to an insert – but an ad that *tells* a reader about a competition and gives a link to your website where you now control the data capture is a wonderful way of taking ownership of readers of the publication in which you have bought space. With this sort of linking device you can begin to initiate Permission marketing techniques, where the potential customer gives you 'permission' to send them information and data about your goods or services, as well as allowing you to do this on a personalized basis (again, if this is a part of your strategy).

By gaining access to potential customers via the web, you already have a foot in the door. Then you can look at your customer acquisition and retention plans via the web, with the advertising space having provided you with the doorway you needed to access this prospect/customer (see Chapter 7 on Customer Relationship Management).

The way in which you choose to use on-line press media is up to you – but don't forget that fancy, whizzy creative treatments are no substitute for good targeting, quality of delivery against promise and sound review of performance!

 **Cinema**

Cinema advertising is definitely impactful. You sit in the dark with only the big screen to look at, the sound is all around you and you truly experience the commercial.

Cinema has been experiencing a massive renewal in the UK in recent years, with more people attending more cinemas for bigger movies than ever! Cinema exhibitors now focus on comfort and service for the cinema-goer. The improved and enhanced facilities, such as advance ticket booking, parking, comfortable seating as well as wine bars and cafés have had the effect of attracting ever increasing numbers of affluent, double-income, working professionals to the cinema.

The fact that cinema exhibitors are able to screen two or three major releases at one time has resulted in more frequent visits to the cinema. Almost one quarter of the population (23 per cent) go to the cinema once a month or more. Cinema-goers are now making an average of eight visits a year as opposed to six five years ago.

With broadening audiences and a significant increase in frequency of visits to the cinema, advertisers can now target various socio-demographic groups in far shorter (six-week) windows than was previously possible.

One of the most interesting factors about cinema for the e-business person is that, even though it is impossible to generalize about the profile of e-businesses, the cinema audience, which is young, well-off and mobile, is likely to be very attractive to many e-entrepreneurs. That said, it is still worth remembering that cinema is cinema, and whether you are e-d or not, the characteristics of the medium remain unchanged.

The true creative characteristics of cinema are:

- High impact, lots of memorability.
- Able to make advertisements 100 per cent relevant to the film-going experience.
- Able to make advertisements 100 per cent relevant to a particular film.
- Often able to run a longer version of a television commercial.
- Sound, vision, movement and demonstration are possible.
- Tie-ins with leaflets at the cinema, or even samples, is possible.
- Because it can be local or national, you can tie in local dealers of a national network, e.g. Ford dealers.

- Can be interactive, e.g. award-winning campaign for British Airways by Saatchi, which used an actress in the cinema audience to converse with an actor on screen.

But there are some drawbacks:

- It is difficult for people to take down contact details.
- Coupons, etc., need to be arranged with the cinema, or you cannot use them.
- It is difficult to remember a web address right through a movie!

The way that cinema is used creatively totally depends on the budget: cheap commercials can look very cheap when compared with the quality of the movie itself!

If you want to find out more about how creativity can affect the effectiveness of cinema advertising, it might be worth visiting the following websites, where you can find case studies:

 http://www.pearlanddean.com
http://www.mediasales.carltononline.com

MEDIA CHARACTERISTICS

There has been a significant increase in cinema attendances from 72.6 million in 1986 to 139 million in 1999 (Source: CAA), with estimates for the year 2000 standing at 142 million and projections for 2001 being 148 million, at the 2992 screens in the UK (Source: CAA/Marplan, Gallup/EDI).

The audience comprises 67 per cent 15- to 34-year-olds, with a 52 per cent male/48 per cent female split, with 66 per cent ABC1s and 34 per cent C2DEs (Source: CAA/NRS, Jan.–Dec. 1999). People are not only visiting the cinema in greater numbers, they are visiting more frequently, with 23 per cent of the population now going once a month or more. Cinema-goers are now making 4.0 visits a year, compared to 2.6 in 1987. Cinema remains the most popular leisure activity for under 35-year-olds, the second most popular for ABC1 adults and third most popular across the population as a whole.

Changes in the traditional calendar of film release dates – historically concentrated in the summer months – mean that cinema is now a highly attractive advertising proposition all year round. Major films are now as likely to be released in January or February as in the traditional summer months. *Titanic*, for example, was released in January 1998 and admissions for that period (January–March) were the highest for over a quarter of a century.

Even though the picture for cinema is very rosy, you should still note that it is difficult to build cover and frequency through this medium: true, the core audience can be difficult to reach in other ways, but you still need to look at a 28-week campaign to build a 65.9 per cent cover (Source: CAA/NRS).

There are two contractors covering 99 per cent of all advertising screens: Pearl & Dean and Carlton Screen Advertising Ltd, with Carlton Screen Advertising Ltd holding the rights to the vast majority of sites. These two bodies negotiate with the cinema owners for the right to offer the advertising time for sale. Contracts are usually renegotiated every year, or whenever cinema ownership changes.

PLANNING AND BUYING CINEMA

There are several ways to plan, and then buy, cinema. Due to the power of Carlton Screen Advertising Ltd they tend to set the patterns, with Pearl & Dean having to put together their own packages. The most common length of commercial is 30 seconds. Key methods of planning and buying are:

- *Screen by screen (or line by line)*: every screen in the country can be bought individually and each screen has its own weekly rate, with minimum exhibition being one screen for one week. The weekly rate would cover one 30-second commercial running prior to each programme shown on that screen during the week.

- *Audience Guarantee Plan (AGP) or Audience Delivery Plan (ADP) – the name depends on whether you book through Carlton Screen Advertising (AGP) or Pearl & Dean (ADP)*: where screentime is booked by ISBA region using a fixed CPT and a seasonal admission base. The rates vary from region to region. This option offers a cost-effective method of covering mass audiences, gives the advertiser a guaranteed admissions target, allows screentime to be scheduled in advance and, because the admissions are independently audited monthly, in arrears, you can sometimes gain some extra coverage!

- *Packages*: various types are available – art cinemas, Disney, Children's Club, film by film. The advantage here is that the advertiser has complete control over the environment within which his or her advert will appear and, thus, allows niche targeting of audiences. Two packages are aimed at children, highlighting their importance as a cinema audience: Children's Club has a higher percentage of young children, with a slightly more downmarket profile than Disney, where there are obviously more accompanying parents. Accordingly, costs will differ.

- *Premier*: this is a niche plan which specifically targets the core 15- to 34-year-old audience. An advertiser's ad would not run during films aimed at attracting an older or younger audience. This pack delivers 60 per cent of network admissions and allows guaranteed audience levels with a fixed CPT and non-pre-emptible space (see TV notes). Rates vary (see AGP notes).

When planning cinema advertising, bear in mind that alcohol advertising needs to be treated with care: it is acceptable for 15 and 18 rated films, but will only be shown

with U, PG and 12 rated films if the audience profile projection indicates that under 25 per cent of the audience will be under 18 years of age. Also, Alcohol Proscribed Film Lists are issued regularly.

RESEARCH

There are three main quantitative sources of cinema research:

- *Gallup admissions monitor*: this piece of research is carried out on a continuous weekly admissions audit basis. It provides data for the AGP/Premier campaign packages. It is carried out on the basis of simply counting torn tickets (80 per cent of sample) and a more in-depth questionnaire to a representative sample (20 per cent).
- *CAVIAR (Cinema and Video Industry Audience Research)*: this analyses who watches which films, where, when and with whom. It is the piece of research sponsored by the CAA and it provides a means of predicting likely audience profiles for forthcoming attractions. This, obviously, aids planning a great deal.
- *IMS*: coverage and frequency evaluation using data from the NRS (see Press), TGI and CAVIAR. What this allows is an analysis of combined media schedules, e.g. cinema plus TV, based on cross-analysed data.

Qualitative research studies are also carried out. Refer to the web addresses for Carlton Screen Advertising and Pearl & Dean to see more research first-hand.

E-APPLICATION POINTS

The main problem faced by e-businesses when considering cinema advertising is the fact the the film is played between the advertisements and the audience leaving the cinema! Seriously, despite the fact that there is now better information than ever before available on cinema audience profiles, and despite the great **general** audience figures, cinema is still not a good place to advertise if you want the target to be able to take note of an address or telephone number – unless you can access a back-up method like leafleting to remind people when they get out of the cinema itself.

If you are using cinema to build brand awareness and understanding with a defined target group, and if you want to do that in an impactful and highly visual manner, then cinema is for you! You can build tremendous credibility for your business if you use cinema to talk to the right people in the right way. Indeed, many high-tech products have done a great job of this over the years, but often by using other forms of communication to back up the cinema presence.

Outdoor

OVERVIEW

Outdoor is more than just roadside advertising hoardings: it comprises roadside, transport (buses, trains, tubes, taxis and stations), bus shelter, shopping precinct, and other peripheral sites like street furniture, parking meters and dustbins. 'Outdoor' is used to refer to all these types of advertising opportunity, as well as the world famous one-off sites that we see at, for example, Piccadilly Circus. Outdoor attracts over £300 million worth of advertising expenditure annually across this range of sites.

There is also a 'sub-section' of 'outdoor' that is now often referred to as 'out of home' advertising. It refers to the sort of advertising opportunity that exists in many strange places: the handle of a petrol pump, the floor of a supermarket, the inside of a shopping trolley – all are out of home, all allow for very focused messages due to the situation, but none are likely to form the main pillar of an advertising campaign and all are areas about which it is difficult to get hard information on rates and data.

For the purposes of this text, let's stick to the 'main line' media choices that can be made in this field – but in reality it is always worth checking out the small campaign ideas that can make a real difference to the success of getting a message to an audience.

The outdoor market had an estimated value of £595 million in 1999, with a 6 per cent of total UK above the line advertising. It was the fastest growing sector at +13 per cent for the second half of 1999 *over* 1998 (all advertising = +7 per cent for the same period).

CREATIVE CHARACTERISTICS

- Sites are excellent for short copy with bold images.
- No sound, movement or demonstration is available, so the words and pictures have to work hard to gain attention in the urban landscape.
- Closeness to point of sale means messages are often reminders of other media messages.
- Coupons are not possible, nor are samples, but phone numbers can be used, especially easily remembered Freephone numbers.

However, in the outdoor scene more than most, the creative characteristics alter for different types of site. For example, sites positioned across the track on railway or London Underground stations can utilize long copy very effectively, as can in-taxi posters; the illusion of movement and demonstration can be given by using the Ultravision style of site that revolves and shows three faces to the motorist sitting at a junction; and so on.

MEDIA CHARACTERISTICS

Different-sized panels attract different advertisers because they tend to be positioned to reach different audiences. The main panel names and sizes are as follows:

- *Six sheet* – these measure 1.2 m wide and 1.8 m high, of which there are 65 000 sites.
- *48 sheet* – measuring 20 feet wide by 10 feet high, of which there are 32 000 sites.
- *96 sheet* – these are two 48-sheet sites next to each other, measuring 10 feet by 40 feet, making what is often referred to as a 'supersite'. There are 3000 of these in the UK.
- *Other* – there are 20 000 other advertising panels in the UK that are not these standard sizes, because poster sites can really be any size and shape that is possible or desired: one-off supersites can be found, planning permission sought and the media world told about the specials that are available. Back-lighting, moving images created through light movement, holograms and real-life posters have all been seen from time to time.

This information comes from the Outdoor Advertising Association's website, which can be found at http://oaa.org.uk

PLANNING AND BUYING

This medium has the beauty of delivering very high cover and frequency figures for relatively low cost per thousand, and can be used either as a narrowcast medium, with campaigns planned to reach a small audience very frequently, or as a broadcast medium, gaining huge coverage of the public.

It is possible to buy just one site or 4000, one bus side or 1000, and with most campaigns being bought in blocks of two weeks or one month, longevity of message is guaranteed, as is geographical targeting. The most common way to buy posters is by package through a specialist, although it is possible to buy line by line, or site by site, from contractors direct. Prices vary a great deal on a site-by-site or even package-by-package basis.

- *Poster specialist* – a media planning and buying company that specializes in planning and buying only outdoor campaigns, often on behalf of agency media departments or even media dependents/independents. They exist off an extra 5 per cent commission granted to them by the poster contractors above and beyond the normal 10 per cent granted to recognized agencies.
- *Poster contractor* – the company that holds the lease or owns the poster site that is for sale. They erect, post, maintain, market and sell poster sites, usually through their own sales force, with a large percentage of their sales being made through poster specialists, although the larger companies increasingly market direct to agencies and clients.

POSTAR

May 1996 saw the launch of POSTAR, the most up-to-date form of poster audience research. POSTAR Ltd represents both the buyers and sellers of posters in the UK, and aims to keep updating its data constantly: it was launched in place of the previously planned OSCAR II.

POSTAR tells the media planner how each poster site is located and positioned, how many people pass each panel and *how* people see those panels. In order to provide this information, the research designers have used computer-modelled traffic counts, a visibility study and a travel survey.

In order to estimate the traffic passing poster panels, local authority traffic counts for 10 000 poster panels were put through a neural network programme and modelled into up-to-date traffic estimates for over 100 000 panels across the UK. Local authorities could not provide pedestrian information, however, so NOP Research performed over 9000 12-minute pedestrian counts over 18 months at poster sites across the country. These were also fed into the neural networks so that estimates could be made. These traffic and pedestrian estimates will be updated annually.

Visibility Adjusted Impacts (VAIs) determine not just who passes a panel, and therefore has an *opportunity* to see, but how the likelihood of *actually* seeing posters is affected by such factors as panel size, angle, distance from the kerbside, illumination and clutter. An eye camera was used in this research, which aimed to establish exactly how we take in the urban landscape, rather than how we think we do. The adjustment scores given to panels are allocated for each panel type (six-sheet, 48-sheet and 96-sheet) and depend on the quality of each panel.

POSTAR's travel survey was set up to gain an insight into the demographics of the audience, rather than just their gross numbers: 7500 respondents were tracked over 80 000 journeys, allowing POSTAR to put together the information that allows them to work out the number of panels needed to achieve given levels of coverage and frequency for national campaigns, or for ITV areas or conurbation campaigns.

Other research

Poster contractors often carry out both qualitative and quantitative research projects to assess the impact and value for money offered by outdoor advertising.

It is worth visiting the contractors' own websites to find out what research they are publishing on their sites:

http://www.maiden.co.uk
http://www.jcdecaux.com

http://www.moregroup.com
http://www.primesight.co.uk
http://www.scoreoutdoor.co.uk
http://www.tdimedia.com

(These are the members of the Outdoor Advertising Association.)

E-APPLICATION OF OUT OF HOME

The use of out of home as a way to direct your potential customers to your e-offering is exceptional – and in particular the poster contractors in the UK noticed a huge increase in demand for poster space by organizations seeking to build brand name awareness and site traffic during the dotcom boom years. That first splurge of activity having subsided, out of home media can still be a great way to direct people to your site, alert them to special offers you might have or tell them about a good reason to visit your offering **today**!

 ## Inter-media decision making

So, with an overview of all the main above the line media under your belt, how can you now start to plan the media you want to use?

Get back to basics:

- What is the nature of your target audience?
- What size budget do you have?
- What is the nature of your task?
- What is your timetable?

In an ideal world you would be able to select the right medium to reach the right audience the right number of times for your product or service to achieve your objectives. Usually, the small matter of budget limitations gets in the way, however, so you need to begin by working within the budget you have. Media planners deal with media budgets, a portion of the overall advertising budget and a portion that does not include production costs. That said, in terms of overall promotional practice you will need to consider production costs as an element of your total cost base.

Which medium is best? Which would complement this lead medium? How can you use this secondary medium to, for example, build further cover, or frequency, or to extend the advertising campaign at a price you can afford? Looking at the sorts of costs involved, what percentage of your budget will you use on each medium?

There are no right answers, only some wrong ones! Give the same budget, the same product and the same task to three different professional media planners and even they might disagree about which two or three media to use. What they will also probably disagree about will be the use of the specifics of each medium.

Intra-media decision making

Once the choice of medium has been made, then you need to choose within that medium. Which television channel, regionally, might be an easy one to answer – where is your product or service available? But should you use Channel 3 or Channel 4? What time of day? Buy TVRs or spot buy? You need to be able to put forward reasoned suggestions given the circumstances as they are. But, again, there really are no right answers, only some that will be able to be argued well because they are based on your knowledge and understanding of the situation and the media choices available. You will be even better armed if you have more than a passing familiarity with real, current advertising campaigns.

You also need to put forward a sensible plan of burst and drip advertising, as explained earlier on.

So, any media proposal should contain the inter-media plan, followed by the intra-media recommendations and the overall timed pattern of the campaign in a timetable format. Cover and frequency aims should be mentioned, as should the reasoning for the selection given the task, audience, timing and budget.

Summary of chapter three

Within this chapter we have covered the following:

An in-depth look at all the above the line media, having established what it is that distinguishes above the line media from below the line methods.

General media issues

In this section we looked at what the commission system is and how it works, and how it's existence defines what is 'Above the Line'.

General media planning issues and terminology were looked at.

What needs to be covered in a media plan was listed.

Specific media covered

All the above the line media were dealt with in detail:

- Television
- Radio
- Press
- Cinema
- Outdoor

For each medium the author dealt with planning, buying, research, terminology and future development issues, in depth, and each section looks at how the medium can best be used for today's e-business.

Inter- and intra-media planning

These two parts of media planning were explained.

Self test questions and opinion development

These are not exam questions, nor are they meant to represent the sort of question you might expect to face anywhere else. They are designed to help you check whether you have understood the content of this chapter. All you have to do is read the questions, give them some thought and maybe jot down some notes on what your response might be. Not all the questions will have factual answers – rather, they might encourage you to think about a topic or an issue and formulate an opinion based upon what is now, hopefully, a better understanding of the topic.

What headings should be used in a media plan?

Name all the above the line media.

Why do you think the commission system still exists?

Do you think it will still exist in ten years' time?

What are the main *media* characteristics of television?

What are the main *creative* characteristics of radio?

Who would you contact to plan and buy a poster campaign for you?

Why do you think cinema audiences are increasing? What do you think would need to happen for them to increase even more?

What are the main differences between planning and buying advertising space in a weekly business-to-business publication and a monthly, glossy women's publication? List the planning differences, the buying differences and the creative differences.

What do you think is more difficult to do – inter-media planning or intra-media planning? Why?

 ## Extending knowledge and understanding

You are encouraged to undertake the following activities to further your knowledge and understanding of the topics covered in this chapter in the following ways:

1 Build a portfolio of examples of campaigns for e-businesses that use:

- only one medium above the line;
- two media above the line;
- three media above the line;
- four media above the line;
- five media above the line.

  Examine the ways in which the different media are balanced. What do you think is the weighting in terms of cost, coverage and frequency for each campaign?

  Do any of these campaigns use *no* other below the line communication methods? Why is that?

2 Visit at least five websites, preferably one for each type of medium. Work your way around the websites to familiarize yourself with how the medium presents itself. Now put yourself in the position of being the manager responsible for selling each of the specific media that you have chosen to e-businesses. Thinking about how your competitors would sell themselves against you, how would you sell your medium (the medium, e.g. TV, and the specific media offering, e.g. GMTV)? Write notes as though you were going to present your sales case to a group of potential space buyers.

Chapter **4**

Below the line
communication methods

Overview

So, as the last chapter looked at commissionable media, this one begins to look at created marketing communications methods, which are referred to as below the line methods, and which can refer to *anything* that communicates your message, other than the above the line methods already referred to! If someone asks 'How many below the line methods are there?', it's rather like someone asking 'How long is a piece of string?' – in that the answer will always be, 'It depends. . .' And it depends on how many methods you want to invent, because the list of below the line, or created methods, can be a s long as your imagination is wild!

From on-pack promotions to hot air balloons, from direct mail to electronic brochures, from an international sales force conference to a notice next to the coffee machine – all these are methods of communication that are *not* commissionable, or already existing media communications methods, and which are, therefore, below the line.

Since it would be impossible to look at all these methods in this book, let's stick to the main categories – but, when you are thinking of marketing communications method selection, always think beyond the obvious, always allow for creative thought, not just in *how* you say it but also in *where* you say it!

What I have tried to do here is to concentrate on the below the line methods, old and new, that are most relevant for e-business uses. But so much depends on what type of e-business you are involved with exactly, that covering all the bases would be almost impossible! Besides, the beauty of below the line is that it is an area full of creative possibilities – in other words, if you can think it up, and it's legal, and you implement it and it promotes your goods or services, or at least informs about them, then you have another below the line method!

Sales promotion – what it's all about, and how it can be used for e-businesses

Sales promotion can achieve many objectives – the main aim being to promote extra sales over a given period of time, within a given budget and with a given incentive to the customer to buy now, buy more, or buy a particular product, service or brand. It is the concept of adding value to a product or service in given circumstances and making that product or service stand out in the customer's mind.

- *Incentivization* – a big word that simply means 'buy me for this special reason'.

There is no end to the exact nature of the value the marketer can choose to add to the product or service involved. Indeed, the fact that it is such a creative field to work in

is one of the reasons why so many practitioners turn to the world of sales promotions. That said, sales promotion must be viewed pragmatically – the purpose is to achieve desired and measurable objectives, as with all marketing communication and promotional functions.

And don't think that sales promotions are restricted to supermarkets and fast-moving consumer goods (fmcg) products. The fields of services, business goods and consumer durables all now use sales promotions effectively. And when it comes to e-business, the possibilities are endless! True, the incentive of being able to access masses of information at once, or order immediately, or to link to associated websites, is already built into many e-business offerings that use the web to inform, promote or sell, but there are additional avenues that have to be explored in order to really add perceived value to the customer and potential customer. Many of what we view as standard sales promotion techniques did originate in the fmcg field, but they are being adopted and adapted with great success by e-businesses.

An interesting exercise is to question how much above the line advertising that you see has as its purpose the communication that a particular sales promotion is taking place – for an e-business or a non-e-business. For example, how many posters do you see that tell you there is a particular on-pack promotion, or how many television commercials tell you about a special offer with a time limit at a given web address? Very often we find out about sales promotion either at the point of sale or through the classic above the line media. Be sure you begin to analyse how much spend above the line is related to below the line sales promotions.

A LITTLE BACKGROUND

The sales promotion industry in the UK is worth about £5 billion per year, and it is growing faster than any other area of marketing services at the moment. Together with its sister discipline, direct marketing (the two are often linked), it is changing the way that marketers seek to win sales in today's increasingly competitive marketplaces.

The one thing to note about sales promotion, like direct marketing, is that it is a relatively new discipline, with few agencies having reached their Silver Anniversary yet! That said, those working in the agencies that offer specialist sales promotion services, which the marketer can choose to buy à la carte, do not view the topic lightly. Sales promotion gained ground in the early 1990s because it is a discipline that can provide easily measurable results against a given budget. With marketers needing to be sure that their promotional budget is producing actual results in the marketplace, the art and science of sales promotion has a particular appeal. It is not based on a 'finger in the wind', but on careful planning and budgeting. We will look at this later.

THE BASIC TECHNIQUES

Now let's look at the techniques that can be used within the field. They break down into three key areas from the consumer's point of view:

- *Free* – the consumer gets something free.
- *Save* – the consumer saves something up to get something back.
- *Win* – the consumer can win something.

Sales promotions are all variations on these themes. Let's look at them in turn and see how they can be applied for e-businesses.

Free

'Free' means just that – the consumer is being offered something for nothing. Now we all know there's no such thing as a free lunch, as do consumers. But in the field of incentivization the 'cost' of the free thing being offered might be as low as choosing a different brand to the normal one. The key techniques in this field are the four that follow, each of which has been analysed to allow the relative benefits to the marketer to be considered.

Free extra product

Giving away your own product is cheaper and less risky than buying in an extra gift, but, for packaged goods, packaging changes will be required to accommodate the extra product – so this can become costly! There are several ways of offering free extra product:

- *x* per cent more in this pack, when the pack is enlarged and the extra amount emblazoned on the website or on the promotional e-mail. Be sure that increased packaging and shipping costs are calculated to weigh the true cost of the promotion – you don't want to just shift more product at such a cut in profit that it *costs* you money to give product away!
- Three for the price of two, or six for the price of five. On the shelves of a supermarket, this means that either an extra product is banded on to the original amount or a special outer is designed (this depends on whether we are dealing with, say, toothpaste or soap, or lager), but if we are talking about e-ordered delivery of product from stock direct to customers then the question of 'banding' does not arise – you can simply ship three instead of two packs, so at least that is one cost you are not incurring.

Also, when it comes to services it is a comparatively cheap incentive to use: you can offer three months' service for the price of two months', or add 10 per cent more coverage, or whatever, at relatively little extra cost, but to the customer it might be just the reward they wanted, or it might encourage them to buy now, or take out the longer-term contract that you want them to.

Free extra product is very common because it offers an instant incentive and reward to those who purchase the product now. However, it is of little value in encouraging those who have never tried the product to try it today – why would you want three of something rather than two if you think you might not like it?

From the marketer's point of view, the costs of the promotion are known and totally controllable because you produce *x* number of special packs and put them into your normal distribution chain, thus allowing for 100 per cent uptake. There is little chance of gaining new customers but a great chance of gaining share of sales in the period when the special packs are available.

The other great advantage from the marketer's point of view is that it allows loyal customers to receive a reward for their loyalty, without endangering brand perception by lowering the price.

E-APPLICATION POINT

An on-line magazine has to work hard to build the subscription list that will become its saleable commodity as far as advertising is concerned. One weapon in its armoury will be enticingly written lead-in pages that are available to all browsers that make them want to read the continuation/more detail in the closed site.

In order to sell subscriptions the editorial team must make sure that what is promised on the front pages is delivered in the subscription site – but how do you convert the browser to commit to more than just the one month that might let them get a taste of whether they like the publication or not? Well, free extra product is unlikely to work – why should someone want to spend nine times more money for something they haven't yet tried – even if it is to get twelve months' worth for the price of nine months?

No, keep the free extra product offer for those who **have** tried the magazine, who can now base their decision to spend more on some experience rather than no experience. It is also a technique that works well to encourage existing subscribers to re-subscribe before their subscription dies! Get in early, reward them for their loyalty and give them a free gift of more of what they like.

Free in/on/with pack

This is another instant incentive and reward for the consumer, and allows anything and everything to be given away free, from space ships in cornflake boxes to Air Miles.

Depending on the type of physical packaging you use (if any), you can place a gift inside, so long as it is safely packaged and meets any legal requirements for, say, food and hygiene regulations. The cost of gifts means that the sort of item found as a free gift is usually very cheap, explaining the popularity amongst children's breakfast cereal manufacturers of this method. It also allows for 'sets' to be produced, encouraging consumers, especially children, to try to collect the whole range. This technique has gained popularity in the games market, where free CD-ROMs of additional games are placed as samples with the game actually purchased: this has the two-fold advantage of not just adding value to certain packs and of encouraging fast sales 'while stocks last', but it also gives the chance to offer a free sample of a product that might then be purchased!

Character merchandise, where a cartoon/film/television series or games characters are used as the inspiration, is particularly popular with children and teenage targeted products. Adults can be targeted by making sure that the gift looks less cheap and nasty by being relevant, e.g. plastic plant ties on a bottle of plant food, a knitting needle measurer in a large pack of wool.

From the marketer's point of view, there is difficulty in predicting the way in which the free gift will, in fact, increase sales solely because of the free gift. There is also the cost of the gift to be borne. Furthermore, not all marketers have the chance to put a gift inside their pack, so you might have to consider an on-pack promotion, e.g. a free emery board attached to a bottle of nail varnish remover. The nail file would need to be specially banded to the bottle, but, as you can imagine, the chance of pilferage or breakage during shipping is high. On-pack, as opposed to in-pack, allows for the gift to be the same whatever the product purchased, so, for example, if you are an on-line gardening supplies company you could offer a free soil acidity tester with the first order placed – whatever that order, you just include the acidity tester.

With-pack promotions, where the gift is held behind the counter and given out with the receipt of purchase, are gaining in popularity for in-store promotions. This can be done at the till point, if well managed and the gift is small, or can be easily handled if the gift is associated with a traditional counter-based purchase, such as quality cosmetics or perfumes. Department stores lend themselves to this sort of promotion and, very often, the free gift will be of high quality (a branded make-up bag with small-sized contents) and even exclusive to one or two department stores. When it comes to e-business it is likely that the 'with-pack' promotion will see the retailer replaced by the shipping company.

Be aware that many on-line sales operations do not hold stock themselves at one central point, but, rather, have it shipped directly from their suppliers to their customers, packaged in their corporate packaging outers. This presents problems for in- or on-pack offers, in that the coordination poses a huge problem. With-pack could actually mean that the gift is despatched from a central gift-holding point, whatever the customer has ordered, and the semantic difference of the gift arriving separately from the products is just that – a semantic difference rather than a perceived difference.

In all three variations on this particular theme, the marketer has the advantage of knowing the exact cost of the promotion in advance, because they set the limit to the number of gifts to be given, and the consumer has an immediate benefit. This type of free gift offer also has the advantage that, if the gift is sufficiently desirable in itself, the consumer may purchase the product for the first time in order to get the gift. Marketers must beware, however, that there is a fine line between finding a gift that has real appeal to the target audience, and dealing with wastage when, say, a with-pack promotion is not taken up as readily as hoped.

E-APPLICATION POINT

Sticking with the on-line magazine example, how might free gifts tempt or reward the reader? Well, free gifts can be despatched to existing subscribers only, thereby rewarding them, and the free gift could be a free three-month trial of a sister publication, of course, thereby offering a free trial opportunity too! If we take the off-line magazine example as a comparison, cover-mounted free gifts are a very popular way of gaining extra sales at the point of purchase. This can work in the virtual world too – a banner advertisement can lead a browser to see that a free gift is offered with this week's issue of, say, *GQ* on-line.

Once the browser has arrived at the site, they can be shown that the free gift can be obtained upon subscribing to the publication for three months trial, and at a specially reduced price too! Of course, the gift has to be appealing to those you wish to reward or attract, and it is always dangerous to give a gift to attract new customers but not to give it to loyal existing customers too, so beware of this potential pitfall. The gift can be physical or virtual – the key is that it must be relevant. This is an ideal point for joint promotions to kick in and deliver an advantage for more than one party – the gift could be supplied by another organization that will be a suitable partner for the promotion – for *GQ* it might be a menswear store that offers a discount to those who can produce the password protected print-out discount form.

Free mail-ins

Usually linked to multiple proofs of purchase (POPs) such as, say, a ring pull, pack opening, a bar-code, or maybe some sort of cookie implanted tracking system that proves purchases made on-line, this type of scheme has great appeal to the consumer only if the number of POPs required seems reasonable.

Slippage is a term used in this sort of scheme: it refers to the fact that many consumers will begin to collect POPs, whilst relatively few will redeem. Slippage is valuable to the marketer – it means that extra purchases are being made within the timescale allotted, but redemption costs can be relatively low, and it applies to e or non-e methods of POP collection.

The balance between pack run/redemption rate/usage/POPs/time lapse is very difficult to calculate, which makes this technique risky for physical sales where special packs are required to allow collection of the POPs (e.g. a special label, or ring pull). Careful analysis of other similar types of promotion is also difficult, unless they were within your own organization, as companies do not usually like to divulge the success of their promotions. Even with analysis of previous in-house promotions, a change in the weather, fashion, or even news stories and scares can make or break a promotion. But, if you are only relying upon the sort of POP that does not demand special pack printing, then you can run this sort of promotion more flexibly and with less risk, in that you don't have to calculate how many packs to print to put out there. That said, you still run the risk of a much higher uptake than you might have bargained for, with a higher redemption rate, so you still can end up in a mess, unless you try to calculate all the variables.

From the consumer's point of view, it should be reasonable to collect the required items within the time allotted, and the gift should bear some value relative to the amount of money being spent. Thus, with ten fizzy drink ring pulls a plastic can cooler would be reasonable, and it would even be possible to collect enough for a set of six, over a couple of months, whilst the purchase of a washing machine, car or several hundred pounds worth of goods through one webstore outlet would be expected to bring a much greater benefit, after a longer period of time allowed for collection, such as free or cheap air flights or holidays, or maybe a good deal of free product or service.

Even when the uptake of such flight/holiday schemes is high, in terms of sending in POPs to get the relevant vouchers, the marketer has yet another variable to deal with – how many consumers will actually go ahead and redeem the flight/holiday vouchers? There are famous, and infamous, stories about how over-redemption can result in chaos; the Hoover debacle is a story that is almost running out of steam in terms of how to organize a totally counter-productive promotional offer, but it still can teach us lessons about what *not* to do. True, over-redemption insurance can be taken out by the marketer, but this is expensive in its own right, and it should be weighed in the balance against the budget size and the chances of exceeding the budget.

For a fully detailed and very illuminating review of the details of the Hoover promotion that went wrong, and the international business implications for the US parent company, Maytag, see the chapter 'Maytag – bungling a promotion in England' in the 2001 edition of *Marketing Mistakes and Successes* by Robert F. Hartley (published by John Wiley). In summary, the promotion was set up to offer free flights for proof of purchase: unfortunately, the cost of the flights outstripped the additional profit from the additional sales, there was not only a huge demand for Hoover's lowest priced items to provide the proofs of purchase, but there was also a very high level of uptake of the free flights, which was probably heightened by the bad publicity that surrounded Hoover's handling of the situation. The problems rumbled on for years, and the damage done to the brand name as well as the finances of Hoover and the potential strength it might have built by remaining a part of the Maytag organization might never be fully understood.

Figure 4.1 The Hoover case

If free gifts are offered in this way then they must be truly free to the consumer. The additional cost of postage is allowed, but that is all. Packaging and handling costs must not be requested of the consumer. These costs will have to be borne by the marketer, so if the gift is heavy or delicate, the packaging and handling costs might make an otherwise attractive scheme very costly for the marketer. Also, where the marketer is having to order gifts from manufacturers, the danger of over- or under-ordering is high – if those special branded coffee mugs are half the price in Taiwan, beware of shipping and manufacturing delays that could lead to irate consumers! Of course, you can eradicate shipping costs and problems by making this a virtual reward for POPs, which, again, could be additional free services or other on-line goods.

With all its plus points, and dangers, this is still a popular technique with marketers. When considering this technique, make sure that the gift is one with which you as a marketer would wish to be associated and, with all the risks you will be taking, be sure to plan to allow for capture and future use of the information you gain about those who redeem. If consumers have taken the trouble to collect and redeem multiple POPs, you should find it worth storing the information they send you in order to talk to them again. The costs of such information storage and manipulation should be carefully investigated, but since data are almost our lifeblood these days, it should be placed at the top of the list of priorities.

E-APPLICATION POINT

Because POPs can be almost free to administer on-line, by making sure that the POP mechanism is built into the site, or bolted on, then the question arises – how to capitalize upon this on an ongoing basis. The on-line community has various 'currency' offerings at present. Let's take a look at one – beenz.com (Figure 4.2).

http://www.beenz.com

Launched in 1999, beenz.com offers a global currency (beenz) that can be earned at sites that sign up to offer beenz, and can be spent at sites that sign up to sell for beenz. The aim is to offer a market controlled POP system, that is popular because it can be redeemed for things that the collector actually wants! If you like, it is almost a virtual form of Air Miles, except that it is not branded as a travel redemption scheme. POPs can be fun on-line – you can use them as an intranet device too: if you want to encourage employees to visit an intranet page every week for a whole year to make sure they are keeping up to date with company news, then let them collect a full deck of playing cards when they visit each week, and let them redeem their deck for something they want!

Figure 4.2 Beenz Meenz?

Sampling

It really is difficult to beat the attraction of a free sample. There is no risk to the consumer and you are allowing them to form an opinion about your product or service based on the best possible type of information – their own experience. It is particularly effective if the product is new in concept as well as just being a new brand. Take instant white tea granules, for example. This is exactly the sort of product that will enter the marketplace with a huge job of work to do just to overcome people's prejudices about the *idea* of it, let alone anything else. How useful, therefore, to let potential purchasers try the product first, at no financial risk to themselves! And what about most of the services that are offered on-line? Again, there is sometimes a prejudice to be overcome – will I really use the Internet to find my. . .weather information, beauty tips, local entertainment information. . .or whatever it might be. So you have to let people try the system free for a while, hopefully letting them discover during that time period that they do, in fact, use the service, and realize they couldn't live without it!

Of course, the way in which you sample will depend on what it is you wish people to try. Tea granules can be contained in sachets and distributed relatively easily on existing packs of an associated nature, e.g. biscuits. Physical samples can be distributed by mail, door-to-door, banded to an existing pack, inside an existing pack, cover mounted on to magazines, fixed within magazines, or even handed out at the point of sale. What matters is that you choose the method that suits the product and reaches the audience you need to reach, i.e. those who have not yet tried the product.

Be aware that miniature samples are expensive to produce, and you will bear negotiable costs whatever your method of distribution. That said, you might have to consider giving a full-sized free sample – a full can or pack of cook-in sauce or a round-trip journey upgraded to Business Class on an airline. But if it's a free sample of a virtual

product or service, then the delivery method for the sample becomes much simpler: you can 'send' a free sample of service to an existing user of another service; you can give temporarily effective passwords to service users so they can access a closed site and try a free sample of the product, service or game you want them to experience.

The use of money-off coupons in conjunction with free samples is very popular. The coupon might be on the free sample or in the associated magazine or newspaper, or it might be a secure document that can be downloaded from the site. Be aware that if you are offering downloadable money-off vouchers they should: (a) have no intrinsic monetary value; (b) have a security device/code built into them which cannot be duplicated (e.g. a running number which is checked and checked off at the point of redemption). This incentivizes the first actual purchase after the free trial, and again increases the chance of committing to a new product, or a longer-term service provision on the part of the customer.

E-APPLICATION POINT

It is often the norm that you have to complete a certain amount of information that will be held and analysed by the marketer in order to access the free sample: certainly this is not unexpected, but the marketer needs to take care that they only ask for the minimum information they really will use – ask for too much and you will turn off the respondent before they enter the site. Get them in, incentivize them to stay and keep asking for more information whilst you track their movements to build a better profile!

Since e-business allows for total interaction, use this business dynamic and ensure that the customer knows you are using it. The potential for personalization within e-Customer Relationship Management (see Chapter 7) means that your sampling offers can be tailored to be most relevant to the individual customer concerned – thereby reducing waste and building the relationship with the customer at the same time.

Save

Self-liquidator premiums

Self-liquidator premiums (SLPs) offer the customer either an exclusive item (a Yahoo mouse mat) or money off a non-exclusive item (a Disney character mouse mat) when they supply *x* proofs of purchase (POPs) plus an amount of money. It is called 'self-liquidating' because the aim is for the promotion to be totally self-funding, with all costs of the gift/postage being covered by the consumer.

The main problem here is that it is difficult to see what you could offer that would be so special that a mass of customers would be prepared to wait up to 28 days for it, having taken the time to gather the POPs in the first place! It is not very popular with customers, but seems to retain its popularity with marketers, which would indicate it must still be achieving some objective for increasing sales of products or services.

The risks to the marketer are high – again there is the problem of knowing what the uptake will be and the associated problem of knowing what levels of gift should be ordered. Gifts that serve little useful purpose other than to shout your brand's name will probably not be wanted by your customers, especially when they can probably buy a T-shirt/sweat-shirt/umbrella today, in the high street, for the same price and without it looking like a freebie!

So beware! This technique is probably best used in conjunction with another, such as running a competition or offering a free gift with an associated SLP. Always try to order goods in the UK, since you might find you need more and thus need a fast delivery time! And don't forget, since e-business is expected to run more smoothly and to be more rapid, the customer is likely to expect a much faster turnaround of SLP gift delivery from an e-business than from a non-e-business.

E-APPLICATION POINT

Never lose sight of the reason for a promotion – if the aim is to sell more product or service in a given time, be sure there is a very good reason for people wanting to buy now. SLPs can be attractive, because you believe you are offering something that the customer will want – but you do need to carry out ample research to establish real needs and wants as opposed to perceived needs and wants. One area where this promotion is unlikely to work is in B2B marketing – free gifts and free extra product work well, but the impulse or desire linked with buying an exclusive or cut-price gift, as opposed to having one for free, is more difficult to kick into action in the B2B market than the B2C market.

Money-off coupons

Consumers love them, marketers often hate them! Why? Well, a money-off coupon has always been simplicity itself – as a customer you cut it out, take it with you when you shop and hand it over at the till to have an instant saving on. . .well, there you have it. The problem of redemption of coupons against the wrong brand or item is known as *malredemption*.

Sometimes it is a genuine mistake – the customer at the checkout really meant to buy Ariel instead of their usual Persil just to be able to use the coupon (this is known as *misredemption*). . .and the girl at the checkout knows they stock Ariel and can't remember which big box went through twenty items ago. Some retailers are happy to let the system continue in this way. Few manufacturers are. The use of a bar-code on the coupon that matches with the correct product can be used to reduce levels of malredemption and misredemption.

The Institute of Sales Promotion works with other interested parties to ensure that guidelines on the design of coupons are updated to recognize advances in technology or checkout practices.

 http://www.isp.org.uk

This website has comprehensive information on how to design a coupon and how to run a money-off or free coupon promotion. The site also contains masses of information of enormous relevance to checking most issues that arise when considering running a sales promotion – on-line or off-line!

Coupons were revitalized in the early 1990s with the introduction to the UK of the coupon booklet which is inserted into a national newspaper or magazine. This means that forecasting redemption rates has become extremely important, because a 1 per cent misforecast could mean that costings are wrecked. Also, bear in mind that money-off coupons need special security – they are as good as cash at the supermarket!

Most coupons in the UK are cleared through the Nielsen Clearing House (NCH). Retailers send the coupons there, NCH arranges payment to the retailer and invoices the manufacturer. NCH produces regular reports for manufacturers so they can monitor their products at all times.

E-APPLICATION POINT

Due to security issues you might find it best to not produce a printable money-off coupon, but to allow money-off links – in other words, if you link into a site from a given point you will automatically go to a sub-section that allows you access to different price offers. This has the same effect as offering money off, but uses technology instead of snipping with scissors, to achieve the same end.

Win

Competitions

Yes, people do really win! But the perception of competitions by the consumer is often that there is little point in entering because it could never be them that would win the car/£10 000/holiday of a lifetime. So entry levels to most competitions tend to be low, even when the prizes are big. Indeed, it is often better to offer a large number of small prizes rather than one big one, because people see their chances of winning something increasing.

However, the main reason that competitions remain popular with marketers is that the cost of the prize is known in advance and will not change, whatever the level of entries. This is a great advantage in that it offers budgetary control but allows the generation of extra sales by requesting, say, POPs to accompany entries. Offering an easy to enter competition on-line means having few barriers to entry, and making it attractive means making sure that the prize or prizes are appealing to the target customers.

The main area that the marketer has to be aware of here is the legal framework within which the competition must take place: the Lotteries and Amusements Act (1976) states that if the entrant to a competition has had to purchase something in order to enter (e.g. provide a POP), then there must be an element of skill within the competition. Enter the tie-breaker element – most popularly a phrase to be written by the entrant or a few questions that can be answered by most people with average general knowledge. This is how a competition differs from the next type of win category.

E-APPLICATION POINT

Once again, the Institute of Sales Promotion (ISP) website can give valuable information that is up to date about what is and is not legal, when it comes to competitions. Don't ever guess – always check! It is worth bearing in mind, however, that whilst laws about what is and is not allowed as a competition change from country to country, if you have a global website, you don't just have to come up with a web competition that is legal, but one that actually appeals to people from many different cultures, with very different expectations about what is and what is not an acceptable prize for a certain type of competition. You will also have to juggle what is normally regarded as 'good taste' in different cultures. True, this is the case for all promotional activity, but it seems to come into very sharp relief with competitions, where the balance between belief, hope, greed and just rewards all come into fine play.

Free prize draws

These often sail very close to the wind, legally! A free prize draw must be just that – totally free to enter, in the UK. No POP can be requested, no newspaper must have to be bought to obtain the bingo numbers within it, and so on. Plain-paper entries, i.e. an entry not on the official entry form that might be printed on the pack/in the magazine, therefore must be allowed. But what about websites? It's very tempting to offer a free prize draw when someone enters your website and all they have to do is give you some personal and professional details to be entered into the draw to get something they fancy getting for free – but don't undermine your brand or your name by offering prizes that are either totally tatty or which never appear to be won. Think about it – do you really want your name to be associated with cheapness (unless yours is the sort of website where tat or kitsch prizes would actually fit the offering and appeal to the target audience!) or with a sort of showmanship that offers prizes but never follows up on who has actually won them?

A free prize draw has the advantage of budgetary control, as in competitions, but if no purchase is truly required it is very difficult to explain exactly how this type of promotion will increase sales! They do work, however, when it comes to getting people to give you more information about themselves than they would if there were no chance of a prize at all.

E-APPLICATION POINT

The Lotteries and Amusements Act is full of pitfalls for the unwary so, in reality, it is always best to seek specialist legal advice when you are planning to run either a competition or a free prize draw. Some large manufacturers' own legal departments might have specialists within them, or else the Institute of Sales Promotion (ISP) can advise. Be very careful to find out what laws you must abide by when running any sort of lottery or free prize draw – take advice, don't guess and don't assume that someone with non-e experience will be well placed to advise you!

Planning to use a promotion

Now that we have looked at the main techniques involved, what sort of objectives can be achieved with them? Well, it is worth saying it again – be realistic when setting all promotional objectives, and be sure that your overall promotional programme is planned to work as a whole, thus each promotional objective is more likely to be achievable. With sales promotions you might want to consider some of the following as your objectives:

- Sampling/broadening customer base.
- Line extension to new/existing customers.
- Brand switching.
- Forward/bulk buying.

- Overcoming seasonal dips in sales.
- Trade or supplier support.
- Creating 'noise' on-pack or at point of sale (virtual POS or real POS).
- Simply building volume.
- Bringing sales forward in time.
- Building loyalty.

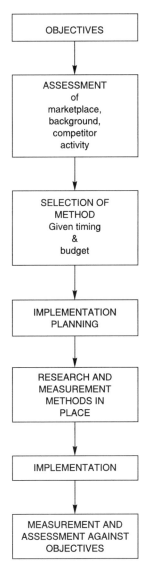

Figure 4.3 Planning promotions

Obviously, in an ideal world you would set your objectives and then your budget, but it is much more likely that you will have a budget figure and have to select the method that will achieve realistic objectives within that budget. Also, remember that you will have to sell the promotion into the trade as well as out to the consumer – there is little point in creating demand for a product that is not sufficiently well stocked!

Whatever method you choose for making your promotion attractive to the consumer, never forget that you have to include the supplier in your plans – if you are not the supplier, that is. Why? Well, other than the obvious point that if you are aiming to sell more then they need to stock more, be aware that some suppliers are only interested in offering exclusive promotions not available to their major competitor, e.g. a book might have an associated give-away on the bol.com website, but not on the amazon.com one.

When it comes to B2B incentives, or even internal ones, the difference between a bribe and an incentive is very clear – the latter being totally above board. Competitions, not free prize draws, are very popular, as are small gifts that are relevant and useful, e.g. the pen with the logo at Christmas, the desk blotter with the logo in the spring, and so on. However, bear in mind that, currently, some gifts are taxable so, unless you want to arrange to pay the tax to the Inland Revenue on behalf of the recipient, you need to make gifts small and frequent, rather than large and annual – don't ever guess what the figure might be, always check with the Inland Revenue *at the time*! Once again, the ISP website gives valuable advice here for UK practice, but, because you might well be operating globally, you will have to research all the countries that are affected.

You should also calculate the tax implications of all sales force incentive programmes. Financial bonuses are an obvious choice, but make sure an expert checks out the implications of the sort of scheme that allows the upgrading of a company car, and so on. The rules change frequently, so the best advice is to check at the time. And don't forget that whilst overseas conferences and exhibitions might prove attractive to some, extra time off might prove more attractive to others! Since bonus and commission schemes are, properly speaking, a form of sales promotion and incentive, they can be mentioned here – especially since a key point about integrating your marketing communications is to check that all communications tools, to internal, partner and external audiences, are in harmony with each other! That said, it is likely that the sales director, rather than the marketing director, will have control over such systems and schemes, so this is where internal liaison will be needed – make sure that there is an acceptable level of incentive against targets that are realistic, though, as setting unrealistic targets means you might attract the wrong sort of sales person and thereby the wrong sort of sales!

The website provided by the Institute of Sales Promotion is a valuable resource in this field, especially as it allows access to legal framework and an advice route. Find it:

 @ http://www.isp.org.uk

Sponsorship as a promotional tool

Sponsorship can be a very effective tool, if used properly and as part of an integrated plan of action. It really is one of the tools that benefits most from being used in conjunction with others. In this unit we will concentrate on four main types of sponsorship:

- Programme sponsorship, as dealt with by the Independent Television Commission (ITC) and the Radio Authority (RA).
- Sport/art/other event sponsorship.
- Individual/team sponsorship.
- Community project/charity.

There's just one tip that goes with any form of sponsorship: many people spend their entire sponsorship budget on the sponsorship itself – *don't*! Allow at least the same amount of money to publicize your sponsorship as you do for the sponsorship itself. This requires tremendous discipline, because it's always tempting to go for the bigger sponsorship, believing that it will draw publicity to it, free of charge, like a magic magnet – but the truth is that this just doesn't happen. If you want your sponsorship money to work for you, *you* have to make it work – you have to use other methods of communication to tell people that you are spending money on the sponsorship, and to explain why – to offer linked competitions, buy in the hospitality suites, get the logos printed on the give-aways and to run the proactive media relations programme that will reach other groups of people who will not be able to actually witness or take part in the sponsorship activity itself.

It is marvellous to have more than the same amount of money as the sponsorship to do all this, but, as I say, you should earmark at least the same amount!

PROGRAMME SPONSORSHIP

The ITC is responsible for overseeing the sponsorship of television programmes, and the Radio Authority mirrors this function for radio transmissions. It is vital that this type of sponsorship is tightly controlled.

Television

The ITC Code has two key principles:

1 To ensure that programmes are not distorted for commercial purposes. A sponsor must not influence the content or scheduling of a programme in such a way as to affect the editorial independence and responsibility of the broadcaster.

2 To maintain a distinction between advertising and sponsor credits. This is to ensure that credits are not used to extend the time allowed for advertising.

The following are not allowed to sponsor television programmes:

- *Political bodies*: this includes any organization whose aims are wholly or mainly of a political nature. (For a definition of a political body, see the ITC Code of Advertising Standards and Practice.)
- *Manufacturers of tobacco products*: this includes any company whose name is chiefly known to the public through its tobacco business, even though it may sell other non-tobacco products and services.
- *Those who cannot advertise on television*: these are listed in the ITC Code of Advertising Standards and Practice.

Providers of the following are allowed to sponsor television programmes, but are subject to certain restrictions:

- *Pharmaceutical products*: pharmaceutical manufacturers may not refer in their credits to brands that are only available on prescription.
- *Bookmaking*: bookmakers (including companies whose principal business is bookmaking) may not sponsor programmes that include coverage of horse or greyhound racing, or the results of such racing.
- *Gaming*: gaming companies (including companies whose principal business is gaming) may not sponsor television game shows that closely resemble the gaming that takes place in bingo halls and casinos.
- *Other restrictions*: no advertiser may sponsor a programme during which they would not be permitted to advertise.

The rules concerning sponsorship and product placement, for example, are complex and can change at any time. It is always best to check them rather than to assume you know what they are! A great way to do this is via the ITC's website, which is kept up to date:

 @ http://www.itc.org.uk

Whilst working within the ITC's rules, it is still possible for programme sponsorship to open up exciting possibilities for the marketer – especially the marketer for an e-business that might benefit tremendously from setting up links and connections in the mind of the potential customer, whilst building name awareness. But be aware that sponsorship is *not* good at building brand understanding – only awareness and image. In the early stages of an organization's life, it might be vital to build understanding as well as awareness and image – so this is when a mix of communication methods, using sponsorship as one of a number of different methods of reaching the target audience, really comes into play. So, ensuring that not only the rules of the code but also the rules of promotional planning are adhered to is the key issue.

Programme sponsorship can help you reach members of your target market who might be difficult, or much more expensive, to reach as a target audience being tackled by your above the line budget. An on-line travel company might want to reach viewers of a gameshow that gives holidays as prizes, but know that their advertising budget is not sufficiently large to advertise in the breaks within the show. Sponsorship offers them a way to reach the viewers, with wrap-around sponsorship credits in return for a contribution to the costs of making the programmes as well as, possibly, the donation of holidays as prizes, for example. Of course, programme sponsorship does mean that the style, content and communication contained within the credits are limited to no more than a simple branding exercise, so should be seen as part of a wider promotional mix, but, that said, the chance is there to build massive brand awareness very quickly whilst using other media to communicate brand image and specific product or service messages in tandem.

Television programme sponsorship was very popular with e-business start-ups during 1999 and 2000, but it seems to have declined since then. It is hard to say why, but the lack of budgets now available to companies that are worth a lot less on the Stock Market these days certainly accounts for a lot less money being spent on TV advertising, and therefore to less money being spent on TV sponsorship too: the link is undeniable!

Radio

The Radio Authority is the body which controls radio sponsorship within the UK. It has a Code of Advertising and Sponsorship Practice which must be adhered to at all times.

Payment, or rewards in kind, can be made in return for the sponsor of a programme having their brand announced at the beginning and end of a programme, as well as at 'appropriate' points during longer programmes, to ensure that the listener knows who has sponsored the programme.

Sponsorships, like advertisements, have to be cleared ahead of broadcast.

The website has full details of the codes:

 @ http://www.radioauthority.org.uk

Once again, the links with shows, formats or presenters mean that you can reach the same audience you would be buying with ad space, but reaching them in a different way with sponsorship; the drawbacks are that, whilst radio can build pictures in the mind, it cannot create any sort of visual awareness for a logo or corporate identity. But since you could be using other forms of communication to get this information across, it might be that the building of name and address awareness and image (by linking with the programme) will be all you need from this form of promotion – in which case it is ideal.

SPONSORSHIP OF SPORTS/ARTS/EVENTS

This is a different type of sponsorship and needs to be looked at separately. Any event can be sponsored – a football match, an athletics meeting, a horse race, a concert, a run of performances of a play, an exhibition of Victorian costumes. Alternatively, a person, team, theatre company, museum or football league can be sponsored. Each type of sponsorship will offer slightly different opportunities to the sponsor, so let's look at each option in turn.

Sponsoring an event or series of events

As mentioned above, any sort of event can be sponsored. It could be a total one-off, such as a specially organized pre-season football match, or an annual event such as the

Once again, there are no right and wrong ways to use sponsorship. What you need is an understanding of the overall promotional programme and a clear understanding of why sponsorship is being used at all. The questions you need to ask are:

- Who will attend the event?
- Is this a chance for corporate hospitality?
- Will our competitors be using the event for hospitality?
- Who else will be exposed to the event? For example, will there be television coverage? Is there interest for press coverage? Radio? National press?
- How will I present myself to these other audiences? Include the name of the sponsor as part of the name of event? Put logo hoardings around the event site?
- Is this event relevant to our overall corporate/brand positioning? Does it add to our positioning programme or is it opening new vistas? How familiar with our name will those people be who are exposed to it?
- Who has sponsored this event in the past? (You will be associated with them in some way by those who are familiar with the event, and your sponsorship will be compared with theirs. Make sure you understand this historical perspective.)

Unless you can answer these questions you cannot decide how valuable the sponsorship will be to you, so you cannot even begin to discuss the financial side of the deal. You need a clear understanding of value to be able to say that a sponsorship is or is not worth £500 000 to your organization, for example. Even if the figures involved are small, say a few hundred pounds to be a sponsor of a local chamber of commerce exhibition to schools, you should still be sure that the money is being spent in reaching the right people in the right way with the right message!

Figure 4.4   Should I or shouldn't I?

Grand National horse race. Sponsors might choose to commit themselves to sponsoring an annual event for only one year or for any number of years they choose, and which the organizers are prepared to accept. The nature of the sponsorship (whether huge amounts of money are involved, as in a golf championship, where lots of prize money is offered, or small, for say a local football match) and the way in which the sponsor is linked to the event are still matters for discussion between the organizers and the potential sponsors. This puts the responsibility for deciding objectives squarely on the shoulders of the sponsor!

Be sure that you sponsor the right event for you! It might be that your sponsorship forms an integral part of your overall corporate promotional programme, or it might be specific to one brand. Be sure you make the right choice.

Another point to make here is that it is the sponsor's responsibility to *check* that the organizer is planning to generate as much publicity for the event, in the right way, as the sponsor wants. Depending on the exact nature of the sponsorship deal struck, it might even be that the sponsor wants their own publicity machinery to be directly involved in the promotion of the event. It is this sort of detail that needs to be worked out beforehand, as there is very little point in arguing about it once the event has taken place and the opportunity has been lost.

Sponsorship of an individual or team

This is a slightly different form of sponsorship which revolves around a person, a yacht, a car, etc.

Your sponsorship could simply be 'in kind', i.e. you simply supply tennis racquets free of charge, or allow the person or team to use your gym or rehearsal facilities free of charge in return for your name being associated with theirs. You could offer your GPS System free to a yachtsman or you could offer free e-mail and on-line satellite conversations and even broadcasts from the journey! The list of possibilities is endless – but this is the category where it is an individual person or a definite group of people who act as some sort of 'team' that is somehow involved. There can, of course, be much more formal sponsorships: a Formula 1 racing car driver will be sponsored by an organization to always be seen on race day wearing a baseball cap with their logo, whilst on practice days he might have another 'hat' sponsor.

Don't forget that 'an individual' might be a whole theatre group, whom you sponsor on an ongoing basis, with the group seeking other specific project sponsors on an ad hoc basis. Then, of course, you would need to negotiate the amount of connection you always receive compared with the amount received by their project sponsors. You might even want to ensure that *x* number of seats are available for you at every performance so that you can use the theatre as a hospitality venue, or even as a perk for your top sales personnel, or best performing dealers.

Once again, be aware that you need a good match of relevance and, here especially, you might find ongoing hospitality potential, or you might find there is no scope for that sort of deal. By sponsoring, say, a yacht, or a golfer, you are tying your reputation very closely to that of one item – a sinking yacht with your logo on the sail might not do your image much good, and scandal or unfavourable press comment is an ever-present threat with individuals. The only pointer here is to be sensible in your initial choice, and monitor whatever or whoever you are sponsoring. If something goes wrong that is nothing to do with your involvement, but your name is in some way associated with a calamity, be sure you have plans in place for how you would deal with this.

Some team sponsorships have now become frighteningly expensive, with some football teams getting so much television coverage that they can demand multi-million pound deals, and get them!

Don't think that all individual/team sponsorships are this expensive, they are not, and there are often people out there who need relatively small amounts of money, that will make a huge difference to them, and can deliver you a cost-effective communication opportunity.

Community or charity sponsorship

A great number of e-businesses have been set up by people who want to give something back to the community – and they do so as soon as they can within the organization's life. This is a great way of making sure that good causes are supported, but, without wishing to be too cynical about it, it really is worth making sure that promotional expenditure goes towards promoting the company – and that charitable donations are seen as something separate. This might seem obvious, but I have met people who want to do good, but end up crippling their own organization because people and resources, as well as money, are being tied up with a good cause, when they should be being used to build and strengthen the business itself – maybe allowing it to do more good at some point in the future when it is better established.

Another point that is worth mentioning, if only because of the very specific nature of many small e-business start-ups, is that often the e-business will have board members who are also involved with charitable works: we are all familiar with the retired finance director who is now doing a bit of business advising e-businesses whilst also supporting his favourite charities. Well meaning though it might be, just because a board member supports a charity, it doesn't mean that it's the best one for an organization to support!

Community projects and charities do offer the chance to do good and build a profile – but only if the cause/charity and your positioning and goals have a good fit: should you support child charities or earth charities? What about education overseas, or animal charities? The answer might be obvious (you're an on-line environmental impact advice line, so earth charities might be your choice) or not so clear – but planning and thought will help. Work through all the implications – both positive and negative – of being associated with this project/charity (a) if all goes according to plan and (b) if everything that could go wrong did go wrong. Then you'll have a better understanding of how hard your money will have to work.

Overall, then, sponsorship can offer value for money and can boost your budget's ability to communicate with large groups of relevant people by associating yourself with something bigger than you could ever hope to produce alone. That said, it is still quite an under-utilized resource in many organizations' promotional programming, so keep your eyes open for novel/impactful sponsorships.

 ## Merchandising

This refers to the way in which, in total, a product is offered for sale. It covers everything from the packaging of the product (in terms of its outer packaging), to the way it is presented to the retailer for sale (whether the products are in trays that can be placed on counters as a part of the point-of-sale display, how the product stacks and stands on the shelving in the outlet), to any and all promotional items that may either be attached to it or form an integral part of the way it is offered for sale. In terms of, say, photocopiers being sold at office equipment retail outlets, in might even include such items as the training/user manual, samples of output from the system for customers to see/use, the development of an in-store 'try me out' system programme to encourage the participation of the potential purchaser, and the literature which makes up the follow-up database building and after-sales service package. Now, you might be thinking, but how is this relevant to e-business? Don't forget, many e-businesses are just an extension of a non-e-business, so it might be that you have to consider packaging and merchandising issues as well as web promotion and on-line sales issues – and the cross-fertilization of access point information could be key to your overall success, so just be aware that all your merchandising offers you the chance to promote your on-line or other e-offerings, and your on-line effort gives you the chance to promote your non-e sales points too!

The important thing to grasp when considering the field of 'merchandising' is that it needs to be relevant to the sales environment concerned, whether that be on-line or off-line, and also needs to add to the appeal of the product or service, rather than be treated as a separate entity. Indeed, it will comprise many elements, with packaging and point-of-sale techniques being the key factors – bearing in mind that the web might be your point of sale, rather than an in-store environment.

OFF-LINE AND ON-LINE APPLICATIONS

When you are a marketer who sells through retail outlets you will only be able to influence a certain proportion of the whole purchasing environment, a tiny part or a great deal of it depending upon the marketplace and the retailing situation within it. For example, let's say you are the UK distributor of a range of restaurant kitchen deep-fat fryers manufactured in the USA. You might find that you make many sales through catalogue sales or direct contract purchasing (to a fast food chain, for example). There will be a portion of your sales, however, that will be made through the specialist retailers who offer commercial catering equipment for sale. How will you ensure that *your* deep-fat fryer has pride of place in the window display?

How will you then ensure that it is always clean, free of grubby fingerprints, and well presented to potential purchasers? How will you ensure that your product will appeal as much as possible at the point of purchase without you having a sales person standing there looking over it 24 hours a day?

It is this type of merchandising question that must be answered every day by marketers. In this instance you could consider a package of eye-catching point-of-sale display stand-up cards with, perhaps, a holder for technical or performance criteria leaflets or range catalogue attached, together with a complementary cleaning kit for the retailer, frequent visits by *whichever* of your personnel happens to be in the area at any time, and even a 'best presented equipment' competition for retailers as an incentive to keep your product in tip-top condition would help too!

But what if your retail outlet is a website owned and operated by an on-line specialist or general retailer, with whom you have signed a deal to supply through them, and therefore you want to appear, at your best, in their virtual retail outlet? Well, the issue of grubby fingerprints disappears for your on-line sales, but you still need to offer the right level of liaison and support to ensure that the photography and presentation of your deep-fat fryer is of the highest quality and properly represents the product offering. You will work with the on-line retailer to ensure that you are always getting the best 'Star Buy' position on the site, and work with them to incorporate feature stories about your manufacturing techniques and sources of raw materials – it is this sort of relationship building that goes a long way to ensuring that your product is easy to find, stands out from the crowd and looks the best it can to the browsing potential purchaser.

Bear in mind that *all* 'real' POS merchandising of your deep-fat fryers will have an impact on the e-purchaser's perception of your brand and of this product in particular – so, just because you might be incorporating on-line sales, through a third party's website, or, indeed, your own, don't think you can ease back on the retail store presentation management!

All aspects of offering your product or service for sale must be given attention; no detail is too small to be overlooked. Let's now focus on two key areas for attention – packaging and point-of-sale techniques.

 ## Packaging

Packaging has to meet certain criteria in order to justify its position within the promotional mix. The outcome of meeting all your packaging requirements should be an item of packaging that protects and enhances the sales appeal of your product.

When amazon.com went to market, they placed particular emphasis on their packaging – not only as a means of identifying what was arriving and from whom, but also in terms of ensuring that the product reached the customer in perfect condition. With product purchasing from e-businesses usually involving third party delivery, packaging is a *vital* link in the chain of delivering ultimate customer satisfaction – indeed, goods damaged in transit will not only irritate and disappoint customers, but they can end up costing the company a fortune in replacement and insurance costs.

There is no definitive list of the attributes of packaging, which will vary from specific case to case, but here at least is a list of factors that should be considered:

- *How will it protect your product during transit?* Depending upon whether the product is frozen, to be shipped overseas, contains easily perishable goods or is very fragile, you will need to use different physical packaging solutions that allow the product to reach the retailer and the consumer in peak condition. If you are an on-line gardening site such as greenfingers.com you will find that you have to be very creative in your packaging solutions. A visit to their site will give you some ideas of the sorts of challenges they face when despatching anything from seeds to saplings to shears to sheds!

- *How will it promote your product and brand when it arrives?* Will you use the pack to 'shout' at the customer with on-pack offers, recipe ideas and so on, or will you only use packaging in this way occasionally, with the normal promotional role of the pack being to please because it is generally well designed/novel/traditional looking?

- *How will it protect your product after delivery, but before use/consumption?* When the product is being stored by the customer, will the packaging protect and keep it safe for them? Will it be easy for them to store part of the pack if they do not use it all at once, and will the product be kept at its best?

- *How will it affect the usage of your product by the consumer?* Does your packaging present itself as easy to open and use? Will it allow good delivery of your product? Is it going to make the job of using your product difficult for the purchaser?

- *How will it remind your consumer of your brand values?* Remember, if you want to continue the brand values you have established through the rest of your promotional programme right up to the point of delivery, you must ensure that your packaging does not let you down at the last minute. Even if your proposition to the customer was 'cheap and cheerful', they will still expect the packaging to perform all its necessary protection and delivery functions, as well as being easy to handle and open.

- *How will it encourage your consumer to buy again?* If all that is left in the boot of a car is the last drop of oil in a well-branded container, then the brand message will be right at the front of the mind of the purchaser when they re-purchase. This is the same for foodstuffs in cupboards, freezers and fridges, or office products and consumables of all types. The packaging is likely still to be an integral part of the product when it is being finished with/disposed of, so make sure it promotes your brand in a way that reminds the purchaser that it was, specifically, your brand.

- *How will it affect the environment when it is finished with?* This is an increasingly important question for the marketer to ask. In some countries, Germany for example, all packaging must now be recyclable by law. We have not reached that point in the UK, but most users of packaged goods are aware that packaging creates waste that can cause environmental problems. Your position might be to shout about environmental friendliness in all aspects of your product manufacture, and so packaging issues will be especially sensitive, or it might be that you simply want to highlight the fact that your packaging is recyclable, or even made from recycled materials. Technology means that many more packaging materials can be made from recycled products and be recyclable, or can just be recyclable.

Obviously, if you are in the business of selling windscreen wiper blades or other automotive accessories, you will have a significantly different set of answers to the problems and issues posed above – in detail, that is, rather than in scope – than a marketer selling aromatherapy oils. Even the dealer mentioned earlier who offers deep-fat fryers for sale must answer these packaging questions, because the fryer that is sold in the retail outlet will probably be delivered from stock in packaging that needs to protect the item in transit and ensure that all parts are there when it arrives at its destination.

Some products are presented for sale with the minimum amount of packaging possible. For example, a range of towels and facecloths might have no 'packaging' as such, other than a swing ticket attached to them that has a price and a bar-code on it when they are offered for sale in a 'real' retail store. Why is this? Well, the best way to make this product appeal at the point of sale might be to let the consumer see and feel the product and, bearing in mind that most people would wash a towel before using it after purchase anyway, there is no need to wrap it up in a plastic/paper wrapper for display. Of course, this approach leaves the way open for the manufacturer of a different style of towel, with a different position in the market, to offer towels for sale wrapped in, say, a cotton drawstring sack, that can be reused as a laundry bag, where the drawstrings are used to hang up the product for presentation at the point of sale with just one unwrapped towel on display for selection purposes. When it comes to the virtual store, there is no opportunity for the purchaser to feel and judge the perceived quality of a towel on a web screen, so packaging needs to be designed in a different way – it will not lead to the impulse purchase, unless it is displayed and made to look attractive – so show the range in their drawstring bags, but also mention in the copy that the bags are waterproof!

Packaging can set your product apart from its competitors; it can be the embodiment of the personality you desire for your product; it can draw the eye of the customer to your product rather than your competitor's, even if it is virtual packaging. Indeed, it *should* do all these things, and if it does not then it is the marketer's fault that a great opportunity has been missed to give one final push to the product, not just to make this sale, but to ensure a consolidation of reasons for the next sale too.

Direct marketing

Direct marketing 'happens' when a client company (the provider of a product or service) decides to set up a direct relationship with the purchaser of its product or service. It may be that the provider, e.g. Nestlé, has a chain of distribution to deal with, i.e. retailers *and* end-users. A direct relationship can be built with both types of buyer – the professional buyer who places huge orders on behalf of their retail chain *and* the end-user who just wants one jar of coffee off the supermarket shelf.

The marketer within the client company needs to make the strategic decision to initiate and build this direct relationship bearing in mind that the relationship must be managed to fulfil the objectives set for it. A key point to consider is that if direct marketing depends upon building a direct relationship with the customer then direct communications are the linchpin upon which direct marketing relies. Indeed, even in the pages of *Campaign*, a trade magazine seen as a traditional advertising title, there is increasing talk of 'direct communications' and the role played by this growing discipline within traditional, above the line advertising agencies.

Here we will consider the various situations within which direct marketing techniques can be used, how to choose the most appropriate method of promoting this relationship, then how to evaluate actual performance. There are few generalities in promotional planning, or indeed in the fields of marketing and marketing communications, but there are some key points to remember when considering the concept of direct marketing:

- All forms of direct marketing are growing very quickly; this can be seen to be mainly due to the fall in costs of computing time and equipment, which allows financially efficient use of data.

- All traditional media can be evaluated in terms of their suitability for use in a direct marketing programme.

- Keeping a customer is usually much cheaper than always having to find new ones, hence the growth in the practice of 'relationship marketing', which is a term which refers to the use of direct marketing techniques to build a long-term relationship with a customer and ensure you get the full lifetime value of their custom.

- Since direct marketing only works to its full potential when you talk to *exactly* the right people in the right way at the right time, the cornerstones of planning a successful programme are research and testing.

- The relevance of direct marketing to e-business cannot be emphasized too strongly – the one-to-one relationship can work wonderfully over the web, and the mass communication with individuals, the relationship of one-to-one, one-to-few and one-to-many that direct marketing requires and e-business allows is just about the most perfect marriage you could imagine.

FINANCIAL PLANNING – OR HOW MUCH IS A CUSTOMER WORTH?

Direct marketing, like all marketing, is driven by economics. In commercial terms, it is necessary to make a profit in order to survive. For historical reasons, not least direct marketing's evolution through mail order and response-driven advertising and direct mail, the economics of direct marketing have tended towards the calculation of immediate returns on investment. This is being overtaken by a more long-term approach which recognizes that it is increasingly worthwhile to invest in recruiting loyal customers and accepting a return on that investment over a longer time (Figure 4.5).

Short-term financial planning, e.g. for a mail order advertisement, would need to cover:

- Cost of promotion.
- Cost of product.
- Cost of distribution.
- Cost of bad debt provision.
- Any other costs (e.g. fulfilment house, insurance).
- Profit.

This type of planning is the lifeblood of direct marketing because it enables you to see the cost and revenue implications of all activity. It provides the groundwork for long-term planning.

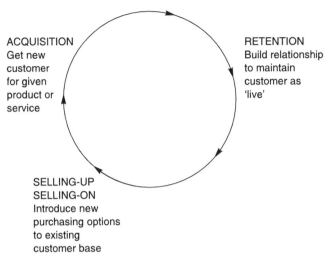

ACQUISITION
Get new
customer
for given
product or
service

RETENTION
Build relationship
to maintain
customer as
'live'

SELLING-UP
SELLING-ON
Introduce new
purchasing options
to existing
customer base

Figure 4.5 Using retention to build business

Long-term financial planning for lifetime value would cover:

- Cost of recruitment.
- Cost of retention, including database costs.
- Profitability.

MEDIA AND COMMUNICATIONS STRATEGIES FOR DIRECT MARKETING

Evaluating media for direct marketing does not differ from evaluating media for other purposes such as reach, CPT, effectiveness and medium for product (need to demonstrate, need for colour, etc.).

It is worth noting that direct marketing media selectors traditionally know how much airtime or space is worth in real terms (measured by the cost per response or cost per order generated) rather than in opportunities to see (OTS) or percentage of target audience reached – hence such things as per item (PI) deals (where the advertiser pays a set amount per response or per sale to the media owner). Traditionally, again, direct marketing media effectiveness is assessed by:

- Front-end (response).
- Back-end (conversion).

And increasingly also by:

- Long-term profitability.
- Retention costs.

The role that direct marketing communications play in doing the general advertising job of awareness and promoting the brand is now also having an impact on media selection.

What are direct marketing media?

Any medium can be used for direct marketing purposes:

- Direct mail.
- Press.
- Television.
- Radio.
- Posters.
- Door drops.
- Telephones.
- Fax, e-mail websites.

What makes a good direct marketing medium?

It depends on what you are trying to do. For example:

- Generating enquiries about a low-cost item would not necessarily demand a medium capable of transmitting a large amount of information.
- Selling a high ticket item in one stage would need a large amount of information and persuasive content.
- If you need to have a form filled in and signed, you have to pick a medium that can deliver your form to the target.

Media applications

Direct mail

Direct mail is expensive, but is highly targetable, flexible and discreet. It is still the single most important direct marketing medium and is used both for business-to-business and consumer marketing. However, it can be intrusive. 'Junk mail' is simply bad direct mail; it is usually both sent to the wrong audience and bad in itself (clumsy offer, creatively amateur). However, there are indications that the public does not distinguish between direct mail, which is more likely to be professionally done, and unaddressed door drops which are likely to be done by amateurs. Much of what is called 'junk mail' probably isn't mail at all.

Telephone

This is the single most important direct marketing medium in the USA. It is flexible, but is relatively expensive, highly intrusive, and difficult to do well (because you need professional training, good staff selection, expert and continuing control – all of which cost money and tempt clients to cut corners).

It's okay for business marketing as business people expect to receive sales calls at work, and see it as part of their job. Because of its obtrusiveness as a medium, it is less good for consumer marketing, unless you are talking to existing customers and can be seen to be providing them with opportunities that non-consumers do not get.

Press

With the press you can use space (insertions) or loose leaf or bound-in inserts (a slightly confusing use of terminology).

- *Space*: the use of space gives you the advantages of relatively short deadlines (except in, for example, gravure magazines), but limits the print area you have available, limits you in the use of colour (in local and national press) and control of reproduction quality. The press gives you a wide reach, and thus it is good for trawling for prospects and customers and through specialist interest groups cost-effectively.
- *Inserts*: whilst publications place restrictions on the size and weight of insert you are allowed, overall you still have more scope for creativity, as your choice of colour is limited only by your budget. You have control of production quality, and you can achieve economies of scale by printing large numbers of inserts to go in different publications. In general, inserts pull in better than space.

Door-to-door

Door-to-door marketing can be very effective because it is extremely economical in terms of unit cost. It is targetable up to a point through Acorn, Pinpoint and Mosaic, or through distribution with selected freesheets (e.g. *London Living*). It is cheap to distribute and can be very cheap to produce. It has a very largely deserved downmarket image, no personalization possible, and is surrounded by lots of clutter – it arrives with everything from double glazing to *Sun* bingo cards.

Broadcast

In many respects broadcast media are still the best way to reach a wide audience. Television allows demonstration of the product and has a high impact, although production costs tend to be very high and lead times very long. Radio reaches more closely defined target audiences and can be very quick and cheap to produce. Unlike

television, radio is not subject to zapping, but radio is typically listened to while something else is being done – it is a background medium. New media such as cable television will probably improve targeting and cost-effectiveness.

Electronic media

This is the real revolution in the field of direct marketing – the ability to communicate directly and even interactively with individuals via electronic forms of media.

The days of sending a fax in place of a mail-shot and seeing this as the height of electronic sophistication seem so far distant and so innocent in their naivety that we must bite the bullet and realize that what we see as state of the art today will doubtless be overtaken by enormous technological advances within a few short years.

The Internet allows direct access to a recipient's home, at the request of the recipient; touch-screen technology allows input direct from user to database and can send an 'order' to the marketer immediately; relatively cheap computer processing can allow the manipulation of huge amounts of data for a much smaller amount of money.

All these aspects of electronic communication, not just the Internet, have affected the way in which, and the speed at which, direct marketing *can* take place – but none of them change the basic concepts detailed above – none of them is a panacea!

FULFILMENT AND BACK-END MARKETING

What do we mean by fulfilment?

- Getting the goods to the customer.
- Getting the right goods to the customer – there is plenty of room for error (usually clerical).
- Making sure that the customer's credit is worthy (or cashing the cheque before sending the goods).
- Data collection and analysis – reordering of stock and management of cash flow as well as monitoring effectiveness of promotions, etc.
- Include customer relationship responsibilities – wrong products, faulty goods, late or non-delivery, etc.

What is the importance of fulfilment?

- You make money out of a satisfied customer; fulfilment is the way you satisfy customers.
- The fulfilment process controls cash flow and, through credit checking, the value of orders. It can make or break a mail order business. Remember that most failed businesses fail through overtrading.

- Accuracy of fulfilment is also vital from the point of view of the cost of wrong orders and returns (the cost of actual goods and the long-term cost of dissatisfied customers).

CUSTOMER RELATIONSHIP MANAGEMENT BUILT ON CARE

Why bother to build a relationship with a customer? Why *is* Customer Relationship Management (CRM) the buzz-phrase these days? Can you distinguish between customer care and marketing?

Let's be honest – customer care is not undertaken as an altruistic exercise. It is done to keep profitable customers and to enhance their value to you; it is therefore central to direct marketing. For example, customer care provides the opportunity of making a service better; telephone/postal research can identify specific areas of opportunity for you. Customer loyalty is profitable; it is therefore worth paying for. That's why it is worth building a relationship with the ones you already have!

There are two main areas of opportunity for CRM:

- *General procedure*: create a programme of communications to maximize customer satisfaction – a two-way flow of information is necessary. A simple example from real life is a pizza restaurant that keeps children's names and dates of birth on computer and sends them a birthday card and the offer of a free pizza if they come in on their birthday, whilst certain financial services organizations dedicate millions of pounds to building computer systems that will allow them to track the whole relationship they have with a customer over many years, thereby allowing them to tailor their offering to the customer as their life-stage, and therefore requirements, alters.

- *Special procedures*: one-off opportunities often occur on an individual basis, e.g. a customer complaint. It is possible to turn a likely loss of customer into an opportunity to increase loyalty, e.g. by having a policy of giving 110 per cent. Outgoing programmes can be tied in with your normal programmes of customer communication (newsletters, billing stuffers, promotional mail, outgoing telephone, etc.). Incoming opportunities (usually complaints) require well-trained unflappable people following clearly laid out general rules and with the option of referring the customer to someone with real authority, who can deviate from the rules, where necessary. There is little point in laying down rules for all special opportunities for customer care because, by definition, they will be different.

Every time you communicate with a customer you pay out money (Figure 4.6). It makes sense, therefore, to use every opportunity you can to ask for another order. For example, bounce back with the fulfilment of an order by using a billing stuffer or sending an order form with a newsletter. Wherever the order comes from, whether face to face, on the Internet or from a printed catalogue, the opportunities for building the relationship with your customer appear at every stage.

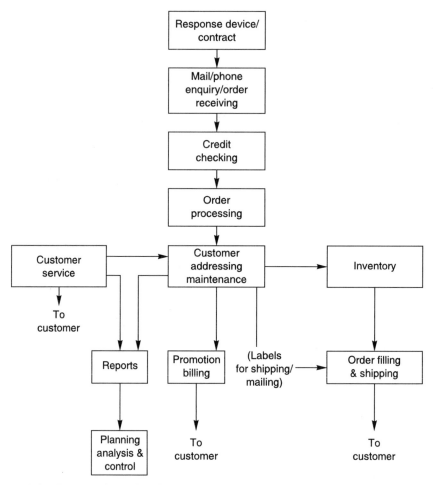

Figure 4.6 An overview of fulfilment functions

When it comes to e-CRM, as one of the areas where there is most 'buzz' at the moment, the Internet is being hailed as a wonderful way to build better relationships with customers, because of the interactive nature of the medium. From the small organization that allows its customers to enter their own orders direct on to their website, to the multi-national fmcg giants, like Procter & Gamble, who have developed corporate and brand specific offerings on the web to enable real interactivity between themselves and their customers, it *is* true to say that the web is being used in a way that no other communications medium has been used in the past – other than maybe the 'Man from the Pru', who was able to meet every customer face to face on a regular basis and *be* the real interaction between the company and its customers.

But even the largest organization forgets at its peril that interactivity cannot be forced, that websites will only be enjoyed as entertainment if they are entertaining, will only justify the housewife's use of time if she feels she gets valuable information or pleasure, and so on. So, although the technology is impressive, the basic rules remain the same – if you are planning to communicate with someone, be sure you know your objectives, be sure you understand the point of view of the audience and be sure to meet their expectations!

See the chapter on CRM for more information (Chapter 7)!

MANAGING A DIRECT MARKETING PLAN

Managing a direct marketing plan is no different in essence from managing any other sort of marketing plan. The basic steps are:

- *Define your objectives.* These will depend on your function: as a client marketing director, you have to start with corporate objectives at board level; as a marketing manager you will have these defined for you; as an agency account director you will probably be given promotional or communications objectives. NB: defining objectives means making them measurable – you must be able to use results to judge success or failure, and as feedback to plan the next stage in the process.
- *Budget for your activity.* In direct marketing this is likely to be a tighter control mechanism than in general marketing, e.g. *x* pounds per sale. Remember the various ways in which budgets can be set. A task budget is the best, but in real life you may not be able to get the budget controllers to accept this.
- *Plan your activities.* Use a critical path analysis that is as simple or complex as the task requires.
- *Feedback and control elements.* Even on discrete and simple tasks, things that you can't control will happen to disrupt your plans. You must put into your plan either specific contingency plans ('Try plan B chaps') or allocate limited discretionary activity to the people actually doing the work.
- *Formal procedures for evaluating success or failure.* Everybody analyses causes of failure to the *n*th degree. You should also analyse successes so that you can repeat them.

 ## Electronic communication methods

There are many e-communication methods – and new ones are being developed almost daily. This section looks at the major forms, but you really do need to keep reading to keep up to date with this topic. Make sure your trade press reading takes you to:

 http://www.revolution.haynet.com

BELOW THE LINE USES OF THE INTERNET

Internal communication

By setting up web pages, sites and e-mail loops that can only be accessed by those issued with the correct password, an organization can set up an effective tool for communication that is either purely internal, or can allow access by, say, dealers and distributors. A purely internal site is called an *intranet*, and an area that can be accessed by, say, a dealer network, is called an *extranet*. More on this use of the Internet is given in the PR chapter (Chapter 5), but this would certainly be classified as below the line communication, as no commission is involved on closed-site communication.

External communication

With the right marketing strategy in place, a marketer can use the worldwide web to offer goods and services for sale worldwide (Cisco Systems now does 75 per cent of its business on the web) – but that is the danger – not all organizations *can* deliver goods or services worldwide, so the whole marketing mix must be reviewed before this step is taken. This would be the use of the web as a channel of distribution, replacing, say, a catalogue for items that are then delivered by some sort of fulfilment service, or through which data can actually be purchased and disseminated, e.g. a research company offering research data for sale through its website, then giving the buyer a password which allows them to actually download the data in question. This would be using the Internet as a direct marketing method as well as a method of distribution.

Other than selling worldwide, an organization can also offer information about itself, either freely or at a price to anyone with access to a terminal. It is essential that such home pages or websites are professionally designed and developed, otherwise they just end up as cyberspace leaflet holders, which is not really what the web is about. This would also be a below the line way of using the Internet, as, again, no commission is involved – you are, essentially, creating a communication method.

It is also quite common to use your own website to run 'advertisements' for your own organization. Early in 2001, reports from research companies specializing in on-line research indicated that on-line ads reached a record level of over 172 billion impressions during the fourth quarter of 2000, while top web media companies stocked 28 per cent of their sites with non-paid self-promotional ads. Apparently, entertainment and society websites ran the highest percentage of self-promotional ads (30 per cent) among ad supported websites.

Another way of communicating via the web is to use e-mails. E-mails might be sent in an unsolicited or solicited manner, indeed, permission e-mail is growing fast. The flexibility of e-mail means that a message can be sent to potentially millions of people for the same cost as communicating with just one – except, of course, for the cost of obtaining the mailing list.

Using e-mail in its unsolicited form can prove to be a big PR mistake, with recipients becoming increasingly hostile towards organizations who contact them constantly in this manner. It makes good sense to allow recipients to opt out of your mailing list by giving them an address to which they can send their address to have it removed once and for all.

This means that no marketer can afford to ignore the web as a potential means of either marketing communications or marketing.

ABOVE THE LINE USES OF THE INTERNET

Using the Internet to promote your goods and services through sites that already exist can be done in three main ways:

Banner ads are the web's equivalent of TV commercials. More specifically, they are rectangular graphics that are static, animated or rich media in form. Banners typically link back to the advertiser's website.

The three main types of banner are:

- *Static banners*: they are what the name implies – static, they don't change or move at all.
- *Animated banners*: once again, they are what the name implies, in that they carry animated graphics with flashing or moving elements. GIF technology, such as Java, is used to create the movement.
- *Rich media banners*: these use flash, video and audio interaction to attract and retain interest – you can even print from them!

The early tools that measured the effectiveness of banner advertising, examples being Netgenesis, I/Pro and NetCount, had the problem that there was no standard reporting procedure. The advent of Nielsen Netratings and Media Metrix are beginning to offer an agreed and standardized form of measuring against objectives.

Sponsorship is when an advertiser sponsors an entire website or section of a website. Sponsorship deals include banner ads, prominent logo placement, exclusives, content and promotions. In most cases, sponsorship allows for a direct link to the sponsor's website.

Interstitials are ads that open a second browser window. Commonly referred to as 'Pop-ups', they appear as static ads or 15- to 30-second multimedia commercials. Interstitials can also be used for customer research, such as surveys or running promotions, to communicate a detailed message.

Sites it is worth checking out would include:

 http://www.enliven.com

 http://www.thestandard.com

 http://www.nielsen-netratings.com

 http://www.mediametrix.com

On-line publications

Buying space in an on-line publication means calling the media sales people at the appropriate publication to buy space in a very traditional manner. Often, space sales have been diverted to a specialist sales house. These are growing in number. The best way to check how to buy space, as well as deciding whether you want to advertise in a traditional manner, e.g. buying a recruitment advertisement, or whether you want to buy a specific link or area of the whole publication, is to visit the advertising sales part of the website in question: this will either give you the data you need or will point you to the right sales house for your needs.

Go to http://www.telegraph.co.uk for an example of how this works – there you will find the Electronic Telegraph site, the first on-line publication which was launched in 1994, and you can then navigate to their advertising sales pages, which will give you good visual examples of the sorts of spaces you can buy from them.

Buying space on other people's websites

Buying banner ads is undertaken through sales houses and companies that specialize in offering sites for sale that the owner of the site might not want to make available themselves because it wouldn't be worth their while.

With this sort of advertising you will buy space by the CPM (thousand hits per page). It is very hard to generalize about space costs, value for money or effectiveness. The Audit Bureau of Circulation is looking at ways to be able to standardize site buying information – but it will be a tough job to get all parties involved to agree. Further reading of *Revolution*, a monthly magazine published by Haymarket Press, is advised, or you can visit their site at http://www.revolution magazine.com

OTHER FORMS OF E-COMMUNICATION

The Internet seems to have *become* e-communication, but it isn't, of course – there are lots of other ways in which new technology is being, and can be, used to build a bridge of communication between either a potential customer, a customer, a client, a supplier and employee, or even a competitor!

Wireless Application Protocol (WAP)

This is the basic building block of wireless communication – handsets are proliferating at the moment, and organizations that make hardware are hoping that the upgrading to WAP-empowered handsets will save them within the saturation stage of the mobile telephone market. WAP is the way in which Internet content can be displayed on mobile devices like pagers, telephones and personal organizers. Some graphics are included, but the information is mainly text based – which means there are a great many limitations to be faced!

WAP is only really one step up from Short Messaging Systems – so we have to be careful about being overenthusiastic about WAP. A great deal depends upon the presentation of data in a WAP-friendly format, which will allow browsers to pick up information that is of interest to potential customers. System owners run TV advertising campaigns telling us how wonderful it is to be able to book flights, shop or order cabs from our mobile communication devices, and for people on the move this offering can be very useful, but in terms of it being a way to get your message to someone about an offering that they can get more details about elsewhere it is great. You can tell customers about offers that are on *today* in *their city*. With WAP becoming standard on most telephones, and other personal communication devices, it is likely that the day of the Smart Phone is coming swiftly – with hand-held sets that fax, e-mail, message, browse, keep diaries and contact details, as well as have a memory that allows sensible amounts of hand-held storage.

So where will this go? Well, I suggest that the development of General Packet Radio Service (GPRS), which is designed to make WAP faster, cheaper and ultimately more packed with the sorts of visuals that people want, will be the technology that allows WAP to grow. By allowing data rates that are faster by three to four times, it can give the impression of real-time linking with the Internet, and could allow the introduction of handset video communication and animation. Beam me up Scotty!

So, with proposed system improvements, such as High Speed Circuit Switched Data (HSCSD) (Orange is working on this) and faster links, better screens and batteries, maybe the potential for the marketer to communicate directly with one mobile person will increase – not in desirability as such, but the changes will come about in what can be communicated and how. A high grade visual image is preferable to a green text message any day, and it means that brand integrity can be maintained.

Moving packets of data around is the Holy Grail at the moment. Systems like Universal Mobile Telecommunication System (UMTS) are being developed, which will allow the constant transfer of data, thereby creating a continuous stream of communication and real-time interaction, so the marcomms professionals for the twenty-first century ignore at their peril the question – do I WAP or not?

Some websites to visit that will help you keep up to date with this field are:

http://www.wapforum.org

http://www.ericsson.com

http://www.nokia.com

http://www.utms-forum.org

http://www.mcommerceworld.com

Interactive kiosks

What's an interactive kiosk? Well, frankly, it's what you make it! It could be a sleek, designer label pod in a department store that allows women to interactively carry out their own analysis of what beauty treatments they might need for their skin type/hair type etc., or it could be a focus for giving out information where there's a high flow of less well-defined traffic – say the concourse of an airport terminal, or at a railway station – or it might even be something that is installed at every operating plant you own, allowing employees to ask FAQs of it. The key here is the interactivity, and this is the key to the communication uses of this tool – it has to be more than a virtual leaflet dispenser, it has to go that extra mile to actually involve the user in an experience that is truly interactive.

It might be that you want to entertain, or inform, or promote, or allow a user to test and sample. You might have a free-standing kiosk that has to operate as a self-contained unit in an alien environment where you are trying to acquire new customers by introducing them to your product or service in an environment where you couldn't otherwise reach them, or you might use one on your exhibition stand. The beauty is that by building a kiosk of the right design for the environment, you can affect that environment, and totally control the input received by the user.

Of course, you can use kiosks if you have a non-e-business, but the great thing about them is, because they are interactive, you can attach them to your e-business effort and either use them, say, just to capture data on prospects or to sell your goods and services there on the spot!

Ways in which kiosks can be used:

- to build awareness and understanding in target geographic locations;
- to allow data gathering from prospects;
- to give samples of product service;
- to interact with clients;
- to facilitate employee communications.

The driving insurance and testing organization in British Columbia, Canada, is called the ICBC. If you want a driver's licence you have to complete both a 'written' test and a driving test. The 'written test' is actually conducted using an interactive kiosk.

Fifty questions, drawn from a much larger bank of questions, are randomly generated for each test: they are illustrated with high quality visuals, offer multiple choice answering and are timed – allowing the respondent to take as long as they like to do the test, but with the results showing the time that was actually taken.

The kiosks are designed to be self-contained units, and as many or as few as appropriate to the test centre's size can be installed. The great advantage is that one administrator can have up to 20 tests taking place in 20 booths at a time, with all the scoring and recording of results taking place automatically.

Not only does the kiosk ask the questions, and record the answers, but it also tells you which part of the British Columbia equivalent of the Highway Code needs to be addressed if you got a question wrong.

Your score, your errors, your timing are all data captured against your provisional licence number, so that when you arrive at possibly a different centre for your test your driving tester can see what you did wrong, how long you took over certain issues and so on. There is a capacity for reducing fraud, as well as cutting costs by streamlining testing.

The ICBC has saved so much money over the last few years, having invested in lots of similar programmes, that every owner of one of their policies received a rebate cheque for $100 in 2001!

Kiosks can also be taken out into the community to publicize changes in the driving code (older drivers often don't even know about these changes until it's too late!) and to publicize road safety in general.

This is a good example of a communications use of a kiosk, that doesn't sell anything, but does fulfil an important PR function for this organization.

Figure 4.7   Kiosk interaction means business – and reduced costs!

Selling, educating, informing, showing, giving, collecting – all are facilitated by the kiosk.

CD-ROMs

CD-ROMs have been around for a long time, and have been used as cover mounts, inserts, give-aways, brochure replacements and methods of distributing high quality video images for many years.

Their particular attraction to the e-business communicator is that they appeal to those who are in any case e-business friendly, because of the convenient way in which they deliver masses of information. Cheap to reproduce in large, and even relatively small, quantities, the CD-ROM allows for data to be transferred in 'hard-copy' format, rather than from a data resource like a website. Their promotional attraction is that it is still appealing to have something 'free' placed in one's hand, rather than having access to

TEN Media is a training organization that offers vocational training for a range of business disciplines – marketing being amongst them. By delivering video programmes, backed up with text data and weblinks on a CD-ROM, they find that they are able to offer their customer base more quality and flexibility than they could via the Internet itself.

Thirty-minute programmes are filmed and produced as though for television, and these are loaded onto CD-ROMs together with the script, lots of background data, complementary documentation and even presentation slides.

They not only use CD-ROM as a way of *doing* business, but of *promoting* business too – they have a promotional CD-ROM that they mail upon request, use as an insert and mail to targeted lists that gives a real sample of what the potential customer would be buying into.

Figure 4.8   TEN Media's use of CD-ROMs

the same data 'free' on the Internet. But, that said, they do carry with them the communication complication of distribution.

Once broadband allows us to access high quality video on-line, and once all the groups who currently have access to a CD-ROM player have access to broadband, then I believe that the day of the CD-ROM will have passed. But, until then, they not only offer a very attractive method of communication, with the chance to print a snazzy cover as well as a visually interesting disc, but they are also a way of running an e-business, as well as promoting it.

The CD-ROM has also taken a newish turn – with the development of different sizes of CD – the business card-sized one being used more and more frequently to replace the traditional card. It can contain the following (with approx. 50 MB CD):

PDF files in English: up to 1500 pages.
HTML pages with average graphics: 500–2000 pages.
Multimedia files: 1–2 hours.
Flash animations: 4–6 hours.
Video files: 5 minutes.
Audio files: 4 minutes, 45 seconds.
PowerPoint presentations: 250 slides.
MP3 music in stereo CD quality: 48 minutes.
MP3 music in stereo FM quality: 96 minutes.
MP3 music in mono voice quality: 400 minutes.

As you can imagine, this makes for an attractive communication tool!

CDs like this can be used to replace tickets/invitations to events, exhibitions and conferences; they can replace brochures and technical data sheets; they could be used to promote any type of business where the potential audience has access to a CD reader. Particularly popular in B2B markets, the applications in the B2C markets are exciting – with relatively low production costs making them an attractive novelty and give-away.

Maybe this is the way that the CD-ROM will save itself as the publishing ability of the web progresses.

e-Mail

Yes, we all get it every day, but don't underestimate its potential!

Recent surveys show that 65 per cent of companies spend 1–5 per cent of their marketing budget on e-mail marketing, with 22 per cent spending over 5 per cent. Clearly, 87 per cent of companies see e-mail as important to their future marketing strategy.

Increasing by almost 100 million over 1999, by the end of 2000 there were 375 million Internet users worldwide – the majority utilizing e-mail. With the number of people around the world using e-mail growing exponentially, reports suggest that e-mail marketing will jump from a $164 million industry in 1999 to a $4.8 billion industry by 2003, and to an estimated $7.3 billion in 2005.

- In 1999, e-mail accounts reached 570 million. By 2002, there will be more than 1 billion e-mail accounts worldwide.
- In 2000, over 7 trillion e-mail messages were sent.
- In 2002, worldwide e-mail volume will reach over 576 million messages sent per day.
- The number of commercial e-mail messages received by a user per year will increase 40 times from 40 messages in 1999 to 1600 by 2005.

Figure 4.9   Some e-mail figures

Masses of research is being carried out into the effectiveness of e-mail, by organizations such as Forrester, Jupiter, IBM and many more. It will only grow if it is proved to be effective – and with ease of tracking making it popular due to the ability to justify expenditure against objectives achieved, we might all find that we are being targeted more effectively and spoken to in a more relevant and personal manner in the not too distant future.

Keep up to date with what's going on in the world of e-mail and other forms of electronic communication by visiting the following sites:

http://www.forrester.com

http://www.isource.ibm.com

http://www.jupitercommunications.com

Summary of chapter four

This chapter looks at below the line media – or created communication methods.

Sales promotion

This section looks at how sales promotions work, what types exist and what they are good at achieveing. By taking an in-depth look at all types of sales promotions and incentives, this section introduces the concept of adding value to encourage either a trial, a sale or a building of loyalty.

Sponsorships

This section examines the different types of sponsorships available (programme sponsorship, event sponsorship, person/team sponsorship), weighing the pros and cons of each one and looking at the sorts of issues that arise in the planning and implementation of successful sponsorships.

Merchandising

This section addresses the issue of the total way in which goods and services are offered for sale.

Packaging

This section considers the role of packaging.

Direct marketing

This is a comprehensive section looking at the difference between direct marketing and direct marketing communications. By considering the planning, implementation and management issues associated with both functions, this section sheds light on the relationship between the two disciplines as well as distinguishing between them.

Electronic communication

This section considers both above and below the line uses of the Internet, as well as some of the other main types of electronic communication.

Self test questions and opinion development

These are not exam questions, nor are they meant to represent the sort of question you might expect to face anywhere else. They are designed to help you check whether you have understood the content of this chapter. All you have to do is read the questions, give them some thought and maybe jot down some notes on what your response might be. Not all the questions will have factual answers – rather, they might encourage you to think about a topic or an issue and formulate an opinion based upon what is now, hopefully, a better understanding of the topic.

What are the three major types of sales promotion?

Your Chairman wants you, as marcomms manager, to organize the sponsorship of an art scholarship at an art college, and to make sure that his son is the first to be awarded the fund. Your company offers on-line purchasing of railway tickets. What possible pitfalls might you have to explain to your Chairman?

How many different types of packaging challenges are faced by an on-line gardening supplies company? Why are there so many? How are they overcome?

For a website of your choice, record all the banner ads you see on it in one month. How many of them are well targeted? How many of them are well executed? Why?

Pick an on-line publication (maybe something like *Revolution*, that you should be reading anyway!) and study the advertisements that appear for one month. What makes them good/bad?

What do you think will happen to the Internet as an advertising medium in the next two years? What about WAP?

Extending knowledge and understanding

You are encouraged to undertake the following activities to further your knowledge and understanding of the topics covered in this chapter in the following ways:

1 Go out and get two examples of each of the three major types of sales promotion, one for a service and one for a product, one of each on-line, one of each off-line. Examine how the promotions were set up, try to find out about them either through the company's own website or through trade press coverage. What were the objectives? Were they achieved? Was the creative good/bad/indifferent? Do you think there is a relevance and appeal to the target audience?

2 Pick a sponsorship of something – something that interests you. . .maybe a football team, a singer, a concert, a school, a golfer. . .by an e-business and find out all you

can about it through websites, the sponsor and the sponsored party. How well does it work? Could it work better? If so, how? If not, why is it so good?

3 Start to collect your direct mail. At the end of two months put it into two piles – that which you think was well targeted and that which was not. For the well-targeted pile, split it into effective creative treatments and less effective creative treatments. Now check how much mail is trying to get you to do e-business with an organization, how much is giving you the choice of doing e-business or non-e-business and how much does not invite you to go 'e' at all.

Chapter **5**

Public relations – more than just a goodwill exercise

Overview

PR as it is practised today is largely a twentieth century phenomenon, although it has been practised sporadically since earliest times. Today, it is the Institute of Public Relations (IPR), within the UK, that we must look towards to begin to understand current practice.

The IPR defines public relations in the following way:

> Public relations is about reputation: the result of what you do, what you say and what others say about you.

> Public relations practice is the discipline which looks after reputation – with the aim of earning understanding and support, and influencing opinion and behaviour.

> It is the planned and sustained effort to establish and maintain goodwill and mutual understanding between an organization and its public.

The key words in the above definition focus on the fact that PR is not something that just 'happens', but rather that it is something that must be planned and controlled. Also, it highlights the fact that PR has at its core the concept of understanding rather than bald promotion. This does not mean that PR is not a valuable promotional method. Rather, it means that it is not a way of pulling the wool over people's eyes, but of communicating with integrity, of educating rather than persuading, of telling rather than selling.

PR is also more than an executive level tool. As with all communication tools, it must be planned for and integrated into the corporate communications programme at the highest level. It is a true management function and should be addressed by all departments of an organization, not just the marketing department.

One of the other unique aspects of PR is that it differs from advertising and many other forms of promotional communication in that, whilst advertising brings the product to the customer, PR brings the customer to the product. PR is a two-way communication process, whereas advertising tends to be a one-way process.

Another difference is that, whilst advertising is placed in the media by buying space and time, PR gets messages into the media through editorial outlets. Stories and items appear because of their value and interest and appear free of direct charge, though there is a cost incurred in putting in the man hours that try to get the stories placed.

PR is also likely to have much wider objectives than advertising. An advertising campaign may have the aim to increase sales by 10 per cent, while PR will have the aim to improve employee relations, customer relations, and educate and inform the general public about an organization.

Public relations has been massively affected by the advent of electronic communication. Based on the premise that Two-Step Communication was much more effective and realistic, public relations and its aim of educating and informing groups who are not just decision makers but who are also decision influencers has flourished for many years. Faced with the new communication models of today, it now has to adapt to new ways of reaching new groups of people. One of the most complicated problems faced by the PR practitioner today is not to get the messages out there – but to monitor what messages are appearing where, and what their impact might be!

The other factor that has affected PR practice is the arrival of so many more ways to communicate – WAP might be a new way to communicate, but it still tends to draw upon existing news sources, so don't always jump to the conclusion that a new electronic method of communicating automatically means a new way to communicate, other than in technological terms. To reach someone with WAP you still have to use existing news gathering/dissemination routes. Indeed, although the points of communication have proliferated hugely, the number of communicators (news media), whilst they have increased, have not increased so much! Yes, it's true that there are many more news media appearing on the Internet, but often news and views are still gathered from central points – news gathering services such as Reuters still gather and disseminate news to be transmitted via many Internet news services.

On-line PR means that you just have more media to cope with when deciding which will reach your target public (i.e. you need to e-mail your News Release about your newly redesigned nursing bra to mochasofa.com – a women's website, as well as to *Woman's Weekly* or *Mother and Baby* printed magazines). Yes, you are likely to have to commission photography that can be digitally transmitted to an on-line publication, as well as being able to send a negative in hard copy to an 'old-fashioned' publication – but *please* don't think that the process of planning, the development of an implementation programme or the need for a communication strategy that will be delivered by the *right* tactics suddenly disappear because we have the Internet!

I hate to appear to be the person who runs around throwing wet blankets at everybody, but, no, the sky is not falling in, the world hasn't gone mad, and it is still possible to communicate with identified target groups in an efficient, effective and measurable manner – even with all the new challenges produced by the Internet. The key to successful e-PR is to keep remembering two things:

1 All communication needs to be planned, targeted, made relevant and have its effect measured.

2 The Internet is one more form of communication (like press or TV) that has to be studied, analysed, targeted and used in the best possible way for the organization upon whose behalf you are communicating, but it has its own unique ability to allow Three-Step Communication, that must be monitored.

If you are planning and implementing a PR programme in the twenty-first century – your job just got more complicated, it didn't just change!

How does PR 'get done'?

PR CONSULTANCIES

These can provide highly specialized, or merely general, technical and creative services, and might be either an individual in the form of the personal consultant who will advise and then 'buy in' creative/technical services on behalf of the client, as required, or a group of specialists working in a consultancy which would be a 'full service' consultancy. These people are able to advise because of their wealth of experience and training. They will have (whether an individual or a large company) a legal and corporate identity of their own, registered for the purpose of the business. There are an increasing number of consultancies offering on-line and in-line PR, as well as traditional off-line PR.

As the management of your reputation brings in the potential millions of communication points that exist on the web, so web consultancies are offering more reputation management and PR consultancies are offering more on-line communication! Sometimes the lines become blurred between web agencies and PR agencies.

There are many sites you can visit to see what's on offer. I suggest:

http://www.netpotential.com

Figure 5.1   Consultancy offerings

IN-HOUSE PR DEPARTMENTS

In-house PR departments may comprise one or many people, depending upon the nature of the organization and the type of PR in which it is particularly active. Small departments are usually made up of generalists, while large departments tend to use people who specialize in various fields, as required. It is often the case that small PR departments will use outside consultancies to help with specialist requirements, or at times when the workload is particularly heavy. In-house departments are manned by members of staff, who will be employed on a salaried basis.

IN-HOUSE PR VERSUS PR CONSULTANCIES

Consultancies have the advantage of being able to distance themselves from the day-to-day problems of the organization, and may therefore be able to bring fresh ideas to existing situations. They also bear the costs of ongoing overheads for large numbers of specialist staff, or have sufficiently wide experience and a large number of contacts to allow them to buy in the services required more effectively and efficiently than those within the organization itself.

In-house departments know the problems and opportunities of the organization better than most, because the information required to build understanding is at their fingertips at all times in the shape of their own internal files and their colleagues' own knowledge.

 ## Some of the 'publics' of PR

The publics of an organization are all those people who come into contact with it or who are affected by its activities (Figure 5.2). In order to understand their relationship

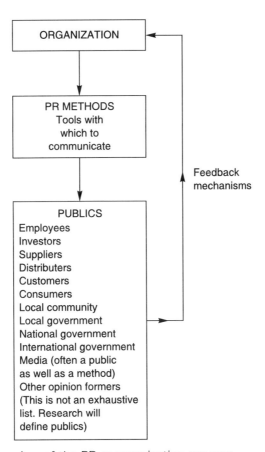

Figure 5.2 An overview of the PR communication process

with us, we organize them into groups and analyse their needs and wants and their opinions of us. An organization's publics vary according to its aims and activities, so the following list serves only as a general guide.

THE PRESS

The members of the press, i.e. journalists, editors, producers, researchers, etc. for print, broadcast and virtual media.

Wants: news (not opinions, unless those of a VIP), facts, a fast response to their enquiries, information of 'interest and value' to their readers/listeners/viewers, an angle, exclusives.

THE CUSTOMER

The customer 'is always right', or should be made to feel so. A customer is known to the organization (dealt with face to face); a consumer is unknown to the organization (deals with intermediary); an end-user consumes or uses the product or service without making the buying decision.

Wants: service, quality/value, knowledge of the product/service (information), reassurance and back-up.

THE INVESTOR

Shareholders, either private individuals or institutions, such as pension funds, building societies and banks. Closely associated is the financial market, which trades in and advises on shareholding, such as stockbrokers, merchant banks, high street banks and their city analysts. These act as city opinion formers, as do the financial press.

Wants: a good return on their investment, both as dividend and capital gain, information on how their money is being/will be used, prospects for the company/market.

THE EMPLOYEE

Organized through trade unions or staff associations. May be shop floor, skilled, professional/technical, administrative, managerial. There are times when the potential employee becomes an important public, e.g. when locating a new factory or when skills are in short supply.

Wants: a fair wage and good working conditions (industrial relations), prospects, security, recognition, knowledge.

THE GOVERNMENT

Politicians and their administrators (civil servants, local government officials, Eurocrats). Politicians include MPs, Euro MPs and local councillors and their political parties. Government authority extends to bodies which enforce regulations, such as the Health and Safety Executive.

Wants: votes, to be kept informed about constituency/ward/department/special interest matters.

THE DISTRIBUTOR

Agents act on your behalf; dealers sell your product, taking a percentage of the price. Wholesalers buy your products and sell them on to retailers. They are the bridge between you and your consumer.

Wants: a good deal, back-up, encouragement, information.

THE SUPPLIER

Other organizations that supply you with raw materials, parts, machinery and equipment, stationery, power, etc. (NB: if your company is a supplier, your customer is a manufacturer or other organization.)

Wants: prompt payment, regular orders, knowledge of how their product is used.

OPINION FORMERS

People and organizations that influence the opinions, attitudes or behaviour of others, e.g. politicians, newspaper editors, pressure groups, the community that is local to your factory or offices, Mr and Mrs Jones, doctors, religious leaders.

Wants: reliable information that allows them to form an informed opinion.

THE ROLE OF RESEARCH

The publics for each organization, and the PR situation, should be assessed before any PR plan is formulated. They should be 'brought alive' using demographic analysis and any personal experience of such relationships (we are all customers and employees). Remember, the headlines are guidelines only and each organization will have special publics (trade unions have members, charities have voluntary workers and donors, a football club needs good relationships with the police).

Because PR does really mean building a relationship with all your identified publics, it is truly a management function, requiring top-level planning and coordination.

However, there are also many executive-level tools that must be understood within this field. We will look at some of these next.

Methods of reaching publics

There is no right or wrong way to communicate with publics. Different publics might well be best reached by certain methods (Figure 5.3), however, so it is important to understand how these methods operate.

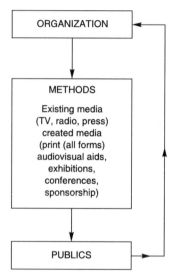

Figure 5.3   Focus on PR methods

THE BRITISH PRESS (PRINT)

We are extremely fortunate in the UK to have an unparalleled range of national daily and weekly newspapers that have a strong editorial content and which allow the PR practitioner to target their messages. We have already seen the way in which the press targets specific socio-demographic profiles in its readership, thus allowing the publisher to have a saleable readership in terms of advertising. Despite the fact that the media relations programme that would be controlled by the PR practitioner does not buy space in these titles, it is of course still the case that the readership profile is of vital importance in the planning of PR coverage.

Regional and local newspapers allow the PR practitioner to communicate with geographically focused groups of readers, whilst consumer interest press, or the trade press, allows a focus on interest rather than location.

How does the press work?

By 'the press' we mean the people who gather, select and report the news. They include:

- *Editors*: these are the bosses. They are responsible for all the news (editorial) that appears in print. Their decision is final. On small or specialist publications, all information should be directed to the editors.

- *Sub-editors*: these edit material received, cutting it to length and/or rewriting it. They also write headlines.

- *Desk editors*: on larger newspapers, editorial responsibility for different sections of a paper (home news, overseas news, sport, etc.) is in the hands of desk editors. If your story is in one of these areas, it should be directed to the relevant desk.

- *Features editors*: these are responsible for the in-depth, longer stories that normally appear in the centre of newspapers. They are often looking for new feature ideas, so a story idea can be 'sold' to them. Some features are advertising features, which means editorial is dependent upon taking advertising space.

- *Feature writers*: these are journalists who write feature articles. They may work full or part time for the publication, or be freelance.

- *Freelancers*: these are journalists who are self-employed, either selling their story to publications or radio or being commissioned, often by features editors. They can be useful intermediaries when a story idea needs to be developed and placed.

- *Reporters*: these may be general news journalists (often juniors) or specialist reporters (especially on radio and television). If you telephone a newspaper you will usually be put through to a reporter first.

- *Stringers*: reporters who work for local papers or radio but who also feed important stories through to news agencies such as the Associated Press or national newspapers. If you think you are talking to a stringer, you are advised immediately to report up the line.

OTHER BRITISH MASS MEDIA

Radio

Much local independent radio news is produced by Independent Radio News (IRN), a separate organization from the radio station itself, which relays news to other stations. However, most stations have their own news editors, so check whether news should be directed to the station or IRN. Radio also employs specialist reporters who work for particular programmes or contribute to the news and cover such subjects as sport, women's interest and science.

BBC local radio stations have their own news editors, but often use the services of BBC Regional Broadcasting for their news and current affairs programmes.

Radio interviews can be conducted live in the studio or by a reporter visiting you with a tape recorder or outside broadcast unit (OBU). In the studio, interviews can extend into 'phone-ins', in which members of the public ring in to ask questions of the interviewee. A 10-second delay is used, so that offensive remarks can be edited out, and the interviewer is at hand to control callers.

Radio also uses pre-taped news items, such as interviews, either produced by the station or supplied directly by outsiders. Freelance radio journalists can often be used to give a professional touch to pre-taped material by using commercial recording studios or equipment, but such material can be home produced.

Before being interviewed for a news item, prepare a sound bite. This is a 20- to 30-second section of the interview which can be edited out of the main interview for use in an overall story. It should contain your main message and stand on its own. This avoids the problems of being taken out of context and means that, if time is short, you can still get your most important point over to the listener.

Remember that radio is a background medium. People listen to it while doing other things, and so listeners are not hanging on every word you say. Repeating your main point is therefore acceptable. If you are giving out details of a forthcoming event, or where listeners can gain further information, provide the presenter with the details in writing, so he or she can read it out a second time. It is always difficult for listeners to remember or take down information from a broadcast, so repeating an address, telephone number, location or date is common practice. Web broadcast radio should be treated in the same way as traditionally broadcast radio.

Television

With the increasing number of television channels available it is becoming more and more likely that there will be a televisual opportunity available via which you could reach one or more of your publics. Niche programming through satellite, cable and digital channels means that you can now reach very specific audiences, e.g. there are The Travel Channel, The Money Channel, The Cookery Channel and so on.

If you are invited into the studio you might find yourself being interviewed by the key presenter of the whole programme, who is often very knowledgeable about the subject being dealt with, often having worked in the field for many years.

Usually, these people are adept at putting interviewees at their ease, and if you have been invited in to speak on a topic, or to comment on a situation, where you are being viewed as the expert then be assured that the questions you will be asked will be designed to elicit information that is helpful and interesting to the audience. If you are there to represent an organization, or even yourself, in a controversial situation, then it is likely that the questions you face will be searching. Yes, some interviewers can be aggressive, and some interviewees choose to respond in kind, but generally speaking, even if a question is asked in a less than pleasant manner it is best to respond in a level-headed way – there are some wonderful examples of interviewees being thought less highly of, or even losing their jobs, because they were not able to deal with an aggressive interview!

Whenever appearing on television it is best to remember that everything you do with your face and body will seem larger than life on the screen, so if you are uncertain, or if you are advising someone who is uncertain about how they will feel when they are in front of a camera, the best advice is to get some media training before making any mistakes you might make in public.

Generally speaking, it is best to wear unfussy clothing, no stripes, small checks or spots (they look strange on camera) and to avoid fancy jewellery that 'dangles' because any movement will be exaggerated on camera. The best advice of all? Seek advice from the producer and take it – they know what they want, they know what their audience expects and they are the ones who can ask you back again to talk about your next issue!

CREATED PR COMMUNICATION METHODS

Created PR material can refer to almost anything – from a corporate brochure to a hot-air balloon hovering over an open day at a police station. Here some of the more common 'tools of the trade' are examined: print, audiovisual aids, photography and sponsorship.

Printed PR material (and virtual print)

Essentially, since you are totally in control of printed PR material, it can be used for any purpose at all. As PR is about informing, printed material is often used with this aim – from one angle or another. That said, what is vitally important is that the PR professional controlling printed material understands print sufficiently well to be able to get what they want. Some of the functions of printed PR material might include:

- Sales information.
- Corporate.
- Explanatory.
- Campaigning.
- Requesting (as in a questionnaire).

As the PR professional is in control of the function of PR material, so he or she is also in control of the nature of the material, i.e. what form it will take. The form selected should be that which suits needs best. Usually this will be fairly obvious. Don't forget that some groups of people will have special needs: e.g. leaflets about pensioners' bus passes should be in large print; direct mail to residents on a cosmopolitan estate should be multi-lingual; international sales force information could be in several languages on an intranet, etc. The general type of formal decision could be one of the following:

- Leaflets.
- Direct mail shots (from letters to multi-part).
- Catalogues.
- Brochures.
- Press advertising.
- News sheets/newsletters.
- House magazines (internal/external).
- Websites.
- CD-ROMs.

So how can you make sure that you get what you want? Here are ten key points for commissioning effective design:

1 First you must establish the use of the material/site.

2 Consider the type of material required (do not use the ubiquitous term 'brochure').

3 Establish the method of transmission.

4 Think of the length of any print or production runs (these can affect design and printing).

5 Establish a rough budget and tell the designer how much is allocated for design (less 20 per cent).

6 Have an approximate idea of how pagination will work.

7 Don't let words do all the work.

8 Don't let pictures do all the work.

9 Give the designer as much information as possible (verbal, visual and written).

10 Give the designer a deadline (at least two days before you are to present the design).

A word of warning: present visuals first (people like coloured pictures) with only a copy outline to clients/principals, and leave the copy for final approval. Do not get copy approval first and then go to design, as this route takes forever and preconceptions are formed on the basis of the words only!

When you are getting a quote for print, the information you should give the printer in order for them to be able to put together a reliable price is:

- Print run (number of pieces to print).
- Number of colours (one-, two-, three- or four-colour process).
- Number of pages.
- Ratio of copy to number of half-tones.
- Size (of page/sheet, with fold to final size).
- Material (type and weight – designer to advise).
- Finish (laminated/varnish).
- Delivery (One address? Consultancy? Client?).
- Run-on price per 1000.
- Provide printer with at least a photocopy of the visual.
- Give the same information to several printers to obtain competitive quotes based on the same criteria.

Audiovisual aids

These must always be:

- Informative.
- Convincing.
- Reinforcing.
- Illustrative.

Forms of audiovisual aid include:

- Flipcharts.
- Overhead projections.
- Slides (carousel/pulsed tape).
- Films.
- Videos (including interactive).
- Computer-generated material.
- Websites.
- CD-ROMs.

The PR practitioner might choose to use audiovisual aids either as a presentation support or on their own. For example:

- Press launch.
- Employee relations and communications.

- Projecting corporate identity.
- Trade relations.
- Training.
- Induction.
- Exhibitions.
- General information.

PR photography

Photography that is submitted with editorial stories is, in fact, a form of 'created communication method' and the rule of thumb is that it has to be as good as that commissioned by, and included in, the media.

Many printed publications now want to receive photographs digitally or at least on disk. On the other hand, some still prefer to receive hard copy, i.e. actual photographs. If you are in doubt, call ahead to check that you will be sending what they want, or check in one of the directories that offers this information. Whatever the desired form of receipt of a photograph there are still some golden rules to be borne in mind when actually creating the photograph itself. On-line publications will want digitally captured and transmitted photography.

Ten golden rules for good PR photography

1 Use professionals *in that field* (e.g. use food photographers for food, studio photographers for studio set-ups, portrait specialists for portraits, and so on. Professional photographers, like all of us, have strengths and specialities, and also see the notes that follow).

2 Think visually from the start.

3 Direct the photography to get what you want.

4 Let the image fill the frame (or crop). Remember that many photos used in on-line publications are cropped to allow maximum use of the page format.

5 Ensure that the composition is tight.

6 Indicate scale (with something familiar, like people).

7 Show the product being used (avoid 'product' shots).

8 Include action if possible. (For on-line publications it is worth checking if they are happy to accept live action footage as well as photo stills – or if they can insert a link to your website where you can offer live footage.)

9 Caption with the facts not the fantasy.

10 Look at photographs that are used in the media, and learn from the different styles that are used in different publications – try to use the right style for that field. If you are using a photographer who is used to working in the field they will also be able to advise, but it's best to have formed something of your own opinion too.

Commissioning PR photography

Also, it is useful to keep in mind the following checklist when commissioning PR photography.

Selecting a photographer. Working with a photographer should be very personal. It is a jointly creative activity and it is vital that you are both on the same wavelength in every way. There are several criteria for choosing a photographer; usually, they are one of the following:

● You already know him or her and have worked with him or her happily.
● He or she has been recommended to you by someone you trust.
● You may have seen and admired his or her work.

Working with a photographer. If you have not worked with the photographer you have chosen, meet them or their agent and look at specimens of their work.

Briefing the photographer. You always need to consider the following:

● Explain the nature of the photographs – editorial (magazine, newspaper, on-line publication, annual report and accounts, print and on-line, exclusive or general coverage), leaflets, local advertising, banner ad or whatever.
● Is it trade (emphasizing quality, finish and size) or consumer (establishing sales points)? What is the lighting and will it create the right mood, directing the eye?
● Is the session black and white or colour, or both? Check proportions. Virtual, real – will you be amending with airbrush work on a real transparency or with a digital paintbrush application on a virtual image afterwards?
● Provide lists of names and designations of people or model numbers or products to be photographed.

Arrangements for the shoot. Considerations should include the following:

● Location of studio.
● Choice of background.
● Position of sun and other details.
● Allow sufficient time to get the models/items/location you want.

I once worked on a photo shoot where we needed a young girl, with flowing pigtails, to be flying a specially made kite over a very green hill with a blue sky with fluffy clouds behind her: that was years before today's special effects systems were available and we waited about eight weeks to get the kite made and have the agreed model available with the right meteorological conditions at Primrose Hill in London – the agreed location! Today, with digital photography, cut and paste and painting/drawing systems, you can capture elements separately and create a great composite that doesn't look any less 'real' than our photograph on location did – you could even get away without having to actually get a four-foot kite manufactured to order! Yes, the skills of the photographer are now married in a much closer relationship to the computer graphics artist: allow teams to grow and allow enough time for them to get the best possible job done for you. It is not wrong to use staged shots, or composites, so long as you are not seeking to *fool* the recipient of the image into thinking something that is untrue: in the example above, we weren't selling the kite, we were coming up with a visually interesting way to announce that a client had just been awarded the BS 'Kite Mark' for a slightly unexciting industrial product – we weren't trying to mislead people into thinking anything, and this should be your guideline when dealing with the challenge of making a possibly 'boring' story come alive with a visually stimulating photograph.

Captions. When photographs are being sent to the press (real or virtual) in the hope that they will be published, it is vital that they carry an appropriate caption. Editors will have expectations that the practitioner should follow:

- Every picture must be captioned.
- For hard copy, the caption should be affixed to the bottom of the reverse of the picture in such a way that it may be read from the front with the picture in view, but doesn't damage the photo itself. For virtual, attach the caption electronically so that it is a part of the same 'document' and the title of the 'document'.
- The caption needs a title to give a quick indication of what the picture is about. If the picture accompanies a news release, then the title should (in most cases) be the same as, or a shortened version of, the news release title.
- Few pictures will stand on their own without some indication of how their subject relates to the text of any accompanying news release. A lead-in can often be a direct quote from the first paragraph of the latter, since this gives the whole story in a nutshell. Double spacing of text is desirable.
- After the title and lead-in, if any, should come a paragraph with the side-heading 'Picture shows. . .' This should say exactly what the picture shows – no more, no less. This is only part of the caption written specifically for that picture.
- As in the case of the news release, the caption should similarly indicate the name, address and telephone number of the issuing organization. The month and year of issue should always be given; it may not always be necessary to give the day of the month.

- The negative number should be indicated or the source.
- Any copyright stipulations should be clearly stamped on the back of the print or included as part of the text.

Exhibitions, conferences, seminars

Sometimes, all three happen together; for example, a major biannual pharmaceutical exhibition will provide the platform for an international conference and various specialist seminars all during, say, four days in Zurich. A PR professional's task is to investigate what already exists, assess whether it meets their needs and plan either to work within the existing framework or, as is often the case, go it alone. What follows here is intended to be a useful summary of points to consider.

Exhibitions

These are mainly trade and business to business, although some are consumer orientated (e.g. Ideal Homes, Clothes Show). They often run in a cycle thus (for each industry):

- Biannual – large, international.
- Annual – large, national.
- Throughout the year – regional/subsector of industry.

Always ask:

- Why are you taking the stand?
- What are the objectives?
- How long do you have to plan?
- What do you want to have achieved after having attended?

If you do not 'fit', organize your own. For example, you want to launch a new commercial boiler at a national exhibition. You are advised that it is not a big enough new product to warrant attention. The solution is to set up your own exhibition of new and existing boilers taken (in a lorry) around regional commercial gas centres, with key specifiers and regional media invited by direct mail to their 'local' exhibition. The result is a high level of attendance, a high and detailed level of product knowledge is gained (across the range), good regional press coverage, *plus* ongoing trade press coverage as new angles developed over the three months of the 'tour'. The cost is not much more than taking a medium-sized stand at the national exhibition!

There are a number of Virtual Exhibitions available now – go and visit one!

 http://www.crm2001online.com

Conferences and seminars

Exhibitions lend themselves best to *showing*. If discussion is needed, then it might be better to use a conference/seminar format, with some 'exhibiting' still being used in reserved areas (hotel foyer, coffee area, etc.). Conferences and seminars are used frequently in two key ways: internal or external.

External conferences and seminars are usually used to bring together dealers, specifiers, key opinion formers, etc., in an environment where information and views can be given and exchanged. Careful planning is *essential*, starting with deciding the purpose, desired outcome and guest list. Many specialist companies exist in the field of conference/seminar/event organization; it sometimes pays to use these experts because they will, for example, be used to planning 'spouse programmes', dealing with travel arrangements, etc.

Internal conferences and seminars are often used to bring together employees who might never otherwise meet! Also don't forget that, whilst it might be a vital element in saving a company, the 'loss' of staff *must* be dealt with carefully for the company to continue to function through its remaining staff, who at least understand the reasons for job losses. If you decide to have virtual corporate gatherings and even meetings, instead of face to face, you lose that human touch, but you can save a fortune in business travel costs!

A colleague who works for a global pharmaceutical organization used to spend as much as two-thirds of his working year travelling the world for meetings! Now that the organization has agreed that some meetings and conferences can take place he only spends half his year on the road – which represents a significant saving in business class flights and fancy hotel rooms for the company, and means just a little more time with his family in Connecticut for the executive!

 ## Applications of public relations

CUSTOMER–DEALER RELATIONS

Marketers need to identify, anticipate and satisfy customer requirements. Marketers use many techniques to enable them to do this, not the least of which is to establish *two-way* communication directly between themselves and their customers.

Examples of the role that a true PR exercise can play might be:

- Customer advisory services. These services allow customers to 'talk' to marketers in a very real sense. The interactive nature of on-line communications and using websites really comes into its own here. Tampax has built an on-line community for teenagers and women to discuss issues that they might be far too embarrassed to talk about openly.

 http://www.tampax.com

- Informative literature, e.g. a brochure on 'towing and touring' supplied by a car manufacturer as a result of an enquiry from a motorist (not with the aim of selling anything) or offered as a way of reducing problems with towing in general, thereby making the motorist and the legislature less likely to complain about towing!

 http://www.sherline.com

- Running an on-pack competition asking for recipes using your product as an ingredient, with winners being published in a book and perhaps invited to cook their recipes on the cookery slot of a morning television 'magazine' programme, or for a women's magazine. You might even link with a TV cookery programme that broadcasts and publishes recipes on the web! Indeed, Dish It Out was developed as a multimedia experience, bringing together the web, the Internet and TV, as well as linking into print media!

 http://www.dish-it-out.com

When it comes to dealers, the marketer is dealing with a vitally important part of the marketing mix – the P for Place, i.e. the distributive outlets. The nature of the marketer–dealer relationship can vary enormously, with scale affecting the PR tools to be used. Generally speaking, however, again the aim is to develop a good, close, mutually beneficial working relationship. The PR tools that might be used here include, for example:

- Literature for information/display.
- Dealer 'training' packs or courses that are downloadable from an extranet.
- Dealer competitions, incentives, that take place in a password controlled web area, etc.
- Events, conferences, seminars, hospitality for dealers.
- Exhibition support for dealers when *they* attend an exhibition.
- Media relations support for dealers.
- Simple 'advice giving' on any publicity matters for dealers.
- Extranet access by password to a part of the corporate website that is exclusively for dealers/partners and might even allow orders to be placed on-line.

For global dealer relations, the Internet and a password secured extranet can represent a huge saving – you just put the information in one place and it can be downloaded globally – think about the implications of this for a global change in legal labelling requirements alone!

EMPLOYEE AND INTERNAL COMMUNICATIONS

All organizations vary in their make-up: a small company with two employees will obviously not need the same tools of PR as one with 20 000 employees. That said, even when people work closely together, planned time away from the working environment can focus the mind wonderfully!

Before embarking upon any plan, therefore, some questions need to be addressed:

- How many employees are there?
- What types of employee are there? Do they all 'speak the same language'? For example, a wages clerk at a chemical plant might not know the first thing about chemistry.
- Where are the employees based – all in one place, spread nationally or internationally?
- What is the corporate structure – a single company, a group, a conglomerate, a recently merged multi-national?

All these questions, and their answers, will help the PR professional decide the *objectives* of internal communication. Are we aiming to inform, educate, interest, reassure, get ideas, build loyalty? All of these? The next question is: How do we do this?

Media for employee relations

An organization can use all sorts of media for mass communication with employees. Some, to be effective, have to be established permanently; for instance, a house journal cannot be switched on according to need, nor can a website, or intranet. Other media, however, can be called into use on an ad hoc basis when required.

Examples in the 'permanent' category might include:

- Annual reports.
- House journals.
- Noticeboards.
- Phone-in information service.
- Intranet site.

Examples of those in the 'ad hoc' category might include:

- Corporate publications.
- Exhibitions and displays.
- Video.

- Film.
- Tape-slide presentations.
- Personal letters to employees.

If starting from scratch, the communicator would list all the categories of information and evaluate the ideal media for each. This analysis would lead to identification of the 'permanent' media required.

Here are a few points to remember if you are planning to produce a newsletter (whether it is printed on paper, or placed on an intranet site, or both):

- Set goals for the newsletter by defining and getting to know the audience you're trying to reach. Don't try to be everything to everybody.
- Make sure a professional communicator, either an in-house staff person or an external resource, is charged with the responsibility for producing the newsletter.
- Don't 'preach' to the readership, the purpose should be to educate and stimulate a genuine dialogue between the company and its staff.
- Write to express – not impress. Use words that communicate your company's message clearly and correctly. Present material in short sentences and paragraphs. Avoid jargon that won't be understood by your entire audience.
- Establish a recognizable format and stick to it, so readers can become comfortable with the content as well as find information simply and quickly. Remember, familiarity is critical in developing readership.
- Develop a solid graphic design. Good design is essential in competing for the attention and interest of your readership.
- Use headlines and photo captions as a way to communicate key points in a story. They're often an editor's best tool in conveying important information. If this is a virtual publication make sure that the page design is as good as any you would use to engage other audiences!
- Don't make the mistake of cramming too much information into a newsletter. Readership surveys repeatedly demonstrate that readers want larger and more legible typefaces, so by providing less in volume, you may actually be able to communicate more.

Ideally, the communicator has the right permanent media for the current situation. However, the ad hoc media should also be kept in mind, with a clear plan of how to bring them into action if required. Letters are a very good and effective vehicle in an emergency, for example, as are staff meetings or cascaded management meetings, but they can sometimes be difficult to arrange at short notice, especially within a multi-national organization.

Increasingly, the idea of using an intranet to communicate internally is being hailed as *the* way to talk to staff. A word of warning: if *all* your staff have access to an intranet (a password protected part of your Internet website), then it might just be the right way to talk to them. Very few organizations find themselves in this position – most have at least a portion of their staff for whom the Internet and the intranet are something they would not normally come into contact with, at least not as a part of their working day. There is some thought that, as home penetration of the Internet via digital television increases, the 'old-fashioned' house journal, which was often mailed to employees' homes, will be seen again in the form of an on-line magazine that is e-mailed to staff members at home – wherever in the world that might be!

That said, the web won't work as a communications tool for factory staff who have no access either at home or in the workplace, will not appeal to, or even reach, many other groups for whom it is not a familiar technology and could cost you a great deal of money, with little effect, if you cannot encourage those who *do* have access to it to visit it! Like all communication methods and messages, your internal communications via intranet must be sufficiently interesting to the audience to encourage them to actually read it, or in this case, visit the site more than once, and, indeed, on a pretty regular basis.

Gaining the reputation that it is 'an interesting site once you get there' is one way of encouraging people to keep coming back, but many organizations give their staff more proactive encouragements to visit their internal communications sites: collection schemes of points of some sort means that you can encourage people to visit every week for a particular time period if you reward them upon proof of, say, one visit per week for twelve weeks, for example. Research could throw light on what rewards/schemes might work for a particular group – never assume that the same will work for everyone!

POLITICAL PR/LOBBYING

All organizations need to be aware of what is happening within government and Parliament that might affect their business either directly or indirectly. What follows is a list of topics for consideration by all organizations and their PR practitioners:

- Current legislation (planned or rumoured) may affect the organization.
- The key personnel, government committees and quangos are involved.
- Special pressure points and how they can be exploited.
- When Green Papers, White Papers, Second Readings, etc., can be expected.
- How best to present your case at each stage in the process.
- Which politicians and officials may champion your particular cause, and what their standing is.
- How ministers and civil servants are likely to react to your proposals.
- How the consultative process really works, and how to influence it.
- How to persuade a select committee to listen to you.

- How to cultivate civil servants and understand their language.
- Where and how to apply indirect pressure (third party endorsements, local press, opinion polls).
- How to get key words changed in a piece of legislation.
- When the House of Lords can help, and how to approach peers.

There are no right and wrong ways to ensure that your lobbying is perfect. There are many PR consultancies that specialize in this field because it is so full of pitfalls for the uninformed or the unwary. It really is worth using a professional who knows their way around this area, because they can, in the long run, not only save an organization time and money by already having the right contact in the right place with the right knowledge, but they should also be fully aware of the restrictions within which they are allowed to operate, which differ within the UK and the European legislature, and can therefore avoid embarrassing and possibly illegal mistakes! Electronic communication has really cut down the time involved with political lobbying, and it might even have saved a few trees along the way, by allowing documents that are usually huge and might have to be printed in several languages to be accessed on websites and not have to be printed all the time!

CRISIS MANAGEMENT

'Crisis management' seems a misnomer, almost an oxymoron: a 'crisis' is something out of control, 'management' means control. Yet hundreds of companies and public utilities have plans worked out for the type of crisis that just might happen to them, so that a management procedure can be swung into action when disaster strikes.

Charities and voluntary organizations are particularly vulnerable to attack from the media when something goes wrong. Such problems are considered 'a matter of public interest' because the organizations receive public money and time, and the money is for the disadvantaged. Possible disaster scenarios are:

- Misappropriation of funds.
- High administration costs/low spend on cause.
- Death, mistreatment or maltreatment of beneficiaries.
- Withdrawal of a major donor or sponsor.
- Criticism by doctors, professional bodies, MPs, etc.
- Patron problems.

In PR terms, crisis management means taking control of the flow of information demanded by the media and the public. If the organization undergoing the crisis is informative, open and honest with the media, they will not need to turn to other

sources (who may be the opposition) for information. Providing as much information as possible, as quickly as possible, will also prevent rumour and speculation. Thus, when planning media handling in a crisis, follow these rules:

- Tell your own tale.
- Tell it all.
- Tell it fast.

In a crisis the press come to you, rather than you trying to attract the press. The journalists and reporters that arrive and telephone are unlikely to be those whom you know and have been carefully cultivating. Pool reporters and home news journalists, who know nothing about your organization, will predominate, and will have a negative, even hostile, attitude towards you. They must be provided not only with any news you have available, but also with general background information on your organization and its work. This should always be up to date and to hand.

If any members of the public are at risk, the press will give this priority – and so must you. In fact, the press can be cooperative in this matter, by getting emergency telephone numbers and advice to the public. They can also be the first to inform you of the crisis (the 3.00 a.m. phone call) and will be prepared to provide you with details, provided you call them back.

Remember that any reporter on the scene will be under extreme pressure on deadlines (with possible late editions being planned) and the 'hold the front page' syndrome will be noticeable. They will also tend to regard the story as their big break – a chance to get a byline on the front page or to obtain the first live report of the story. So find out their deadlines and call them back/provide statements, etc., in time – and remember that the one who broke the story to you should be the first to get the information.

If the press don't get what they want from official sources, they will get it any way they can. This is why it is vital that all press calls and enquiries go to the PR office or crisis management team and to no others. Telephonists, receptionists and security staff must be briefed/trained to do this.

Finally, never say 'No comment' – the public will automatically assume your guilt and other people *will* comment. Remind your legal advisors that saying you are sorry is not an admission of liability. Announcing an inquiry and promising to publish the results shows you to be an honest broker, not a failure. If you don't put right publicly what went wrong, you will never restore your public image. The faster you put your image right, the quicker the problem will be forgotten.

Crisis management – a basic survival guide

Pre-crisis:

- Expect crises – every company has them.

- State the worst possible scenario.

- State the next worst possible scenario.

- In utmost confidence, talk to the very senior management in the company for two reasons:
  - If it's a real crisis then they should know about it.
  - If it isn't worth bringing to the attention of the senior management, there is a question regarding its seriousness.

NB: one man's crisis is another man's salvation (e.g. closing a factory in the prosperous south east to open up a plant in the north east is not everyone's crisis).

At this stage, managers should look seriously at whether all possible steps are being taken to prevent the hypothetical crisis.

- Set up a crisis management team of senior people. If it is a vital problem it must be handled by a very senior director with the PR person advising on communications strategy. The PR person must not be put up as the spokesperson, however trivial the company may consider the matter. The most senior director of the company must act as the only spokesperson.

- Set up the physical machinery (e.g. faxes, telephones) to cope with communications. Have, for example, telephones ready, but don't label the area the 'Incident Room'. It could be equipment in routine use that could be made ready in an emergency.

- Set up an emergency reporting procedure for when an incident is seen to be likely. Don't allow staff to remain silent until it happens, but beware of panics and beware of crying 'wolf'.

- Make sure that your website newspage (if you have one) is updated with all the latest information, and make sure that the same information is given to real journalists who have taken the time to really come to the site of the problem! Make sure that you give them Internet access at your crisis centre (most will have laptops which will give them access either through mobile phones or over a land-line, so make sure there are enough lines for them to all be on-line as well as on the telephone!).

- Finally, set up a system for payment of immediate needs, without prejudicing any future compensation claims by victims.

Planning the use of public relations

The six-point plan that follows was initially put forward as a framework by the late Frank Jefkins. It has now become widely accepted as a sound basis for PR planning, and could in fact be used for planning in all promotional fields. The RACE acronym underlies all PR planning (Figure 5.4).

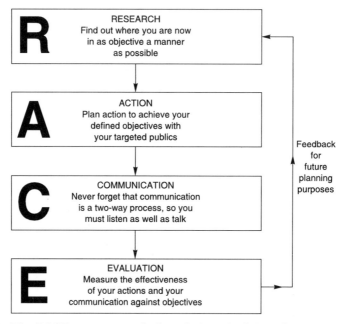

Figure 5.4 The RACE acronym underlies all the principles of PR

POINT 1 – APPRECIATION OF THE SITUATION

This means that the following questions need to be asked:

- What is the current situation?
- What do people know or not know about it?
- Are there any misunderstandings?
- Observation.
- Press cuttings/media monitoring.
- Statistics:
  - National.
  - Internal (sales, etc.).
  - Industry (competition/exports).
  - Financial/economic (share price).

- Trends (inferred and stated).
- Opinion polls (qualitative and quantitative).

Other factors affecting the situation include:

- Industrial relations.
- Weather.
- Customer appreciation (complaints and praise).
- Prices.
- Economic/political situation.
- Opinion leaders.

Are there any negative thoughts such as:

- Hostility?
- Prejudice?
- Apathy?
- Ignorance?

How can these be changed to positive thoughts such as:

- Sympathy?
- Acceptance?
- Interest?
- Knowledge?

A warning – all can't be done at once and the change needs to be continuous.

POINT 2 – DEFINING OBJECTIVES

This is where you spell out the objectives of your programme. Is the aim to change attitudes from x to y? Are you wanting to increase knowledge within your public from x per cent awareness to y per cent awareness? What objectives would a PR programme aim to achieve? List them. Categorize and prioritize them.

POINT 3 – DEFINING PUBLICS

List and define which publics you want to reach:

- Internal: staff (production, promotion and sales, senior, middle and junior management).

- Associate:
  - Suppliers.
  - Distributors.
  - Retail outlets.
  - Shareholders.
- External:
  - Customers.
  - Potential shareholders.
  - Potential employees.
- Local/community:
  - Neighbours.
  - MPs.
  - Local council (members and officials).
  - Pressure groups (ad hoc protest groups, residents associations, national groups).
  - hambers of commerce/Rotary clubs/Lions clubs.
  - Schools and colleges.
  - Hospitals and health authorities.

Remember that you communicate with *people,* so it is essential to look into the above categories to identify the appropriate individuals. This can be done by:

- Trade publics:
  - Job title/function.
  - Company.
  - Industry.
  - Location.
- Consumers:
  - Age and age group.
  - Sex.
  - Neighbourhood and location.
  - Housewife/working wife/with or without children.
  - Head of household/chief wage earner.
  - What they read, watch and listen to.
  - Car owner/motorist.
  - Possessor of durable goods.
  - User of retail outlets.
  - Level of income.

The more of these factors that are known the easier it is to pinpoint the target, and yes, they are advertising/marketing techniques, and yes, they are valid in PR. Remember, very few organizations actually communicate with 'the general public'.

POINT 4 – SELECTING THE METHODS

This is the chronological order in which you should communicate with the media to make sure that information is distributed at the right time and place to have maximum impact. It is no good sending out a press release and hoping it sticks – media relations have to be planned.

Suggested order:

- If it's hard news then the *immediate* media: TV, radio, daily press, on-line news media, on-line interest media (this might mean many different publics are reached, so be sure to do your targeting planning thoroughly well in advance!).
- Financial media (if raising investment, but not in place of contact via the financial management of the company/organization).
- Internal newsletters/house magazines (to reinforce routine management procedures, formal and informal communications do not replace them).
- Trade, technical and professional media (again, in addition to and not as a replacement for normal business discussions and negotiations).
- Special interest magazines (such as *Ideal Home*, which have long lead times).
- Television (other than news, as programmes have a long lead-in time).
- General interest monthly publications.
- Current affairs weekly publications (such as *The Economist*, if appropriate).
- National Sunday newspapers.
- Local weekly publications (including Sunday newspapers).
- National daily publications.
- Radio (unless a programme or longer item is possible).

Constantly review the media you are contacting – the item may be appropriate in other sectors. Negotiate placement (which you can do if you have a plan). Do not always blanket mail. Think of particular editors, journalists, correspondents and freelance writers, and discuss their requirements. Don't distinguish between actual media and virtual media *except in that* virtual media are likely to be taking advantage of their ability to constantly update news, so information you give them might break there long before elsewhere – be aware of this and make sure you plan accordingly.

Media relations techniques include the following, i.e. the ubiquitous press release is not appropriate for every occasion:

- News releases.
- Press statements (written and oral).
- Photo opportunities.

- Product releases.
- Case histories.
- Briefings.
- Interviews.
- Media entertaining.
- Press conferences.
- Articles and features.
- Competitions and prizes.

The essential substance can be obtained (not be made up) from the following:

- New products.
- New technical developments/technology.
- Application of products and technology.
- Corporate developments.
- Issues and controversies.
- Introduction of standards, regulations, laws, etc.

Other means of communication can also be used. There follows an overview of which method is useful for achieving which type of objective.

Printed material

Printed PR material might have the following purposes:

- To give sales information.
- To build corporate image.
- To be explanatory.
- To be campaigning for a cause.
- Merely requesting (as in a questionnaire).

Forms of printed PR material include the following (they can all be actually printed or virtually created, or both, as appropriate):

- Leaflets.
- Mail shots (from letters to multi-parts).
- Catalogues.
- Brochures.
- Press advertising.
- News sheets/newsletters.
- House magazines (internal/external).

Always select the form which best suits the purpose.

Participatory media

Participatory PR media (or methods that need human involvement for delivery) include the following:

- Seminars.
- Workshops.
- Conferences.
- Exhibitions.
- Displays.

Again, select the form that best suits your needs, budget and timetable, and make sure that you choose real or virtual, or both, as best suits your needs and the access points of your target publics.

Audiovisual material

Audiovisual presentations might be in the following forms:

- Flipcharts.
- Overhead projectors.
- Slides (carousels/pulsed tapes).
- Films.
- Videos.
- Computer-generated material or websites.

Sponsorship

Sponsorship might be a method you select, but always ensure it has been well thought through:

- It must be relevant.
- Participation should be taken on a sound basis.
- It can be expensive.
- It can be inexpensive.
- It can be ineffective.
- It can be effective.

If you let your heart, or your principal's heart, rule your head, make sure you have a healthy budget.

The question then arises about how and when to ensure integration of on-line and off-line PR effort – well the answer is that all effort should be integrated, not just PR effort, so all PR effort at the very least should feel the same, say the same and work towards a common goal.

POINT 5 – DEVELOPING A BUDGET

There are a number of ways of constructing a budget, but the main ones are:

- Finger in the wind.
- Top-down, i.e. see what you've got and work within it.
- The task method, i.e. decide what needs to be done and price it.
- Historic plus, e.g. 10 per cent more than last year.
- Percentage of sales/receipts.

The methods are not mutually exclusive, but it is best to be realistic, i.e. don't put forward a proposal with a huge budget. Remember, the four main elements of setting a PR budget are:

- Labour – salaries/PR consultant's fees/PR practitioners and other staff that might be involved.
- Office overheads – these are mainly fixed and can easily be calculated.
- Materials – stationery, print, etc.
- Expenses – these must be controlled at all times.

POINT 6 – EVALUATION

There are three key points to remember here:

- It is important to measure the effectiveness against the objective (if the exercise fails to meet the objective, it is a failure).
- It is important to take soundings before as well as after to establish changes.
- Evaluation should be continuous (to review progress and preview future activity).

Evaluation/assessment methods can be either quantitative or qualitative.

Quantitative:

- Column centimetres (measure them).
- Ratings/readership/site hits (count them).

- Enquiries received (count them).
- Quality scored (score it).
- Increased interest generally (measure it).
- Increased sales/receipts (know past levels and present levels, and measure the difference).

The main problem with quantitative methods of evaluation, when used alone, is that they only measure what has happened, and not the effect or the understanding of why it happened – so you might have sold more, but was it because you were on a well-hit web page for two weeks, or were there other factors?

Qualitative:

- Opinion polls (to gain insight into attitude changes).
- Peer group/competitor attitudes (carry out depth research).
- Media interest/sympathy. This may not result in immediate column centimetres, but can be judged on a one-to-one basis and bodes well for the future.
- Effect of total positive and negative media coverage.

A good example here of understanding why both quantitative and qualitative research is needed would be the following: you have had a huge number of opportunities to see your good news message about your past year's performance *and* your great plans for the future – you have achieved high quantitative ratings through your press, TV, radio, on-line news and face-to-face coverage, but then your CEO is on Radio 4's *Today* programme for two minutes, and blows the whole effect of the good news by uttering one thoughtless phrase that belittles all your customers and suppliers at one blow! The outcome of *all* the coverage, good and bad, might be heavily weighted in *quantitative* terms towards the good, but because of the *qualitative* impact on a huge group of influencers (the listeners to *Today*), your overall *impact* is negative!

Think this can't happen? Gerald Ratner pretty much brought down his very successful high street jewellery retail chain by uttering one phrase at a luncheon given for a 'friendly' audience of businessmen: he referred to his company's product as 'crap'. The national press picked up on this. Buyers stayed away from his shops in droves – who wants to give or receive 'crap' as a gift or a memento of a special occasion? He had to sell out to the Samuels chain shortly afterwards!

Publics will not judge you on column centimetres, be they virtual or real, they will judge you on a much more subtle balancing scale than that – so the professional PR practitioner should always research the *impact* of what they say, as well as the appearance of it!

On-line research is both secondary and primary.

1 On-line is an important source of secondary information because so many libraries and information databases are in electronic form accessible at your desk.

2 Primary research on-line is well established with large panels of users and respondents. Commercial research companies have on-line panels to examine products, services, issues and ideas.

3 On-line research includes:
 – Perceptual tracking and analysis of company/product/service/issue/trends.
 – Instigation of discussions in newsgroups/forums/elsewhere for feedback: these are less than focus group but still valuable, especially if discussion participants are among the target audience.
 – Competitor information.
 – Soliciting user reactions to products.

When do I use it?
Perceptual and competitor tracking should be a part of your public relations tools.

Tracking is vital too. It is important to repeat that finding information is not enough without careful interpretation and recommendation.

Instigation of discussions in newsgroups and user reactions to products should be done carefully based on the product, service or issue you are researching. One must remember that newsgroups and forums are self-selected sites, and they do not represent a statistical cross-section of a population. Therefore, the choice of the site in which to instigate a discussion is as important as the discussion.

Before taking an active role in newsgroup discussions and soliciting user reactions, you need to do advance work. One part of advance work is to analyse the newsgroup or forum in detail to determine the kind of people who show there regularly, their temperament and civility, and topics they usually discuss.

Figure 5.5 On-line research

Many organizations exist to sell research services that do just that; here are a couple of useful addresses:

 http://www.metrica.net

 http://www.pre-fix.org.uk

SUMMARY OF PR PLANNING

The main stages in PR planning are:

- Situation analysis including the problem.
- Objective setting.
- Target audience definition.
- Methods.

- Budget.
- Evaluation.

In theory, the budget should be decided when the programme is finalized. In practice, the client (or employer) may say 'Here's the cash – that's it!'

In a more detailed sense, here are some notes on planning:

- Set margins for the operation.
- Estimate the working hours and other costs.
- Select the priorities.
- Assess the feasibility of carrying out the declared objectives.

A six-point PR planning model would be:

1 Appreciation of the situation.
2 Definition of objectives.
3 Definition of publics.
4 Selection of media and techniques.
5 Planning of a budget.
6 Assessment of results.

You must always take into account:

- Hostility.
- Prejudice.
- Apathy.
- Ignorance.

What you are aiming to achieve is a transfer from this stance to the following:

- Hostility > Sympathy.
- Prejudice > Acceptance.
- Apathy > Interest.
- Ignorance > Knowledge.

Remember, investigation is required to arrive at a helpful appreciation of the tasks involved and solutions needed. PR is about effecting change, not just creating favourable images.

Visit some agencies on-line to see what they are up to:

 http://www.nelsonbostock.com

Nelson Bostock is a London-based PR agency that offers PR and Marketing Communications services to both e- and non-e-businesses. This site is newly updated (as of June 2001) and will lead you to their clients' sites, many of whom provide e-services that the PR practitioner would use!

 http://www.bm.com

Burson Marstellar is a global reputation management organization. Its website reflects its scope and range of activities as well as its corporate ability to work in the modern e-world.

 http://www.hillandknowlton.com

As part of the global communication giant WPP, Hill & Knowlton offers a full range of PR services.

 ## Summary of chapter five

Within this chapter we have covered the following:

The background to, the reasons for, how to plan and how to implement a public relations communication programme.

Overview

This section describes what PR is and can do.

How does it get done?

This section looks at who does what internally and externally for PR.

The publics

This section takes a look at publics and what they want.

The methods for communicating

This is a comprehensive review of a large number of above and below the line communication methods and how they are used for public relations purposes.

Applications of PR

This section looks at how PR is applied in a range of real circumstances.

PR planning

This section addresses the specific issues about writing and implementing a PR plan that will work!

Self test questions and opinion development

These are not exam questions, nor are they meant to represent the sort of question you might expect to face anywhere else. They are designed to help you check whether you have understood the content of this chapter. All you have to do is read the questions, give them some thought and maybe jot down some notes on what your response might be. Not all the questions will have factual answers – rather, they might encourage to think about a topic or an issue and formulate an opinion based upon what is now, hopefully, a better understanding of the topic.

What is PR?

How would you say it differs from advertising?

Why do you think PR is made fun of so much?

What do you think the IPR could/can/does do to change that?

Name four possible publics and their needs from an organization that wants to build mutual understanding with them.

Name three possible PR objectives.

How could you use TV for PR instead of, say, advertising or sponsorship?

Answer the same question for radio.

How would you describe on-line PR?

Name the possible crises that could be faced by the following:

- an on-line, global charity to help children;
- a company known for buying its raw materials in the UK;
- a cricketer and his sponsors;
- a nuclear fuel plant;
- a company that makes children's furry toys;
- a website that offers cut price sportswear.

What are the six points in a six-point plan?

Why do you need six? If you had to add a seventh that related just to e-PR, what would it be? Why?

 Extending knowledge and understanding

You are encouraged to undertake the following activities to further your knowledge and understanding of the topics covered in this chapter in the following ways:

1 Visit the IPR website and work your way through it. What does this say about PR in the UK today? What interesting links are there? Do you think it could do a more professional or proactive job? Why do you think the IPR is needed? Spend some time working around the site, and try to visit other PR Association sites too, e.g. the PRCA in the UK, or for Ireland or the USA. By using a search engine and a bit of imagination you can find many. How do you think they compare?

2 Try checking out several PR agencies' own websites, remembering they are in business to help others manage their reputation and image – what do you think their sites say about them? A great site I found is http://www.soc.american.edu/friedheim/pr.html, which has been set up by US college students to make links easy! But if this address doesn't work for you, don't worry, you can still surf and find lots of agencies – good luck – you might be amazed at what you discover.

3 Keep up to date with your PR trade press reading – whether it's on the web or on paper. What are the big issues *today*? What's their background?

4 What qualities do you think it would take to become a great PR practitioner? How many types of practice are there? Would you need to be a very different sort of person in each field? What do you think?

5 Try to find a PR plan for your own organization/one of your choice. What does it tell you? What does it tell you if you don't have one? Why not write one yourself?

Chapter **6**

Managing implementation

Making sure you have the right resources – internally

There are two types of resource you will need to be able to implement your marketing communications programme: your internal resources and external resources. It is normal for the *internal* resource to be your first consideration when assessing your resource requirement situation.

The internal resource available to you might be adequate to carry out all the marketing communications functions you need. This might especially be the case if the functions are being managed by you and implemented by a team of specialists either in your office, in your country, or even just within the organization across the world.

Thus, your starting point is working out what your communications programme is going to be, assessing the skills of the staff available and hoping that there is a match! But even if there is a match in skills, there also has to be a match in terms of workpower available for the size of the task – in other words, have you got enough of the right people to do the job? This is often where a problem arises, especially if there is any element of seasonality in the business, thereby producing peaks and troughs of activity for the marcomms team.

If you have an opportunity to mould a team for the future, through recruitment, then here's a useful tip: work out what you will need in the team one month from when the new person would join, and six months from when the new person would join – if there's a difference, recruit someone who can grow to be what you *will* want, or who, indeed, has the skills you *will* need already. It is important to look ahead in terms of team development, knowing that you can buy in short-term resources when you need them.

SPECIFIC ISSUES

One of the most contentious issues being faced by many marcomms managers today is the question 'Who owns our website?' and the equally contentious issue of 'Who manages our website?' The battle lines are usually drawn between the IT department, marketing and corporate affairs or PR departments. So who *should* own and run the corporate website?

Well, as a writer on marketing and marketing communications I am sure you would expect this author to say 'The Marketing Department' without hesitation, but actually I have a different suggestion: why not get the marketing department to lead a team effort? Often there are other issues that need to be dealt with on the website, such as investor relations, customer communications or internal communications, and there might well be technological advances about which the marketers will have no knowledge but which could greatly alter the content, or method or type of communication available through this valuable tool. Thus, a team effort with user focus remaining the emphasis being kept in mind by all team members might do the best job. But leadership skills will be put to the test, as will communication skills, so a good programme of continuous communication and discussion, with clear guidelines about responsibilities and no-go areas, needs to be put in place from the first opportunity. I suggest that marketers take the lead in this area because they are the keepers of the 'identify, anticipate and satisfy customer requirements profitably' ethos.

Making sure you have the right resources – externally

HOW DO MARCOMMS MANAGERS CHOOSE THE RIGHT EXTERNAL SERVICE PROVIDERS?

There is no simple answer to this question. Indeed, as you read the trade press and see the way that advertising, public relations, direct marketing, sales promotions and all types of accounts move from agency to agency, you might begin to wonder whether any client ever does choose the right external service provider (hereafter referred to, in the interests of brevity, as 'agency', but without the implication that this refers to just advertising agencies – you might equally apply what is said to web agencies, PR agencies, sales promotion agencies, design agencies, etc.!).

This general movement aside, both clients and agencies have an interest in an account remaining with the same agency for a reasonable period of time, as this allows the client–agency relationship to develop a depth that can lead to truly great advertising. However, the job of constantly reviewing the ability of an incumbent agency to deliver work which meets objectives, and the reviewing of the alternative agencies available, takes a great deal of valuable time on the part of the client, or marketer, so it really is worth attempting to choose the best possible supplier in the first place.

Thus, as mentioned earlier, when considering your needs internally, you need to have decided, broadly speaking at least, what types of promotional effort you will be requiring. Remember that even if you go to a full service agency, if it is an advertising agency you are likely to get an advertising solution to your marcomms problems, if you go to a below the line agency you will get a below the line solution and so on. Possibly the business to business communications agency, or a real, honest to goodness through the line agency (and they are few and far between) are most likely to offer you a true range of communication solutions.

Figure 6.1 shows the sorts of tools you might want to consider for certain objectives.

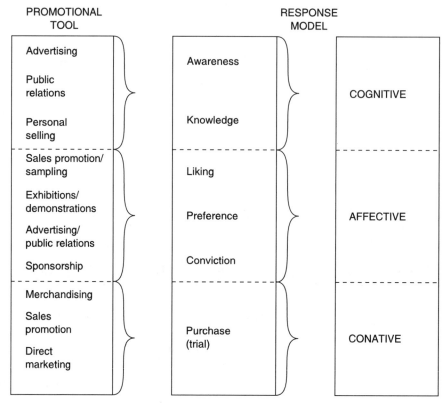

Figure 6.1 The role of different promotional tools in the promotional mix – advertising in context

Once you have decided what type of supplier you are looking for, or, indeed, what range of suppliers you might need, then you can begin the process of selection, appointment and management. I suppose I should add a word of warning here – most e-business communications agencies are new, young – staffed by enthusiastic, well educated, bright, knowledgeable people. But experience counts for a lot in all aspects of life and business, so you might be tempted to look for the sort of supplier, in this field of newness, that has a few people in it with a few grey hairs. It's not true that because you are older you make better decisions, the truth is that, if you are intelligent and prepared to learn, you are likely to make fewer mistakes the more experience you have.

Now, whilst it *is* true that no one has masses of experience in this field, and with new methods of communication being developed almost daily it seems, then you can't really expect more than a few years' experience within new communications disciplines; you should accept that sometimes the questions and issues being posed and raised are old ones – it's just that the answers are new! With that in mind, it really can help to have someone around who has been dealing with these questions and issues for a long time – they know some of the short cuts it's worth taking, and some that it's not, they know pitfalls and understand pressures – true, they might not be as technically advanced as some of their younger colleagues, but with an open mind and an astute business brain, there's no reason why experience in marketing communications has to be discounted in favour of digital know-how!

What follows is not an exhaustive 'how to' list, but rather a basic checklist for a client who is trying to choose an agency – of whatever type (the word 'agency' is not being used to refer exclusively to an advertising agency, as mentioned before). There are two lists, one which deals with the process one might follow and one which looks at the criteria one might use when choosing. I would give these as checklists no matter whether you run an e-business or a non-e-business: best practice is best practice! All you need to do is make sure that you *apply* these hints and tips to the specific circumstances you face today.

The process of choosing an agency

- Decide what your needs will be: full service; specialist on-line PR back-up; e-CRM and fulfilment, etc.
- Decide the type of budget you will have: all with one supplier, or how will it be split?
- Look at the output you like: which agency's name keeps cropping up, who is winning awards for *effectiveness* (not just creativity!)?
- Which agencies do your competitors/admired rivals use: are they rumoured to be moving accounts, if not might you be big enough to woo them away over time?
- Which agencies produce work for those organizations, outside your own field, whose communications have the spark you want for your own?
- Check with a trade publication for campaigns that use the type of communication tool you believe you will be using.
- If at this point you find you have seven or eight agencies to choose from, you could find out whether they have a show-reel of their work, a portfolio that they could send you, or if their website is their showcase – thus avoiding the need for them to send along a team to mount a full 'credentials' presentation.
- Build a list of about five agencies that appear to offer the range of services you need, handle the sort of size of account where yours would fit well, and produce work you admire.
- Invite these agencies to give a 'credentials' presentation – this is the agency's chance to show you what it does for existing clients and gives you a chance to meet some of the agency personnel.

- Select two or three agencies that you are now happy with as your final selection.
- Brief these agencies so that they can mount a real 'pitch' for your account.
- During a pitch presentation, always look out for an agency that has met the criteria of your brief.
- Award the contract and tell the loser(s) of your decision.
- Agree any press announcements with the agency.

The criteria for choosing an agency

- Know what you want.
- Look for an agency that can offer the services you need.
- Be sure that the size of agency is right. If your account is small, try to get an agency where it will be mid-sized; small accounts can fall to the bottom of the priority list.
- Is the agency well located for you, your other offices, etc.? Although electronic communications mean that you do not need to be breathing down each other's necks, it makes sense to use an agency whose location makes it accessible to you, and good staff/suppliers accessible to it.
- Has the agency got the sort of track record with its past/existing clients that matches what you are looking for?
- What is the staff turnover at the agency like? High turnover of staff is not good.
- Is the chemistry between your team and their team good?

The Incorporated Society of British Advertisers can offer good advice when it comes to selecting an agency, and has produced a publication called *Choosing the Advertising Agency*, which can give further guidance, and which contains principles which can be applied to choosing any sort of marketing communications agency.

These days it is even possible to retain a consultant who will do all the initial searching and screening for you, but this can be costly. However, the marketer's own time costs money, so if time is tight and a consultant is being considered it is worth costing the true value of the time it will take the client to find a new agency, compared with the cost of having the initial stages contracted out.

Whatever process is worked through, it really is the client's responsibility to have a basic understanding of the services they will need and, similarly, a basic under-standing of who does what at an agency, thus allowing any decision to be based on better knowledge. So let's take a look at today's full service advertising agency structure, so you can get to grips with who does what.

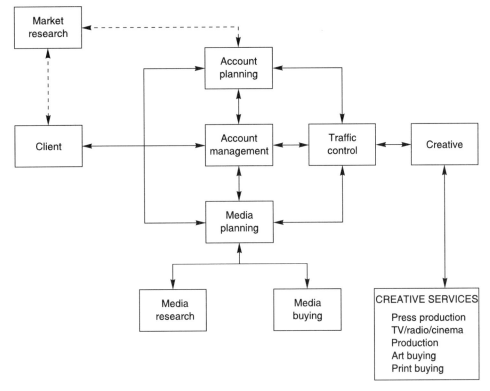

Figure 6.2 Full service agency structure today

Advertising agencies: who does what?

The full service advertising agency has evolved over many years into what we see today. That is, due to the requirement of marketers to have access to a centre of excellence, full service agencies still exist and are growing in strength and corporate weight worldwide. Many full service agencies have realigned themselves to be of maximum attractiveness to e-businesses: if you are moving from bricks to clicks you might find that your existing agencies are offering small, young, specialist teams to help you address the e-challenge; equally, full service agencies are finding that they are offering e-services to e-clients as they attract pure e-businesses – so a full service agency is often a real option for an e-business today, even if you are quite small. But don't forget, as mentioned earlier, if you are small you might fall to the bottom of the pile in a big agency that handles big accounts (often they will take smaller e-business accounts than you might think, because of the strong belief in growth potential), so be careful to choose the right *scale* of full service agency, as well as one that offers 'full service' on your terms, not its own!

Account handling

Account handlers are the point of contact with the client, and the conduit through which all communication between the client and the agency flows. They are carriers of information from the client to the agency, translators of client language into agency language, internal coordinators of accounts within the agency, and the people responsible for presenting the agency's work back to the client. They need to be listeners, interpreters and coordinators. A team player, the account handler has a vital role in ensuring that the client gets what they want, because the agency has a true understanding of what is needed.

The different layers of account-handling responsibility will vary from agency to agency, with the titles bestowed upon the handler being dictated by both corporate culture and the needs of the client. For example, a marketing executive would quite happily deal with an account executive, whilst a marketing manager would probably prefer to deal with an account handler whose title also included the word 'manager'. Advertising agencies that have their cultural roots in the USA often carry the term 'Vice President' across the Atlantic and use it here in the UK.

Account planning

The account planner will often have a numerate background, or will at least be an expert interpreter of research and numerical data. This function comes very close to the client's own marketing planning, with many of the same market tracking surveys being on-line as within the client's own research department. The account planner will research, investigate and put forward proposals for action to the rest of the account team based upon market, audience, attitude, media and creative treatment research.

Media planning

Media planning is a vital function within an agency. The means of putting the message in front of the right person at the right time is key to the overall promotional and communication task. Within media departments there is usually a central research and planning function, with specialist planners and buyers being called upon as necessary. For example, whilst a generalist planner needs to take an overview of the campaign requirements, it makes sense to have specialist buyers who build firm relationships with either television or press media sales forces, for example, thus ensuring that the best buying deal is obtained for the client, with the planning requirements having been agreed at the outset.

A detailed knowledge of all above the line media must be complemented by free access to on-line media research data, allowing detailed planning to take place. Also, the account handler will ensure that the media planner has a full understanding of the range of other media being used by the client at the time of the campaign in question.

The creative effort

Within the creative department of a full service agency, there are those who are conceptually creative and there are those whose abilities are more practical.

The creative team

This term specifically refers to the art director and copywriter, who often work as a team for many years, if not for the whole of their careers. It is vitally important that there is a deep level of understanding within the team because they are the key players in the success, or otherwise, of a campaign. Often, teams that have worked together for years see their relationship as a sort of professional marriage, with each knowing the other so well that their thoughts often fly off in the same direction together at the same time.

Indeed, whilst one will be responsible for visual concepts and the other for the verbal message, it is the synergistic effect of the two elements together that makes a campaign work. The team that works well together will produce harmonious advertising almost automatically, and can attract clients to an agency because of its reputation for producing outstanding creative work.

Traffic managers

These people are responsible for ensuring that each stage of the creative process is fulfilled at exactly the right time to allow advertisements to be finally prepared and reach the media owner in the right format at the right time to appear as specified in the media schedule. Timetabling of an entire campaign is essential, and the traffic manager will liaise not only with the creative and media departments, but also with the account handler, ensuring the total internal coordination of the account.

Other services

Gone are the days when agencies could afford the overhead of their own television commercial production teams, or a stable of illustrators or photographers. The early 1990s saw the last of the in-agency film production units move off to become, at first, a profit centre within the agency and then a totally separate entity. Often, production departments devolved from agencies with a 'buy-out' of equipment from the agency by the original staff, who then set up as an independent production company. Many producers and directors still work on a totally freelance basis, being contracted in by independent production houses, who themselves work for agencies on a project-by-project basis.

Photographers, illustrators, composers and musicians tend to work as freelancers, usually using an agent to represent their work to agencies. Within an agency the art buyer, or in some cases the art director, is responsible for reviewing, say, photographers' portfolios on a regular basis, ensuring that the agency knows exactly how to get hold of the best food photographer, or the best trick photographer, or the best fashion photographer at very short notice. With specialist abilities being the order of the day, agencies need to call on those with the required skills on an infrequent basis – the freelance system works well in this environment.

As mentioned earlier, you might find that specialist e-teams are available to e-businesses: the e-team will tend to be made up of a Hands-On Account Handler, a New Media Guru, an Electronic Creative Whiz and a Technical Genius.

Flippant? Well, I do know one man who has New Media Guru printed on his business cards (he has a great sense of humour and his cards are firmly tongue in cheek, but it does reflect on what some people in the New Economy think of themselves – especially when they take themselves too seriously!), so beware of people who tell you that they can predict where it's all going, where it will be tomorrow and why you should get there ahead of the pack. If you are going to build a comprehensive knowledge of e-communications methods you need to be working with energetic, knowledgeable people who will take the time to listen to your communications problems *before* they rush towards you with communications solutions!

Just because you *can* doesn't mean you *should*, so be sure that the additional services you see offered, or are offered, are, in fact, services that you are likely to use or want (and are therefore prepared to see being carried by the overhead towards which you would be contributing).

When all is said and done, any full service agency works with a client company to plan, execute and monitor the effectiveness of a communications campaign. Generally, this means that at least a part of the effort will go into an advertising campaign that uses above the line media. However, most agencies will have either specialist departments, devolved sister companies or links with other specialist providers of sales promotion, direct marketing and public relations functions at least, if not the full range of other miscellaneous below the line promotional services.

As already mentioned, this is particularly the case in the business-to-business specialist advertising agency, where the use of below the line tools is important and often uses more of the budget than above the line services.

Agencies are in business to do business. If they are to survive and thrive they must provide the services their clients require. Thus, as clients' requirements change, the specific services offered and the way in which they are delivered will vary within the largest and the smallest agencies.

BUYING 'À LA CARTE'

As mentioned earlier, all the functions offered by a full service agency (account handling, account planning, media planning and buying, creative conceptual work and production facilities) can be bought direct by the client from independent companies or even freelance individuals. This is referred to as buying 'à la carte'.

From the client's perspective the advantage of using a full service agency (of any type, because the full service versus à la carte buying of services applies equally to PR as to advertising) is that you have immediate access to a whole range of experts who are able to bring a fresh and unjaundiced point of view to bear on your problems. However, it is a very expensive way of operating if you do not intend using all the services on offer – your fees are having to service the overhead, so you might as well use the facilities!

This has to be balanced with the huge amount of extra time that the client who chooses to buy each element of service individually must dedicate to the task. Sometimes it is easy to lose sight of the fact that the internal cost of staff who coordinate matters in-house is as real a cost to your company as the fees paid to an agency. The client should weigh up the objective pros and cons of using a full service agency as opposed to buying à la carte, as circumstances change and alter with time.

An understanding of basic approval procedures is also required. If you are the client you will want to know what is going on and whether it is meeting the brief you have agreed. How do you do this, without getting in the way? Quite simply, you work with the agency before they begin to implement your programme to ensure they know when to seek your approval:

- It is usual for all creative concepts to need approval.
- Finished artwork/animatics (for commercials) need approval.
- Finished commercials need approval.
- Media schedules need approval.
- Literature proofs need approval.
- Prototype gifts/samples/give-aways need approval.
- Event plans need approval.
- Exhibition-stand designs need approval.
- Packaging and point-of-sale mock-ups need approval.
- Web content needs approval.

The best guideline is to approve the brief, approve the plan, approve the rough/mock/model/prototype and approve the finished item before it is shown/displayed/run/despatched.

It is the client's responsibility to make it quite clear that they require sight of any promotional item or method at each given stage. You might want to lay down rules that allow nothing to go beyond each stage without your signature on the artwork/contact report (a contact report acts like minutes taken at a meeting between client and agency).

Promotional output begins with the agency putting into action the promotional programme as agreed. However, another integral part of the whole promotional process that certainly has to be planned in from day 1 is the system of monitoring that will measure the effectiveness of what it is you are doing.

As the overall controller of a promotional programme, it is your responsibility to ensure that each part of the promotional programme, each promotional tool, has in place its own monitoring system – a system that will monitor how effective that particular tool is being in achieving the objectives set for it. So, you need to measure the increase in sales levels in March if your on-pack promotion aimed to get proofs of purchasing being collected in March for redemption in April; you need to measure attitudes to your organization's environmental stance before you run your 'plant a tree' scheme, as well as after it, and so on. The method you need to use to measure effectiveness needs to be selected for and tailored to each promotional tool and each promotional objective.

BRIEFING

When it comes to briefing your full service agency there are essentially three types of brief that allow the information needed for a successful campaign to be passed around those who need it:

- The client brief.
- The media brief.
- The creative brief.

The briefing system has grown up in the field of 'traditional' full service agencies, and most of the terminology and expectations have been drawn from that area. With new media agencies, digital communication agencies, global virtual agencies, etc., this author suggests that you stick to the tried and trusted methods of making sure that you, the client, give the information that your agency/agencies need (whatever their title or type) to be able to do the best job they can for you.

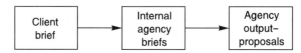

Figure 6.3 The overall briefing process

The client brief

A poor brief in the first place from the client will waste the agency's time and can cost both the client and the agency money by leading, ultimately, to poor output with poor results. The damage can be long-lasting and potentially disastrous for all concerned.

A brief is not a document that is merely handed over to an agency, it should be presented to the agency by the client in a briefing session which is designed to allow the agency to ensure that it has all the information it requires in order to meet the brief it has been given. Thus, it is worth stating that the briefing session demands preparation by both parties, so that the client is able to give the information required of them by the agency.

The agency representative, usually the account handler, will be looking to leave the briefing session with a document and appendices that give the agency all they need to know, as well as an impression from the client of the way they see the project working. That is not to say that agencies like clients to write the headlines and do the media selection even before the brief leaves their office! An account handler will try to stop the client doing these things, and should also resist the temptation to do them themselves, even if the client starts to press for a 'top of the head' response.

The brief is the start of the creative process.

Certainly, it should contain all the relevant information. At the end of the brief, the creative team should be clear whom they're talking to, why they're talking to them, and what the advertising must say.

But it should also be a stimulus to creativity. A good brief will contain insights into the product category, the marketplace, and the thoughts and feelings of the prospect. It will carry hints of likely directions, it will offer a promise that is easy to dramatize, and generate enthusiasm for the task.

A good brief is one that the creative team cannot wait to start work on, because they sense the opportunity to do great work.

If you master the art of good briefing, you will receive better creative work from your agency and earn the respect and loyalty of your creative colleagues. You will be the person whose jobs are consistently done well, and on time, and budget, because people enjoy working with you.

Ultimately, good briefing is one of the highest skills in agency management. This is not to belittle presentation skills, or the ability to negotiate. But the quality of briefing has a direct effect on the quality of the creative work.

And the quality of your marketing communications determines your company's reputation and prospects. So let's look at this process from the 'inside'. We need to get an understanding from three different perpectives:

1 What the agency is looking for.

2 Using an agency briefing form.

3 Briefing an agency team.

What the agency is looking for – the account handler's viewpoint

So there you are, briefing the agency on a campaign. Sometimes they're terrific written briefs covering the whole marketing background. Sometimes they're not so terrific written briefs, as they cover the whole marketing background but completely miss the key points that the agency need to know.

There is one golden rule when writing a brief. Always imagine that you have to actually create the response. Imagine that at the end of the meeting, you have to go back to your agency, shut yourself in the office and produce a great campaign. You. Not the agency, not the creative team. And if you can't do it, well. . .

That way you know what information to put in.

When taking a client brief, there are two things you, as the account handler, have to do:

1 Collect the basic background information.

2 Begin to develop the promise.

Background information

This sounds easy, but isn't always so. You often have to dig out the information. It may help to structure your notes around a checklist called POMMMM.

Product	What *exactly* are we selling?
Objective	Why are we advertising?
Market	Who are we talking to?
Media	How will we reach them?
Message	What must we say?
Measurement	How will we know it's worked?

If you've covered these fully, you've got the background. Give the agency everything you can lay your hands on!

- A copy of the brief.
- Brochures/literature.

- What did the first website look like?
- Let them take the product back with them.
- Research? Who did it? Where is it?

Don't pretend you know all the answers if the agency wants to dig a little deeper.

- Who can tell them?
- Can they meet the technical people?
- Go out with a salesperson?
- Visit a distributor?
- Is there really no research?
- Can they have sight of the marketing plan? (Is it confidential? Can they sign a secrecy agreement?)

All the time, think how you would feel if you had to sit down and write the ad.

- You would like the product to play with.
- You would like the literature to read.
- You would like some good, relevant background reading.
- You would like a good, clearly thought-out brief.

Developing the promise

Digging out the background information is only part of the job of developing an agency brief.

A good briefer is schizophrenic. Your brain has to be divided into two compartments – both working flat out. One compartment is digging out basic facts, the other compartment is looking for clues that will help the agency.

When delivering a brief, you can literally divide your piece of paper in half:

Facts   Clues

In the Facts half, you can note down any background information. In the Clues half, scribble down the little points that come up which you feel may help to develop the promise and create the ad.

The trick here is to talk to the agency; anecdotes lead to great ads. Get excited. Ramble on a bit about the product, market, competition, big contracts, funny stories – anything.

And spot the Clues.

- 'Well, we lose out on price. But if you take all the costs into account, we're cheaper.'

- 'In the end, they're all terrified of choosing the wrong one.'
- 'The bloody brokers take the easy way out. They just sell the product they understand.'

Sometimes a client throws out a clue that goes further than helping to develop the promise; they come up with an idea for the advertisement as well.

For example, David Ogilvy was taking a brief from Rolls Royce, and was told that the car was so quiet, the noisiest thing about it was the damned clock! He went on to create a famous advertisement that used this fact to sell the car's uniquely quiet running!

It's not always easy to collect facts and pick up clues simultaneously. But always remember: you have to write the ad.

It does wonders for sharpening the brain.

Using an agency briefing form

An agency might have a very detailed briefing form, or not.

The briefing form should provide a way for you to order your thoughts, and present your arguments. It should be treated as an aid to analysis and communication, not as a kind of tedious examination form.

Often, an agency will suggest that their client uses it as a 'blank' to complete prior to briefing. Here is an example of what such a document might contain as prompts/information for a client, so if you are a client you can use this to help you prepare, or if you are an agency you might want to give this to a client to complete (amended with any special requirements, of course).

Product/service

What is your company selling? What is the market buying? There are two important questions here.

The first, 'what is your company selling?' asks for a factual description of the product. For example, Bosch is selling a drill.

The second asks for a judgement. In the case of Bosch, the market is buying a hole. To give another example, Redland is selling Rosemary clay tiles but the architect is buying a building material with warmth and character. It might be that you are offering an intangible and even virtual service – so what exactly is the market buying? Better information, or easier sales?

- To help the creative team understand 'what we are selling', find relevant information: brochure, photographs, press releases, pages from the website. If possible, bring the product itself into the meeting.

- To help the team understand 'what the market is buying', look for relevant magazine articles and research.

Role of communication

Why are we communicating? Let's look at advertising for a moment – there are many roles that advertising can fulfil. Some examples are:

- to reinforce existing behaviour;
- to overcome prejudice;
- to generate response;
- to get the brand on the candidate list;
- to boost company morale;
- to change perceptions;
- to improve distribution;
- to increase brand or company awareness.

You should be clear what the advertising, or other form of communication, is expected to achieve today, and in the long term.

What do we want people to do? Send off the coupon? Circle the reader enquiry number? Call a Hotline? Fax their business card? Look up the website? Check a particular web page every day? Ask for our brand at their distributor? Specify our brand by name? Not veto our brand when someone else suggests it?

You should be precise. How many hits will count as success? What is the perception now, and what change is sought?

How will we know it has worked?

Wherever possible, you should ensure that a system of measurement is in place before the campaign breaks. Without this, you *will not know if the campaign has worked*. Accurate data are the only good foundation for subsequent campaigns.

Target audience

Demographics, attitudes, function.

1 This heading recognizes that communications aren't hitting job titles but people. For example: Security Manager, C2, aged 40–55 years. Ex-policeman, passed over for promotion. Spends most of his shift reading, mainly spy novels and thrillers. Bored with his job. Feels that company security could be better, but people only want his opinion when things go wrong.

Suddenly, we're talking to an individual.

If the agency has a clear picture of the lifestyle and attitudes of the prospect, they can address him in his own language.

2 It is the expectation that fmcg and B2C markets will be tough to tackle, but don't forget that B2B markets are complex too. The person who specifies the product will probably not be the person who buys it. There may well be other 'influencers', including the end-user.

For example, in the case of a fork lift truck:

Truck Driver	Identifies the brand
Works Manager	Selects the brand
Purchasing Manager	Negotiates the price
Managing Director	Signs the cheque (and vetoes if he hasn't heard of the brand)

Make sure that the agency understands who's involved and how they interact (for example, should the advertising give the Truck Driver some arguments he can take to his Works Manager?) and make sure you understand the different intra-media decisions that have to be made in order to reach them (your tracking research might find that cheque signers visit a different part of your website than the specifiers do).

Competitive frame

Who are the direct competitors – how are they positioned?

Don't just list competitive companies. This will mean nothing to the agency. Instead, paint a picture of the market. Who are the 'best' companies (i.e. the ones you most admire)? Who are the 'worst'? What makes them best and worst? Where does your own brand stand on this spectrum?

Who are the indirect competitors? What are the environmental factors afoot? Share your 4U Audit.

What is the prospect currently thinking/using?

1 Most communication is about changing perceptions, or reinforcing those we want. To do this, the agency must know the starting point. Does the customer know that this type of product/service exists? Is he satisfied or dissatisfied with what he's using at the moment? Does he have a negative view of our brand ('too pricey', 'too old-fashioned', 'too complicated', etc.)? Challenging preconceptions can lead to great creative ideas.

2 Bring along samples of previous advertising/PR, etc., and competitor advertising and communication. If an agency knows what communications in this market usually look like, they can create an unusual one.

3 Make sure you consider all the competition, including indirect competition. (For example, the 'competition' to automatic mailing equipment is a room full of company employees folding paper and licking envelopes, or a comprehensive e-mailing facility.) Does the prospect have to compromise or improvise without our product or service? This can be a rich source of creative ideas.

4 Look in the trade magazines for 'burning issues', especially the editorial and the letters page. Is there a market trend the agency should know about? Or some impending legislation? Is there a preoccupation with cutting costs or raising quality? Maybe this can be integrated into the communications argument.

Single-minded proposition

This should be the single most compelling thing we can say about the brand. You should evaluate different propositions and aim for a killer.

A killer proposition is both *motivating* (it gives a powerful reason to purchase our product/service) and *differentiating* (it sets our product apart from others).

Imagine you are face to face with the prospect. What is the one thing you could say to him to make him want to know more?

Could he save his company time or money? Is there an urgent problem he can now solve? Or an opportunity he's missing? Is there some good news he hasn't heard yet? Or a danger he should know about?

The important thing is to concentrate on product benefits, not product features. As the saying goes: 'People do not buy 1/4-inch drills because they want 1/4-inch drills, but because they want 1/4-inch holes'.

Why should they believe it?

You must be able to substantiate the promise, otherwise your agency will produce work that is glib and unconvincing. To quote David Ogilvy (for the last time) 'We tell the truth but we make the truth exciting'.

Other significant benefits/factors

Including practical considerations, mandatory inclusions.

Here you should list other important benefits that will help to form the body copy. You should also mention mandatory inclusions (standard disclaimers, Queen's Award logos, exhibition stand flashes) that cause so much grief when they're mentioned *after* the ad or site has been created.

Tone and mood

What are the values of the brand?

Every company has a unique personality.

For example, Diversey Lever is bringing a new vision to cleaning and hygiene systems. Instead of merely pushing products, they offer total cleaning solutions, via a talented workforce.

The agency needs to understand your company's distinctive tone of voice. Is it relaxed and humorous? Challenging and aggressive? Caring and compassionate? Lyrical and romantic? And so on.

How to brief the agency team – as an account handler

Understanding the internal point of view from the agency's perspective is important to the manager of marcomms work – the more you understand the issues that will be faced by your suppliers, the better a manager of that service provider you can be. So let's take a look at the viewpoint of the account handler within an advertising agency – what do they have to bear in mind to do the best job they can for you, the client, within their own organization? And how can you help them to do the best job they can on your behalf? Account handlers *are* human beings, so each one will handle internal briefing in a slightly different way, that almost goes without saying, but it is important to remember that you, the client, have a responsibility for helping your account handler to be able to be as good at his/her job as possible – you can do this by arming them with the information they need, when they need it!

Each type of account handler (PR, SP, Web, etc.) will also be facing a slightly different briefing situation, so the exact nature of internal briefing will vary from agency type to agency type – but these are the basics that you need to understand.

The account handler is the conduit between the client and the agency, and has to get the agency team to perform to the best of their ability – here are some notes that would be valuable to an account handler, or, indeed, anyone directly briefing creative and media teams!

By now the account handler should have collected all the *facts* and *clues*. Let's talk directly *to* the account handler in question. . .you've compiled a brief that's informative, imaginative and stimulating. Now, don't throw it all away!

Never, ever, apologize for a brief. Never say 'I'm sorry, we've got to do a quick ad for so and so'. The chances are you'll get poor creative work, and you'll deserve it.

Here are a few pointers:

1 Make the brief special. Fix a special meeting. Don't just turn up with an armful of papers and say 'If you've got a minute, can I brief you on this?' If you squeeze

briefs in as 'AOB' and don't take the job seriously, neither will the agency. There's no rule that says you can't brief in the morning over a bacon sandwich or in the evening over a beer!

2 Show the agency that you're enthusiastic about the product. Bring the product/ service and its application to life. Tell stories, paint pictures. Use your presentation skills to bring a bit of theatre to the brief. Remember, it's part of the creative process.

3 Have lots of relevant information: videos, magazine articles, competitive ads and literature, copies of the candidate media. Agencies can never have too much *relevant* information.

4 Brief problems not solutions. You should never ask the agency for a specific type of execution: a testimonial, an editorial style ad, a product demonstration. It sounds reasonable but it leads to mediocrity. It's better to concentrate on the problem that advertising must solve. If you can find 'originality' in the problem, you'll help the agency to find an original solution.

5 Insist the agency make a recommendation. The agency should give you what is, in their judgement, the best possible solution. They should believe one of their ideas to be better than the others (should they not?), and in that case why would they ever show you (or want you to see) their second best. Of course, you may want to know why other solutions were rejected, but insist on one recommendation.

6 Show that you appreciate the creative product and the agency's role. Don't show the agency your secretary's idea for the ad.

7 Radiate confidence in your team. Confidence breeds enthusiasm and it takes enthusiastic people to produce great creative work.

8 Open up the briefing process. You may have technicians, product managers and sales people who are in love with the product. Their enthusiasm is contagious. Organize an agency visit to some satisfied customers. It's amazing what agencies can do when they really believe in a product. Conversely, it's hard to create great advertising when your heart isn't in it, or you can't understand why anybody would want the product.

9 Give the agency team time to digest information, evaluate different solutions and consider implementation. Terry Lovelock was given ten weeks to write the Heineken slogan 'Refreshes the parts other beers cannot reach'. Give your team at least ten working days. You wouldn't put a new product on the market overnight.

10 Don't be stingy with praise. If you think an idea is elegant, ingenious or witty, say so. You won't appear uncool. Every agency has a portfolio of favourite ads that never ran. They get used to taking knocks, the way that professional footballers do. So it's nice to get some praise instead. Praise is very motivating.

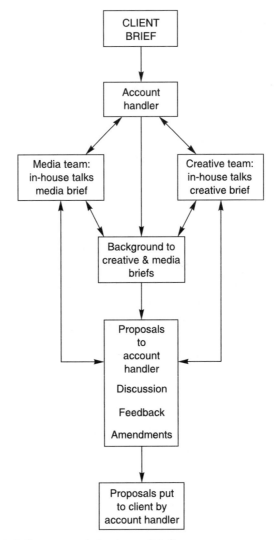

Figure 6.4 The briefing process in more detail

Everything that is mentioned as being necessary for briefing an advertising agency applies equally well to briefing all other types of marcomms service providers – but with some specific amendments according to specific needs.

If you're dealing with a PR agency you might find that the person who is the account handler is also the person who will actually write the articles and news releases, talk with journalists and even organize conferences, etc. for you – so you are actually briefing the person who needs all the information, directly, rather than dealing with a 'go-between'. This means that it is easier to discuss the heart of the matter, but it doesn't mean that any less effort should go into the brief preparation or the briefing process itself.

MANAGEMENT ISSUES FOR SERVICE PROVIDERS

You will find that the trade associations for each of the disciplines (the ISP for sales promotion, ISBA for advertising, etc.) will be able to offer guidance on the content of contracts that should be set in place when you appoint an agency of any sort. Both parties will benefit from a contract being in place, as this will form the basis of the expectations each party will have of the other as they work together.

Contractual agreements

Some organizations have standard Terms and Conditions for appointing suppliers, but often these are not adequate for the requirements of the marcomms manager. If they have to be used, then they should be used as a basis for the contract. Some other items that should be considered as additions (in a covering letter, which allows them to become a part of the contract) are outlined below.

Contact report procedure

It is normal for the service provider to supply reports of *all* contacts between the supplier and the client (including telephone calls, but excepting any written communication – rules vary about whether the receipt of an e-mail should elicit a contact report response and it is difficult to generalize: if an e-mail is sent then it could count as a written communication, and therefore not require a contact report response, it becoming a part of the contractual relationship itself, but it would be best to take the advice of your own legal department on this issue).

These contact reports should be generated, often transmitted electronically these days, within 24 hours of the occurrence of the contact, and should state clearly, and succinctly, the content of the contact. It would be normal for the client to have a further 24 hours to query the content of any such report, but if they do not, then the report becomes a part of the contractual agreement.

An example of how this works in favour of *both* parties would be if a telephone conversation takes place between the client and supplier, and the client tells the supplier to go ahead and spend £20 000 on a particular item. The supplier sends a contact report saying that the client has approved £30 000 worth of expenditure (maybe a simple typing error). The client has 24 hours to get back to the supplier and change the figure to the lower amount, or else the supplier can go ahead and spend the higher figure. It just all makes sure that everybody knows what is going on at all times. After all, most marketing communications implementation takes place with tight deadlines, and mistakes are easily made – this process is there to try to prevent miscommunication or misunderstanding from becoming a huge problem.

Account team personnel issues

If the client has appointed a supplier on the basis of a particular account team and their presentation of their efforts, the last thing they want to happen is for the people they thought they would be working with to disappear to work on other pitches or other accounts! That said, there are rules about not placing restrictive contracts on people and not allowing them to go about their business in a reasonable manner, so you have to be very careful about wordings here. Your main aim is to make sure that the supplier knows who you want to work on your account, by name and in what capacity, that if one or more of those people leave the agency or need to be reassigned, that you, the client, will be informed and will be able to have some say in selecting the replacement, or at least being able to have a 'trial period' for anyone new who is assigned to your account.

Marketing communications is often referred to as a 'people business', and it is true that the personal relationships involved are very important when it comes to building the most successful campaigns possible. This item addresses this issue.

Review periods and content

One of the best ways to manage the relationship is to keep reviewing progress: this should be done even when there is no output on the account. But, again to benefit both parties, the nature and timing of such reviews should be made clear: not only does the supplier need to know how much time and effort they will have to put into the review preparation and presentation procedure, but the client needs to make clear why they need to review what they want to review, when they want to review it.

Day-to-day management

If relationships are important in business it is because communication is important. And communicating within the client–agency relationship is vitally important, because if either party does not understand the other then a great deal of money can be wasted on work that does not achieve the desired effect.

If a client has several agencies to deal with it is likely that the workload with each might ebb and flow, but that occasionally there will be a massive workload with many suppliers at once. This can mean that the client ends up repeating various tasks across suppliers. So why not brief suppliers together? No reason really, and many clients will do this. The other advantage that this has is that it allows all the suppliers to see how their work fits together.

Day-to-day working relationships are likely to ebb and flow with workload: and the agency has a responsibility to proactively try to develop the relationship too, so the responsibility lying with the client is mainly responsive and professional.

However often communication takes place, and whether it is professional or social, building understanding of needs, wants and desires will always lead to better work – the better the client is understood, the better the supplier can supply! So the golden rule is to keep communication clear and all should be well.

REGIONAL AND INTERNATIONAL FACTORS

Throughout this text the main emphasis is on UK national marketing communications campaigns. Of course, not all campaigns are like this – some are local, some regional, some national, some international.

When you are setting promotional objectives you must, of course, define the geographical area within which those objectives are to be achieved. This will guide you in your selection of promotional tools.

When it comes to the international factor, it will again be fairly straightforward, when looking at your objectives, that you are supporting your products in, for example, the USA and the Far East, or you are not. Having established within your objectives where you need to support what product/brand, it is then the responsibility of the person managing the promotional programme to deal with that country/those countries on exactly the same basis as the UK, i.e. decide objectives, budgets, timescales, seek and appoint the appropriate agencies and establish planning and implementation guidelines for each programme. The way in which international promotional programmes are handled is no different to the way described in this text when talking about the UK. What will be different will be the specific nature of the balance of the promotional mix selected and how each tool can and should be used within the country in question (see Figure 6.5).

Generally speaking, most large UK-based agencies of all types either have branches, sister companies or affiliated agencies in most countries worldwide. Even small agencies usually belong to international groupings of agencies nowadays. That means that there is no excuse for not using the indigenous population for all your promotional planning and execution. This is especially important when it comes to the creative treatment for your promotion. Beware of mere translation – it might seem like a logical solution to a pan-European campaign for example, but literal translation is a very dangerous tool. So much promotional communication depends on nuance and interpretation that it is worth considering getting creative work totally originated

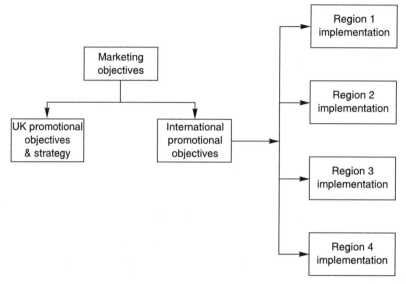

Figure 6.5 How central control works to ensure that international promotional programmes have local relevance

in each country for each country. If this is not possible, say due to budgetary constraints, or not desirable, because you want a truly pan-European campaign, then carrying out pre-campaign research in each country will at least establish if the population there is receiving the messages you believe you are sending!

CONTROLS AFFECTING YOUR COMMUNICATION OUTPUT

Whether you are communicating just within the UK, or globally, what you can do and how you can say it will be constrained in one of two ways – either by law or by some sort of code of conduct.

Of course, laws will differ from country to country, as will codes of conduct, or guidance, so it is a good idea to get advice in each country on what is allowable, as well as what is desirable. But since it will always be the client organization who's name will be connected to any problems that might arise, it isn't enough to tell your agencies that they have to abide by the rules – the client must check that the requirement to do so is in the contract, that they constantly ask the questions that get the right answers and that the agency is making them aware of when they might be 'sailing close to the wind'!

The UK has seen a spate of advertisements that have courted controversy with the specific aim of generating press coverage, thereby leveraging a relatively small advertising budget to create a lot of 'media noise'. For certain brands it could be argued that this has worked well, FCUK being a case in point, where controversy is very much a part of the brand proposition and sits well with the target market. The Benetton organization adopts a similar strategy, using its advertising to raise issues it feels should be discussed within society. Some say that this stance has created a unique presence for the brand, others raise the point that it can turn as many people off the brand as it turns on – maybe not too popular if you run a store trying to sell broad appeal youth clothing!

Laws and controls can change overnight, so a printed book is not the best place to reproduce such information. But at least a marcomms manager should know when to stop and ask the question, even if they don't know the answer, and they should also have some idea about where to look for that answer. With this in mind:

1 Check everything with your legal department, if you have one.

2 Know where to check the law and codes: generally, each trade association for each communications discipline (e.g. ISP, IPR, PRCA, DMA) will be able to give advice and guidance on not only which laws apply, but also what the self-regulatory codes of conduct say too!

An example of such back-up would be the website offered by the Advertising Standards Authority at http://www.asa.org.uk

Generally speaking, advertisements must be legal, decent, honest and truthful, as should all marketing communications tools.

Specific laws and codes might change, but the rule of thumb must always be to be open and honest with those you seek to communicate with, or influence.

Summary of chapter six

Within this chapter we have covered the following:

The issues concerned with managing and implementing marcomms programmes, using internal and external resources.

The right resources – internally

This section shows how to assess what you have already against what you will need.

The right resources – externally

This section looks at how to assess what external resources you will need, how to find them, how to brief them, how to assess their pitches, how to appoint them and how to manage them. It contains comprehensive checklists and contact points as well as practically useful documents such as: What should be in a brief?

This section can be used when dealing with any type of marketing communications service provider, not just advertising agencies.

Self test questions and opinion development

These are not exam questions, nor are they meant to represent the sort of question you might expect to face anywhere else. They are designed to help you check whether you have understood the content of this chapter. All you have to do is read the questions, give them some thought and maybe jot down some notes on what your response might be. Not all the questions will have factual answers – rather, they might encourage you to think about a topic or an issue and formulate an opinion based upon what is now, hopefully, a better understanding of the topic.

How many people work in marcomms for your organization (or one of a friend/relative)? What do they do? How are they structured? Who do they report to? What does this tell you about the way that this organization views marcomms?

How many agencies does your organization/one of your choice use?

What do they all do?

Do they do it well?

How could they do it better?

If you were to work in an agency, what job would you like and why?

If you were to work on the client side, what job would you like and why?

Why do you think agencies (of all types) are now positioning themselves as 'integrated marketing communications agencies'?

If you were to set up an agency, what would it offer, to whom and why?

Why do briefs matter?

Extending knowledge and understanding

You are encouraged to undertake the following activities to further your knowledge and understanding of the topics covered in this chapter in the following ways:

1 Visit some websites for the following types of agencies (use a search engine to help you find them – you might want to use several search engines and compare how

they hunt out what you need) and find out what they offer and how – what does this tell you about them and how they see themselves?

- Advertising agency.
- PR agency.
- Sales promotion agency.
- Direct marketing agency.
- Media agency.
- Website agency.
- Integrated marcomms.
- Business-to-business agency.

2 You are an account handler at an agency that has just lost a pitch for a piece of new business taking an existing client from bricks to clicks. You have a chance to ask the client who has turned you down five questions that will help you plan better for the future – what would your five questions be and why?

3 If you were to set up a small, business-to-business marketing communications agency, what business issues would you have to deal with? How would you operate? Where would you set up? Who would you hire? How would you market yourself (not *sell* yourself, but *market* yourself)?

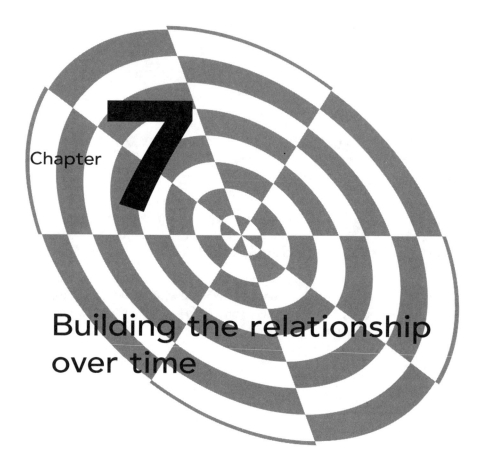

Chapter

7

Building the relationship over time

Much of what has been said so far implies 'getting in touch with' a target audience, or public. We have considered planning, what tools are available, even which tools are good at which jobs. What we now need to consider is how to *build* a relationship with a customer, getting them to ascend the 'ladder of loyalty' and thereby gaining maximum 'lifetime value' from them. e-CRM is one of the most exciting aspects of e-business today – and one of the most challenging and rewarding!

 ## Getting them in the first place

A great deal of marcomms effort and money is spent trying to get potential customers to visit a site and then try a product or service for the first time, and, increasingly, we are seeing more time and money being spent on keeping the customers who have been gained, and in making them not only advocates, but also truly valuable aides to marketing to their peers!

Let's get this into perspective – the ladder of loyalty shows us how true lifetime value can be gleaned from customers.

THE USUAL SUSPECTS

There have to be a very large number of Suspects, in order to end up with a significant number of customers, clients and advocates. So the 'casting of the net' for Suspects will tend to be pretty wide, with Suspects usually defined in general target groupings, such as:

> Males, B, C1, 55+, living in the North of England or Scotland, with traditional tastes, a down to earth approach to life and a preference to spend money carefully, seeking value for money in a beer, not seeking kudos.

Though this profile speaks of lifestyle as well as demographics, it is still very general in terms of targeting. It will be adequate for above the line media planning, it will even allow for regional upweighting and below the line communications planning. But all that this level of promotional effort will achieve is something of a hand-raising, or testing of product, effect, if you were, for argument's sake, launching a new beer.

Mass communication is generally used to get Suspects to nominate themselves as Prospects – to put themselves into a grouping that says 'I am interested' rather than 'I might have been interested, but in fact I am not'.

Suspects are grouped in different ranges, from primary to secondary to tertiary – in other words, from hotter, to warmer, to cooler! With Suspect groups being so broad ranging and generalized, it is unlikely that all members will have an equal propensity to be interested; thus, we need the differentiation within this overall group.

Relationships can get very stale, and suffer because of it – a competitor might suddenly look very attractive to your customer because they are offering a new incentive, whereas you haven't offered them any real reason to keep coming back to your website time and time again.

How can you keep the relationship alive – without changing so much that you are no longer the organization they wanted to have a relationship with in the first place? **DRAMA – that's how!**

DIALOGUE – an organization should offer customers ways to talk to them – every message sent should allow for a response. Every unsolicited communication from them should receive a swift and *relevant* response. The organization *must* show that it listens and can talk and tell too!

RELEVANCY – the beauty of e-CRM is that mass communication can be personal and made relevant to the recipient; indeed, the customer's expectation of relevance will be so high that it is dangerous to send bulk messages that are not tailored to that one person's/company's needs.

ACCURACY – e-CRM opens the door for poor information management, as does any other form of direct communication – but this time the problem might well have originated with the customer themselves, e.g. they mis-spell a name, enter digits incorrectly, etc. when data are captured. Data must be checked, must be updated and must be kept 'clean'. Equally, any information you give to customers must be double checked (as in all good communication) to ensure total accuracy.

MAGIC – this is what makes the difference! The extra dimension that makes people want to be your customer. There is much talk of Customer Delight – go one better and aim for Customer Amazement! The Internet allows for special effects, deliveries of technically advanced packages of information presented in very appealing ways – animation, sound, interaction, prizes, incentives, collection schemes – these are all pretty much expected by customers nowadays, so what will you do that is different? Will it be your creative execution? The links with famous personalities whom you sponsor or hire? The very personal touch of a one-to-one advisor, the best free software downloads available? *Magic* is what should be the goal – and never guess what it might be, carry out research to find out what your *customers* want it to be – there is little point in offering a two-week holiday in Tahiti to every customer you have, because it is unlikely to appeal to them all…don't forget the *relevance* rule, and use the *flexibility* to be able to offer prizes to selected groups or individuals (e.g. people with children of different ages would agree that Disney World is either a great idea or dreadful!).

ACCESS – 'I feel like we're drifting apart!' Don't let your relationship wither due to lack of contact, but also be sure you are not smothering the relationship with over-attentiveness! If you have a scheme to get your customers to visit you regularly (let's say they have to visit you every week for a year to collect all the cards in a deck of cards to be able to get an opportunity to have a free trip to Las Vegas, you must keep them going with spot prizes, because a year is a very long time to wait!), then be sure there is something worth seeing when they do visit! Getting someone to access your site is one thing – entertaining them, informing them, having what they want when they get there is something else – and cannot be ignored. One further point about access – customers will get used to the way a site works – change it and they can get lost and frustrated very quickly, so if there are some small changes, designed to get them to browse more widely across your site, make sure they are well signposted, and if there are *big* changes, make sure you make your customers feel special by telling them about the changes clearly and well before they are in place.

Figure 7.1 Dynamism in a relationship!

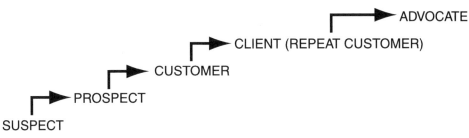

Figure 7.2 The ladder of loyalty

In e-business terms it is likely that you will be selecting mass communication methods such as on-line banner advertising, hotlinks and search engines to get Suspects to at least be aware that you exist. Once they know who you are and where you are, and have followed the link, or at least decided to give you a look, you want to do your best to get them to *enter* your site – this is where you need to consider your entry barriers or data gathering barriers at site entry. The more people you turn off from entering the gateway, the fewer Prospects you will gather from your Suspects. If you have kept to the Three-Click Rule and keep your initial login data requests to a minimum you might ease people into your domain, where, by careful tracking and staged questioning, you can find out more about their interest in your offering a bit at a time, rather than boring or frightening them initially.

But don't forget – the better your thinking at this stage the less wasteful it will be when you cast your mass communication net. If you have used non-e-media to raise awareness of a new offering, or of a reason to try doing business with you *now*, then it might well be that those coming to your site to investigate further are prepared to go the extra mile in terms of the hurdles they are prepared to leap to find out about your offering, but not everyone will feel this way, and there is an increasing level of negative feelings about having to answer detailed questionnaires just to enter a site.

One further factor to consider is that many Suspects choose to remove themselves from your range of possible contacts, by placing themselves on what's called a Preference List. Visit the DMA website to read more detail about their Telephone Preference Scheme, their Mailing Preference Scheme and so on. Basically, these are ways of removing your personal details from a contact list and must be borne in mind.

 Web contact: http://www.dma.org

 ## The role of targeting

Because it can be expensive to contact Suspects, there is a refining process that can be undertaken to narrow down the targeting: a good and sensible place to begin is by building an understanding of your existing customer base, finding out what these people, or, indeed, companies, have in common, and trying to find more people, or companies, like them. This might sound like common sense, but it is, in fact, what underlies a great deal of target market planning!

Once you know the type of person you are looking for, then you can decide on the best tool available to reach them. It might be that there are only another 60 organizations in the whole world with whom you are seeking to do business, in which case the use of a very direct form of contact, such as a telephone call, an e-letter or brochure, an e-invitation to an event (either a virtual or a real event), etc. would be suitable. With business-to-business marketing and selling, it is often the case that a sales force will be involved, and this very personal method of representing your organization's offering can be effective, but with the increasing number of organizations choosing to do e-business-to-business marketing, it might well be that your website becomes your sales presence as well as your communication presence.

It might even be that your Prospects have already told you they are Very Hot, by entering into a Permission Marketing relationship with you.

PERMISSION MARKETING:
Any form of marketing where the recipient of the marketing effort has requested that they receive the marketing effort. The marketing effort might be sales orientated (in the form of a sales offer) or purely communication based (in the form of an updated newsletter highlighting company, brand, product performance).

Of particular relevance to e-CRM, as Permission Marketing denotes the readiness of a Prospect or a Customer to continue at least a communication-based relationship with the marketer.

Figure 7.3   What is Permission Marketing?

 ## The role of branding

That is when mass communication methods have to be assessed. Yes, it is true that there might be a mailing list for your Primary Suspects in existence somewhere – you might even be able to afford to use it! – but a direct mail item is rarely enough to turn a Suspect into a Prospect all on its own. Indeed, many Suspects will only respond positively to a brand name with which they are very familiar, even if they have never tried the product or service, nor know someone who has. Many e-businesses have a strategy of saturation banner advertising *just* to make sure that their brand name is known by those they might contact via another method. Brand familiarity breeds trust – even if it is only enough trust to elicit a first visit!

That is why so much time, effort and money is spent building brands that have a personality that will communicate the values and proposition of the offering to a mass

THE INVESTMENT IN A BRAND is an argument that was accepted as vital to success by many investors in start-up and rapid growth stage e-businesses – to such an extent that the amount of the total investment that went into brand building off-line advertising was often many times the level of investment in the rest of the business.

In many cases this proved disastrous, with a name that was known resulting, but no business delivery to back the brand identity.

Brand means identity *and* reality – a name will only be built into a brand when the company delivers what it promises.

Figure 7.4   The major e-business panic!

audience very rapidly. Of course, this is an expensive exercise, with millions of pounds, dollars, yen and lire being spent every year trying to build associations between a brand name and logo and a specific positioning strategy.

The strength of this perceived relationship between a Suspect and a brand name has enormous value. Indeed, so great is the potential held within brand building that the international accountancy fraternity has now accepted a number of Brand Valuation Models into its accepted methods of valuing a company, or part of a company's assets, when it is selling to a buyer who wants a valuation based on more than manufacturing equipment owned and stock held!

The true value of a brand is, of course, its potential, and this is the problem – no matter how well a brand *has* performed in the past, how it will perform in the future is a matter that will be controlled by its future management, and how future market conditions will affect it.

It is *this* aspect of Brand Valuation that is now exciting the financiers of e-businesses: with the stock markets around the world readjusting their valuations not only of e-businesses, but also those other businesses whose viability relies upon the e-ing of the world (the Tech Stocks as they are often referred to, meaning technology companies such as telecoms, cabling, etc.), it is the strength of the business *delivery*, along with the strength of brand awareness and understanding that has to be weighed.

However difficult it might be to position, build and manage a brand, it is still an important factor in bringing Suspects towards a Prospect position: it does this by allowing Suspects to form opinions about whether the personality and offering of the brand will fit with their needs, wants and desires, by allowing them to at least begin to decide whether they want to put themselves forward as a Prospect.

Thus, when it comes to building a relationship with Prospects, and then Customers, an e-business is showing a dedication to its most valuable resource. Frankly, I believe that the awareness and understanding of a brand identity, the ability to deliver the brand promise and the efficiency with which customer relationships are managed *will be* the three most important measures of likely future success, and therefore market value, for e-business and all business in the near future – and if they aren't, then they should be, because if an organization only pays lip-service to marketing, rather than every member of staff living and breathing customer focus, then frankly, it probably deserves to lose out to a competitor that really does put the customer first!

Prospecting for gold

A Prospect is not a Customer – a Prospect is still a potential customer, someone who *might* become a customer, who has, maybe, something in common with many of your existing customers, but who has yet to buy from you.

Sometimes a Prospect needs to be able to try the product or service you are offering free of risk (which usually means free of charge!). As such, you might have Prospects who have no experience of your offering and Prospects who have some experience of your offering – it is likely that those with experience (and the marketer would be responsible for ensuring that it was a good experience) would be seen as 'hotter' Prospects than those with none.

It might seem odd to think of Prospecting as part of Customer Relationship Management, but it is. If you deal fairly and well with Prospects you are increasing your chance of them becoming Customers. You will also have set the tone of relationship that your newly acquired customer will expect from you – so be careful to ensure that the promises you make to convert Prospects to Customers are promises that you can, and do, keep to your Customers.

It might even be that your best Prospects are *lapsed* customers. BT has an ongoing campaign aiming to convince those who have moved to their competitors to 'Come Back' – offering free reconnection as an incentive. Whilst this is indeed an excellent incentive to those who wanted to try the competitive offering, but who now might be swayed to return, those who never went away in the first place, those who have remained loyal customers, can feel somewhat aggrieved that they won't get free connection if they want an extra line, but that those who have not been supporting BT all this time now get a service for free for which they themselves have to pay! So you do have to be careful that you do not set up a system of seeming partiality.

So, you have your various types of Prospect, as outlined below.

Type:

- Lapsed customers who have had bad experiences of your offering and are very unlikely to return, but might if you can convince them that you have changed.

Potential marcomms:

- You still have their contact details, so contact them directly, in a very personal way: (a) be sure you have all the facts about why they left – have you checked all incoming e-mails, etc. and possibly (b) try to find out why they left you/haven't done business with you for *x* months. Since this is a group that is highly unlikely to return, unless you give them facts and data that show why whatever turned them off you in the first place has changed, you must make any communication direct, personal and relevant. Personal messages backed up by mass communication work well, so make sure that if you have had recurring problems that have led to customer defections, that you not only address the reasons, but then tell people what you have changed and why they should reconsider you!

Type:

- Lapsed customers who didn't have a bad experience of your offerings, but who wanted to try an alternative – they might return if you remind them that they enjoyed dealing with you, and give another, more rewarding reason, to do that now!

Potential marcomms:

- If you give them an added incentive to return, as well as trying to tie them into some sort of loyalty scheme (maybe building points, so they don't go off for a better quick deal to one of your competitors), then this will help enormously. Collecting schemes can either be individual to your business, or you could join one of the web-wide schemes that exist to link various sites with a common reward, that can then be 'spent' across those sites.

Type:

- Those who never have been a customer, but who have had some sort of free (or risk reduced) trial of your offering, which was (hopefully) a satisfactory experience, and who now need to be converted from 'trier to user'.

Potential marcomms:

- This needs some sort of push, some incentive to convert *now*! Often financial (i.e. lower price to subscribe/buy now), it can be more complex – e.g. money off another site or even another business's goods or services that are relevant. Contra-deals and deals of all sorts of cooperative marketing can, of course, take place between e-businesses in the same way that they do with other business, so think about ways that you don't have to go it alone all the time – maybe a link with a travel site would be a good incentive to buy for your target group, or maybe a discounted subscription to an on-line magazine on a closely related topic?

Type:

- Those who have never been a customer, have knowledge of your offering and feel positive about it, so might be prepared to try it at a low risk or risk-free level.

Potential marcomms:

- As above, but with a free trial to get them to the stage described above, then take them forward as suggested. You might need to use off-line media to bring the free trial to their attention.

Type:

- Those who have never been a customer, have no knowledge of your offering so need to be made aware of it, hopefully in a positive way.

Potential marcomms:

- We're back to off-line communications methods here, being used with the aim of building awareness, and on-line methods building awareness of the name, with hyperlinks, hotspots and banners being used to give a chance to jump to the site and start on that free trial offer ride.

Type:

- Those who have never been a customer, know of your offering through third parties who have had bad experiences – so will need a lot of convincing to try it even for free!

Potential marcomms:

- Offer them not only the chance to have a free trial, but also to be rewarded if they bring in a friend as a buyer/member, etc. This means that they become advocates very quickly, and psychologists tell us that if someone is told by another person that something is bad, then they discover for themselves that it is good, they are most likely to try to convince the person who told them that it was bad that it is better than they thought – so you might end up gaining two customers!

Obviously, each category of Prospect poses a different challenge for the marketer, and for the marcomms manager, with different objectives and tools being set and used. Offers and incentives should be tailored to best meet the needs of the target group, and the method of communication should be chosen to get the right message through to the right number of the right people at the right time. This is a very important factor in terms of marcomms planning: get too many people asking for a free use of your system at the same time and you might end up with an overworked workforce who cannot deliver what the brand promises, maybe by way of site maintenance or query response, for example. This means you could end up with a large number of disappointed people who had raised their hands to move from Suspect to Prospect –

AOL runs television advertising campaigns globally that tell non-AOL users about cost comparisons, special offers, upgrades of software and new reasons for going on-line with them.

By using television to raise awareness and give directions to the website they are increasing their Prospects. By giving a free trial of AOL for a short time-period they give Prospects a chance to become convinced they will enjoy doing business with AOL. They can then offer incentives to join at the end of the free trial period that make it a very attractive prospect to do so, thereby increasing their conversion rate from Prospect to Customer.

Over-servicing free trial users, communicating benefits at a very high frequency rate and giving incentives to convert works well.

Figure 7.5 Getting them to try!

and that's not good! So be sure you monitor and manage the number of those who are using what you offer free of charge – and never let their needs overtake those of your existing customers – because word of mouth (even electronic chat) gets around very fast, and disgruntled customers will communicate a more powerful message than any incentive to convert you might be able to offer!

Aiming to score a conversion

Once you have found and categorized your Prospects, you can decide what it is that is most likely to convert them to Customers. Is it the promise of a three-year warranty, or free petrol for 3000 miles, or a weekend for two in Paris, or a money-off voucher for their next holiday? Is it 10 per cent off their next purchase, or this one? Is it that chance to save for money off something of their choice? Is it access to a layer of your site reserved for highly technically adept VIPs? All of these are examples of incentives that *might* work to help convert a Prospect to a Customer – but you must be sure to choose the right one.

What is it, other than your offering alone, that will get them to buy, buy now, and then buy again? Is it a lower price, or easy payments? As you can see, sales promotions can be seen at the fore in this area, and the chapter that looks just at promotional offers should have given you some creative ideas of how to offer what, to whom and why! But promotional offers alone cannot do the job of converting a Prospect to a Customer – there has to be a reason for the Customer to want to be a Customer, other than the specific offer itself, or else they will move to one of your competitors as soon as your competitors offer a better promotion.

But even when you have converted a visitor into a user, your challenges are only just beginning in some ways. You might offer goods or services with either a very short or a very long repeat purchase cycle. Whatever your offering, getting a customer turns into keeping a customer very rapidly.

LONG REPEAT PURCHASE CYCLE CRM

Thus, CRM for long repeat purchase cycle products and services differs significantly from that which works best for short repeat purchase: long repeat purchase cycles would be anything longer than, say, a month.

The forms of tool used in long repeat purchase cycles vary from simple letters, direct to the customer (permission e-mail), to very special offers on related goods and services that come about from being an honoured member of an owners'/users'/customers' club.

The aim with this type of programme is to treat the Customer as though they are a Prospect for the next purchase, but to keep emphasizing all the advantages of being an existing Customer – making them understand what they would lose if they were to choose another supplier next time they buy.

Basically, you need to choose the type of communication method that works for the target audience, in this case your Customers, and then make sure that the content is relevant and interesting and the appeal is high. Otherwise, why would they miss it if it stops – or, worse still, they might be glad when it does because the communication is too frequent or too irrelevant! Don't forget that, just because you are an e-business, it doesn't mean you can't offer a non-e form of communication, if that's what your Customers want! The chance to meet your representatives at an exhibition might be just perfect, for example.

It is tempting to think that frequent communication with Customers is the best way to keep them 'warm', but, in fact, the best way to keep a Customer satisfied is to deliver what your product or service promised in the first place (so, no matter how good your customer retention programme, you will lose Customers if your offering fails to deliver!) and keep in touch with them at a frequency that is right for them, with information, entertainment and rewards for their custom in the right balance.

Getting the right balance is something that not even the most experienced marketer can guess at – it is vital to carry out research, and to go right back to basics and *ask the customers*!

Indeed, one of the most vital elements of any successful CRM programme is the ways in which the Customer has the opportunity to talk back to the marketer – and to know that they have been heard! In other words, it is not enough to allow for feedback and comment loops – the whole communication programme has to be designed to work in both directions. By allowing you to talk to your Customers, by allowing them to talk to you, and by telling them you have heard them and by showing them that what they say matters to you by telling them when their comments have been acted upon, *then* you will begin to build the most successful CRM programme you can.

Lakeland Plastics is a mail order, and store-based, retailer of kitchen and homeware equipment and supplies. Its sales catalogue is available both in a printed format and on-line at http://www.lakelandlimited.com

It is engagingly written, contains good, clear photography of the products for sale, and also contains quotes from satisfied Customers, sometimes telling of the unusual ways in which they use certain pieces of equipment – often giving Prospects an additional incentive to purchase a certain item! They also carry requests from Customers to help them find replacements for old items they might have had from their grandmother's kitchen – so Lakeland often introduce a modern version of the item to their range. When items arrive at the Customer's home each parcel contains a hand-signed note from the packer who put the package together, and the company's returns process is very simple.

As an example of e-CRM in practice, it is a good one!

Figure 7.6   Keep them coming back!

Little touches often mean the most to customers: the birthday card from your insurance company; money-off vouchers for dry cleaning a week after the wedding date; information on how to help toddlers learn best when baby is a year old! They all say 'we care' to Customers. So, even if all your business isn't all e-d, you can still use e-CRM to make sure you keep in touch. Some use technology to keep track of complex data that makes sending birthday cards to thousands of people on the right day each year seem simple, whilst some small organizations just keep a simple card file index! The *way* you do it isn't what the customer is interested in – it's that you bother!

FMCG CRM

And what about the fmcg customer – the person whose name and address you might not have because you don't deliver to their door – they simply pick up your product from the supermarket shelf?

Well, increasingly it is possible to use the shopping profiles generated by supermarkets' retailer cards to gain a better understanding not only of your Customers' profile, but also to know what else they buy when they pick up your products – thus allowing you to learn much more about how cross-brand promotions might work for you, or when to contact Customers to best remind them how much they enjoy *your* brand just before they go shopping – every week, or month!

So, not only is it now possible to *get* the name and address of someone who might be a regular purchaser of your brand of tea, or biscuits or toilet tissue, but also to get that information about those who are *not* your customers, so you can approach them with an offer that might capture them for yourself!

That said, you can also use club membership schemes to build databases, run promotions that require at least one proof of purchase so that you capture addresses that way, or you can buy lists of shoppers on a broader scale for associated products (shampoo for conditioner, moisturizer for hand cream, etc.). Thus, you can build a relationship with your own customers either through your own brand's relationship with them and the opportunities you have with your own product or service for getting them to give you information about themselves that allows you to contact them with more, relevant data at a later stage, or via other customer database lists. This is also e-business, so don't discount it!

Servicing the Client – right every time!

If the Customer is always right, then the Client is the person, or company, who is right time after time after time! The key difference between a Customer and a Client is that the repeat purchase relationship is established with a Client.

Whatever the specifics, these are loyal Customers, their business has been valuable to you for some time, and you want it to continue to be that way. You need to nurture these Clients, seek their opinion and input into your product and service development processes, ask them *why* they are loyal, learn from this and try to benefit from what you learn by applying the lessons to other, 'not yet Client' groups of Customers.

They are likely to feel they have a close and binding relationship with your brand, your offering. They are the purchasers you are least likely to lose to a competitor, but it is dangerous to become complacent about their love for you! Many Clients can feel as though they are being taken for granted, whilst attention is lavished on Prospects and new Customers – it is very important to build a special part of your CRM to deal with these, your VIPs!

People who have shopped at a store for 50 years are appalled when change is proposed. And if that is the use of some new-fangled technology stuff, called the Internet, then the crime can seem even worse! So be careful that you don't alienate good Customers *when* you offer something that will turn on new customers.

Estimates vary about how much more it costs to get a new Customer than to keep an existing one – and of course this will depend on how much it costs to get one in the first place – but one thing is certain, it *does* cost more! So making the most of what you have is important.

You might simply want to repeat-sell, you might want to up-sell, you might want to take the Client on to the next level, that of Advocate. Whatever the objective, you must treat the Client in a different manner than the Customer, or they will gradually lose the incentive to stay.

Speaking up on behalf of Advocates

When a Customer believes in you enough to keep on buying from you, when they feel valued as a special Client, they will want to pass on that warm glow to others – and you can help them to speak up on your behalf by encouraging them to do so, either directly or indirectly.

Direct methods include 'member get member' schemes, where the original Client will get some sort of reward for introducing a new Customer (maybe money off their next bill, or a gift voucher, etc.), whilst indirect methods would be advertising campaigns or direct mail that encourage the original Client to want to speak out about their long relationship with your organization because it will show them to be clever/prudent/ discerning, etc.

Advocacy can be a simple referral by example, 'I got theatre tickets/a flight/car rental at a great price from this site', or complex, 'I am a profesional Business Presenter and I recommend this presentation equipment'. The marketer must decide just how important Advocacy is to their proposition. To some it is so important that they even *buy* Advocacy, in the shape of Professional Endorsement. Whenever a golfer endorses a golf club, or a footballer a pair of football boots, all Suspects, Prospects and even Customers and Clients are aware that money has changed hands and that the golfer or footballer in question is clearly being paid for their visible support of that brand. But, even so, there is a built-in belief that the golfer/footballer would never use a product that would diminish their ability within their sport, so the product *must* be good after all! That's why billions of pounds are spent globally every year on professional endorsements for products, and that is unlikely to stop!

Many celebrities have been recruited to speak up on behalf of start-ups, and some very high profile names (Her Majesty The Queen amongst them) have found their own business reputations being called into question as the businesses they have backed or invested in have gone either through tough times or the actual floor!

But the real Client, the real loyal Customer, makes a truly wonderful Advocate, and many marketers have spotted this and utilized its potential. In Canada, a company called Subway found a young man named Jared who lived on their low-fat sandwiches for months, and increased his exercise, losing a huge amount of weight and saying that the Subway product had changed his life! Jared has inspired thousands of others to do the same sort of thing, and he now stars in the company's TV advertising as an example to others to take advantage of Subway's low-fat offering. An Advocate who is shouting very loudly indeed, and an example that should and could be emulated in the e-world!

Other Advocates come in the form of those who endorse products but without payment changing hands. In the UK, it is claimed that Delia Smith can make or break a company, or even a whole system of food production, if she says yes or no to a product on her cookery programmes. She is almost single-handedly responsible for the huge variety of olive oils we now find in our supermarkets, she popularized the sun-dried tomato and cranberries exploded into UK supermarkets when she included them in several recipes. It has even been claimed that just one of her television programmes that showed how to boil and poach eggs meant that three times more eggs were bought in UK supermarkets during the week that that programme was shown than would normally be the case! Yes, Advocacy even for the humble egg can work wonders! In North America, Martha Stewart represents the same sort of domestic goddess profile – but her range of goods on sale is more far-reaching than even Delia Smith could imagine. She cooks, organizes homes, decorates them, raises chickens, gardens and gives advice on most types of domestic challenges. She also has a hugely successful e-business at http://www.marthastewart.com – built on the back of herself as a brand. When Martha speaks, America and Canada listen!

Some products or services almost miss out the Client part of the ladder and leap straight from Customer to Advocate: getting your carpets professionally cleaned is not something we do every day – maybe we only do it once every five or six years, and we might have moved out of the area in any case – but that carpet cleaner will need the Advocacy of satisfied Customers if he/she is to build a reputation based on recommendation, and recommendation is very important in all types of areas – hairdressers, cleaning services, garages, decorators, plumbers, dentists, etc. – they all rely on personal recommendations to get a great deal of business. So Advocacy works on many levels, from word of mouth in the local supermarket to multi-national endorsement campaigns, but they all have one thing in common – it is all about people who know the company's offering speaking out on its behalf. In other words, they are going beyond being mere users, they are becoming a part of the promotional effort itself.

 ## Summary of chapter seven

Within this chapter we have covered the following:

How marketing communications works to build a relationship with customers over time.

Getting them in the first place

This section looks at why it is worth keeping customers and introduces the ladder of loyalty.

The role of targeting and branding

These sections look at why it is important to get the right customers, and how to attract them.

Prospecting for gold

Here we look at how to get Suspects to identify themselves as Prospects, and what to do with them when they do.

Aiming for a conversion

This is where turning Prospects into Customers is considered.

Servicing the Client

Here we consider how to keep Customers coming back time and again.

Speaking up for Advocates

By making sure that those who use you speak up for you, you can open up a whole new form of communication!

 ## Self test questions and opinion development

These are not exam questions, nor are they meant to represent the sort of question you might expect to face anywhere else. They are designed to help you check whether you have understood the content of this chapter. All you have to do is read the questions, give them some thought and maybe jot down some notes on what your response might be. Not all the questions will have factual answers – rather, they might encourage you to think about a topic or an issue and formulate an opinion based upon what is now, hopefully, a better understanding of the topic.

What is the ladder of loyalty? What does it mean?

How can you decide who your Suspects might be?

List three types of marcomms activity you could undertake to get Suspects to nominate themselves as Prospects for:

(a) a brand of biscuits;
(b) a brand of beer;
(c) a new family hatchback car;
(d) a new office stationery company;
(e) a printing company that specializes in self-adhesive label printing;
(f) a new emergency generator that would be suitable for building sites.

How would you use e-CRM for each type of business?

For a company selling cars, how many levels of 'hotness' do you think there might be for subdividing Prospects?

What sort of customer services should the following types of companies offer, and why:

(a) a make-up manufacturer (selling direct to teens on-line as well as through high street retail outlets);
(b) a disposable nappies manufacturer (dealing with retailers);
(c) an accountant (now needing to do as much business on-line as possible);
(d) a dry cleaning company (real, with a very simple website);
(e) a health centre (real, with on-line help services);
(f) an on-line college;
(g) an on-line lingerie shop.

List the things that could *stop* you being a customer of any e-brand/retailer/company you use at the moment. How do they prevent these things happening?

How could you encourage people like you, who are loyal to the above e-brand/retailer/company, to speak out on behalf of the brand/retailer/company?

 ## Extending knowledge and understanding

You are encouraged to undertake the following activities to further your knowledge and understanding of the topics covered in this chapter in the following ways:

1 Have you got a bank? How long have you been with them? How hard would it be to move away? How easy would it be for you to switch bank? How could other banks tempt you and help you to move? Take some time to investigate the different targeting, services and customer relationship building programmes used by banks today – ask friends and relatives about their banking experiences to add to your own, and use the Internet to compare offerings, as well as the tone and style of what the bank sees as its image. Has your bank handled the introduction of e-banking opportunities well, or poorly? How has it done it, compared with its competitors?

2 Have you got a car? If not, work with someone who has – you need someone who has bought a car (new or previously owned) from a dealer. Break down the whole Suspect onwards relationship you/your friend have had with the brand, the dealer, the model and the specific vehicle. How did you/your friend move from Suspect to Prospect to Buyer to User. Are you already an Advocate? A Client? Why? How does the manufacturer communicate with you as a customer? How does the dealer communicate with you as a customer? How did the manufacturer and dealer use e-opportunitites to communicate with you?

3 I recently had all my carpets professionally cleaned by a small local firm – just one man and his son, with his wife taking the telephone bookings. Not only did I get great, fast, efficient service, but I received (two weeks later) a Thank You card from the family, signed by all, to acknowledge my custom, and saying they hope I mention them to friends. Low cost, not complicated – but it works. Find as many examples of great customer relationship management as you can that *do not* involve complex, high cost data mining, etc., then think about how these simple lessons from 'real' life could be adopted and applied to 'virtual' life.

4 How much of the paper direct mail you receive is part of a CRM programme, and how much of it is trying to get you (a Suspect) to become a Prospect? Start sorting all your direct mail into 'purpose' piles, and see what you find! Now do the same for your e-mail. You might be surprised at the differences you find!

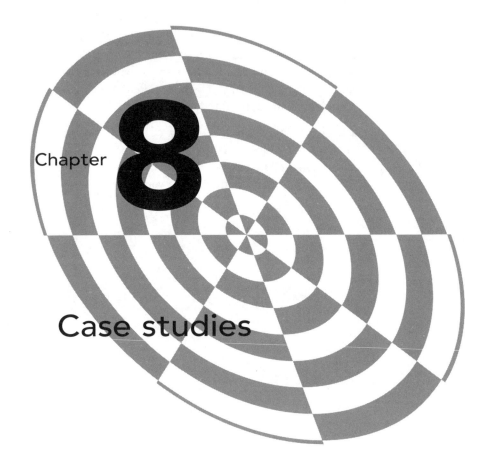

Chapter **8**

Case studies

These case studies have been developed especially for this textbook. They feature real organizations and real communications programmes with their results.

CourseLeader

THE BUSINESS BACKGROUND

The company was formed in July 1999 by John Elliot and Andy Hasoon. They both recognized the critical business need to radically improve the efficiency of the IT training market, which has historically been paper based and fragmented. They believed that, through consolidation of data and suppliers, centralizing business systems and distributing information through the Internet, a total solution for IT training could be found.

The highly fragmented nature of the global IT training market makes it ideally positioned for aggregation via the Internet. CourseLeader has developed tools, applications and services that provide a complete end-to-end multi-vendor solution for sourcing, ordering, approving, procuring and administering IT training solutions.

The company's business model has been specifically designed to satisfy the IT procurement needs of national and multi-national companies. It revolves around an e-commerce strategy where companies can access CourseLeader's proprietary searchable aggregated database of independent training providers, which allows prices, content and availability of courses to be compared, selected and booked on-line.

To complement the e-commerce aggregation strategy, CourseLeader has adopted a direct sales and customer service model which sets it apart from its competitors and will be the key to successfully penetrating the corporate IT training market.

The business went live on 1 October 1999, and launched fully on 29 November 1999. Since commencing operations, the company has attracted a highly credible management team, and signed partnership agreements with over 38 leading IT training companies in the UK.

Corporate objectives

- *Profitability* – to meet investors' expectations and deliver profit to all stakeholders.
- *Customer focus* – 100 per cent complete customer approval in a customer-led organization.

- *Universality* – to be a truly global solution, multi-cultural, multi-lingual and multi-currency.
- *Market leadership* – to take lead market position for the quality and flexibility of its training portfolio.
- *Become a benchmark* – to be a benchmark in the industry for reliability.

Market information

In 1999, the top 15 training providers in the world represented only 20 per cent of the total worldwide estimated revenues, while the top 15 training providers in Europe represented only 22 per cent of the total estimated European revenues. Small regional training providers generate the remainder of the revenue. In North America alone these are estimated to number some 10 000–30 000 (source: IDC).

The large number of IT training vendors, along with the diversity of the content provided, has created a demand for training aggregators that can provide a comprehensive multi-vendor training solution, as well as cost savings on the procurement side. CourseLeader is well positioned to lead this transformation by offering a highly customized, scalable solution which can be easily replicated across Europe and the US.

Outsourcing

An increasing number of companies are also outsourcing part, or all, of their training activities to outside consulting firms or training companies in order to reduce their overall education, training and administration costs. In 1999, 24 per cent of all corporate training was partially outsourced, with outside vendors (e.g. Oracle, Productivity Point International) taking more and more of the traditional inside training department budget. IT training is estimated to account for around 60 per cent of the total outsourced training market in the US (source: WR Hambrecht & Co.).

Market sectors

The IT training market consists of two main sectors: instructor-led training (ILT) and technology-based training (TBT). In addition to these two sectors, a small percentage of the market is captured by text-based training (TXT).

CourseLeader sees the long-term future of training as *blended learning* (training will become a little used word). In a blended learning environment, a personal learning programme will have a number of objectives. These objectives will have been determined as a result of an appraisal, skills gap analysis or by testing.

To achieve a learning programme, the candidate will receive learning modules in whatever format is most appropriate for the skills to be learnt and as time (both professional and personal) constraints dictate. Typically, this would blend the learning technologies of:

- Instructor-led training.
- Self study using TBT.
- Tutored or assisted self study.
- Recorded courses.
- Synchronous learning.
- Private reading.

Each learning object would have a measured outcome and allow for a planned and assessed progression from one objective of a learning programme to another. Candidate progression would be managed and tracked in a Learning Management System (LMS).

There is a dominance of instructor-led training in the marketplace, which will remain over the next few years, but the market share is expected to decline in favour of the increased popularity of TBT. Over the period 1999–2004, IDC forecasts TBT to grow seven-fold in Europe, where it represents a smaller relative market share compared to the US, where the market share is expected to almost double over the same period to represent over 50 per cent of the entire US IT training market.

The most popular and fastest growing form of TBT is e-learning, which combines the benefits of instructor-led training with electronic learning to produce a highly interactive medium.

Market research suggests that this form of 'blended' learning is expected to be the preferred solution adopted by most companies. The CourseLeader solution is specifically designed to address this expected demand.

Key market drivers

The key factors impacting on the demand for IT training can be summarized as follows:

- IT skills shortage. In the UK alone, the shortage of skilled IT professionals is predicted to increase to over 300 000, while in Europe this shortage is predicted to reach 1.7 million by 2003. In the US, 70 per cent of the top 1000 IT consuming companies cite lack of trained employees as their number one barrier to sustained growth (source: IDC).
- Increasing trend towards business outsourcing.

- Emergence of Application Service Providers (ASPs) and other hosted solutions in the learning industry.
- Impact of the Internet on business, including the increased focus on new technology implementations and the search for effective Internet strategies.
- The direct spend in the IT software and hardware markets.
- Greater corporate focus on employee training, by re-skilling, up-skilling and cross-skilling.

Critical success factors

- *Breadth and depth of product offering* – strong partnerships will be critical in meeting corporate customer demand for delivery of best-of-breed training.
- *Blended learning solutions* – customers are increasingly seeking customized training solutions. The key will be applying the right technology and delivery mechanism to the right learning environment.
- *Flexibility* – customers will demand increasing customization of service offering.
- *Quality* – corporate customers will increasingly insist on the assurance of training quality to meet their business needs.

Other influences

- *Certification* – companies view certification as a key attribute in validating their expertise and, as a result, are willing to pay more for certification-related training. Certification paths can be confusing and irregular in the marketplace, so both companies and individuals need clear, simple guidance through these certification paths.
- *Move to e-procurement* – as companies move more of their purchasing on-line, they will force their entire supply chain to react.
- *Emergence of Learning Management Systems* – which will enable companies to monitor and manage employees' learning cycles. These systems will tie in with enterprise applications ensuring organizational knowledge management is maximized.

THE MARKETING BACKGROUND

Target audiences and marketing organization

CourseLeader's training solution is not industry-specific. It is a meta-model that can be applied equally well to any market or market segment.

For sales and service reasons, however, they use a vertical market schematic.

Their sales staff is divided into five key vertical markets. Each team consists of business development managers and account executives who have been assigned to a particular vertical market on the basis of their experience and knowledge of that market.

Their account managers thoroughly research the client's business before it is engaged. The business development manager within each vertical segment is then responsible for managing the account team's client knowledge base.

In servicing vertical and specialist markets, the account teams uses a Customer Service Management System (CSMS) – SalesLogix – to monitor client relationships. This helps in building a strong knowledge of the client's business sector.

A specialist CourseLeader market intelligence coordinator regularly delivers relevant market information concerning the client to the alliance manager and the corporate training portal manager. This ensures that all customer-facing staff within the organization are thoroughly familiar with the client's business.

This systematic, professional knowledge management therefore guarantees focus on the client's business objectives.

Overview of offering to target groups

Individuals.
CourseLeader (CL) has been designed to give individuals all the information they need to make decisions about training quickly and easily. In essence, they give advice on the *public courses* with the leading companies in the industry, but more importantly courses are rated by customers' peers as a further endorsement. CL aims to give access to cheaper training solutions than customers could find in their own time, such as *Internet-Based Training*, free *careers guidance*, information on *getting qualified* and *news* and views from experts. And by listening to feedback, CL aims to ensure they give all the information needed to find the right training solutions. When an individual registers on the site, he/she will automatically qualify for discounts. The more courses bought the bigger the discounts achieved.

Corporates/organizations.

- *Personalized Corporate Membership Packages – a portal for partnership*: PCMs offer the organization a system where all the features of CL are offered on a corporate website and branded with the organization's logo and colour scheme, which in turn offers their clients added value as part of their website. Customized training solutions and discount structures will be based on buying power. Furthermore, exclusivity packages can be offered to market sectors.

- *Intranets*: provide organizations with the opportunity to run a customized service on a corporate or organizational intranet.

- *Strategic Partners*: joint PR/marketing initiatives and revenue streams.

IT recruitment.

- *Contractor – via MSB*: through the PCM with MSB CL.com will benefit from a £2 million marketing campaign to advertise the new contractor package, together with 360, a financial planning company. There are 100 000 IT contractors out there with 2500 on MSB books.
- *Graduate – via Trotman plc*: Trotman will be the core supplier for careers advice and provide access to approximately 50 per cent of the graduate IT recruitment market. CL will have access to IT career titles, pychometric testing and advice from the top 100 companies.

Training companies. HP Education – the education arm of Hewlett Packard, Azlan Training – the largest certified network training organization in the UK, Sun Education Services – Education arm for Sun Microsystems, Informix, Oracle Education, Horizon and NETg. In addition to branded microsites on their homepages and discounts, other initiatives will include sponsored seminars.

Software/Hardware houses.
Third party advertising.

Amazon.co.uk
A £20 book voucher on the completion of evaluation forms by users or £20 to Cystic Fibrosis. Referral fees.

e-Commerce partners.
Itportal, Commercenet and Silicon.

Competition

www.bookacourse, www.trainingdirectory.co.uk, www.nowtraining.co.uk, www.learninguniversity.com, www.trainingdeals.com

Competition is defined as any website offering on-line IT training. No one at launch was offering the comprehensive one-stop shop technical IT training concept. Bookacourse.com, however, had developed a fairly comprehensive directory and there had been rumours that they might relaunch with a superior product.

CourseLeader competitive positioning/USP

The amalgam of an IT training and Internet company, CL knows the business and the technology.

CL will always be 'people-centric'. Margins may be less, but turnover will be greater.

CourseLeader, the brand

- *Vision*: 'When consumers think IT training they think CourseLeader.'
- *Mission – CL's pledge*: 'By understanding and listening we can give you a solution for buying IT training that is easy, cost-effective, and always ensures you receive the quality solution you need to enhance the running of your business every day!'
- *Proposition*:
  - CourseLeader will be the one-stop shop for technical IT training requirements.
  - The new e-commerce solution for technical IT training.
- *Brand values*:
  - Independent.
  - Up to date, accurate
  - User-friendly, easy to navigate, simple.
  - Best prices, cost-effective.
  - Fastest website.
  - Widest portfolio of courses.
  - Exemplary customer service, cuddly, quality service.
  - Maximize solutions.
  - Human.
  - Fun.
  - Family.
- *Brand visual*:
  - Use of primary colours on site: less corporate, less threatening, fun, childish.
  - The use of fast forward.

Marketing objectives

1 To launch the product and the association of CourseLeader with the procurement of IT training.

   CourseLeader = procurement of IT training

2 To promote a multi-lingual, multi-currency site with true global capabilities: now ready for launch.

   CourseLeader = a global solution to the procurement of IT training

3 To communicate the careful and planned development of the portal for integration into ERP, CRM and learning management systems.

   CourseLeader = a global, managed solution to the procurement of IT training

4 To become the industry standard in quality assurance for IT training.

   CourseLeader = a global, managed solution to the procurement of quality IT training

5 To expand their capabilities to include all needs of a corporate integrated learning environment.

CourseLeader = the preferred learning solution (our mission)

Marketing strategy

Their core strategy is to achieve the above-mentioned objectives by facilitating the procurement and management of learning by electronically delivering services to their corporate client base. The company was established with the view that there 'had to be an easier way' to manage training. Figure 8.1 indicates where CL aimed to sit in the training procurement market.

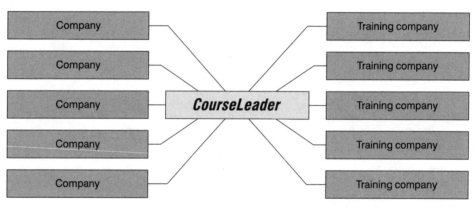

Figure 8.1 Desired position

The CL market offering

The complete CourseLeader Product Profile includes the following.

● *Public course booking service*: CourseLeader provides an on-line booking service, offering the public course schedules of the leading training companies. Companies and employees that use the site have access to over 1706 course titles in the UK and over 5800 in the US, which creates over 5500 and 45 000 scheduled courses, respectively.

● *Corporate solution*: CourseLeader offers a unique intranet and/or corporate web solution called the Corporate Training Portal (CTP). This is essentially a client-branded, customized version of the CourseLeader website. The CTP can be customized to include customer approved courses and locations, and incorporate specifically negotiated discount structures.

- *Requests for proposal (RFP)*: CourseLeader responds to RFP for large corporate IT training solutions. CourseLeader will enter into tenders alone or in conjunction with existing and/or potential partners.

- *Internet-based training (IBT)*: CourseLeader offers 250 NETg Internet-based training course titles from the market leading e-learning company NETg. This is currently being expanded to over 600 titles, including every possible language available in the NETg product range. These courses can be purchased on-line with a credit card.

- *On-site training*: CourseLeader has set up a comprehensive on-site training solution for tailored courses. It works in partnership with training companies and consultants to offer a combination of authorized and non-authorized training solutions.

- *Consultancy*: CourseLeader provides consultancy to companies looking to define their training needs and in establishing CTPs.

- *Additional value-added user services*: the customer service operations provide assistance with the booking process, post-course follow-up, delivery of partner performance guarantees and course feedback. In addition, CourseLeader provides on-line information on topics which cover advice on careers and qualifications, updates on technology and IT developments and issues.

The benefits of the CTP solution for the procurement of training are as follows:

- A total managed solution (so managers are freed for more critical deployment).
- Complete customization ensures the relevance of the portal.
- One invoice a month means reduced administration costs.
- 100 per cent quality guarantee.
- Less time wasted in negotiating, sourcing, invoicing, etc.

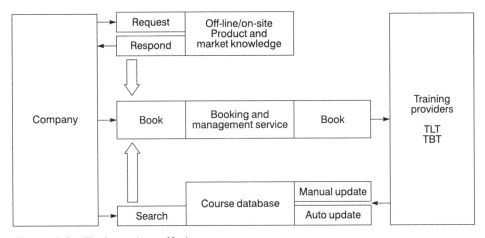

Figure 8.2 Their market offering

Managed Service Option

Features

- Automated
- User-friendly
- Fast search
- Up to date
- Over 5500 classes
- Easy directory structure
- Course content on site
- Pre-approval
- On-line booking

Benefits

- Total managed solution
- Customization
- Integration with existing systems
- Reduce admin costs
- Save time/money. End of catalogue fatigue
- Information streamlined

Figure 8.3 Benefits of the Corporate Training Portal

- Reduction of sourcing booking and procuring (paying) has been reduced from an average of 7 hours to 7 minutes.
- Consistent service levels.
- Delivery is 24/7/12/365.
- Administration is reduced to almost none.
- Time is saved: the CTP reduces sourcing, validating and procuring to a single process.
- Money is saved: collective bargaining means that the client can get the best discounts.
- Course information on the whole range of IT training is streamlined.
- No more ringing around, repeating the same questions.
- An end to catalogue fatigue.
- Accuracy and reliability of course information guaranteed.
- Quality is assured since training providers are thoroughly screened by CourseLeader.

MARKETING COMMUNICATIONS

The website

As with most e-businesses, the website is a key communications tool in its own right. They have built, and continue to build, a comprehensive course catalogue listing training courses, classes, venues and providers. Each course outline is resident with their system and presented in a standard format (allowing for speedy access and ease of comparison). This course catalogue is built in three ways.

- Direct links to training partners: they have a link to the training partners' internal database and registration system.
- Web crawl: they have developed intelligent agents that trawl their training partners' websites to extract the relevant information from them.
- Manual input: their data management team re-enters the data from information provided by the training partners.

As part of the cataloguing exercise, each course is categorized by a keyword and its position in their hierarchy.

User interface

CL provides access to the course catalogue through a web-driven user interface that allows users to search for, select and request a training course. The user interface is customized for each corporate customer and they call this customized interface a Corporate Training Portal (CTP). Within each CTP, the following elements are customizable:

- User interface (logos, colours, etc.).
- Training providers listed.
- Manufacturers listed.
- Locations listed.
- Other learning products available.
- Pricing.
- Booking form information.

Search: they have a search and browse mechanism that allows a user to find the most appropriate training course.

Select: in a traditional e-commerce environment this would be called a shopping basket, but gives users the ability to select the course they want to take. CL made a business decision that only one course can be booked at a time.

Book: users fill out the required information (this can be tailored to each company's requirements) and select how they would like to pay. For most CTPs, this is an account purchase, although CL does have the ability to take direct payment for credit cards.

Fulfilment

The end of the booking process results in an electronic message being sent from the website to CL's e-bookings system. This is a workflow application developed in Ultimus and allows CL to model complex workflows for the booking, approval and confirmation process. They have found that each company's authorization and notification procedures are unique, and as such they model the requirements of the company within the workflow application. Although the procedures differ from company to company, the general steps are:

- Receive booking request.
- Make provisional booking with training provider.
- Confirm availability of provisional place.
- Request authorization(s).
- Receive authorization(s).
- Confirm place on course.
- Issue invoice.
- Issue joining instructions.

An example of a workflow for another customer is shown in Figure 8.4.

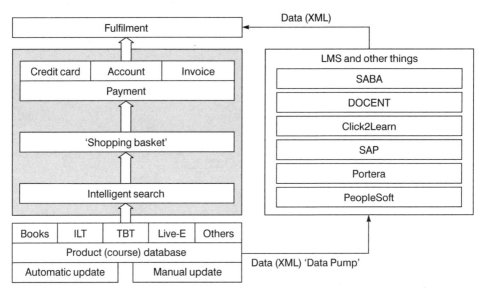

Figure 8.4 Integrating the model

Their three-tier model is designed to integrate with an in-house Learning Management System (LMS), where the LMS takes the place of the CTP website. In this scenario, the catalogue populates the LMS and the workflow system takes booking/cancellation, etc. requests from the LMS.

This formed the basis of a comprehensive CRM opportunity, which CL took by the horns – communicating with individual customers and partners based upon their on-line activity.

Service level agreements

Another factor that CL believed could work for them both as a business proposition and as a factor that communicated a dedication to service and customer care was the decision they took from the start not to produce traditional service level agreements (SLAs). All CTPs were to be governed by their standard contract and then they would work with each client to define the service level required by that specific client. CL exists to make the procurement and management of training easier – the criterion they set themselves was 100 per cent satisfaction and any deviation from this would mean that they would not have not met their own standards, which are equally as important as their customers' and investors' expectations.

SLA reports are typically produced on a monthly basis and are reviewed by the account management team with the client. CL's sales and delivery staff are constantly engaged in reporting back on the training needs of their clients, providing feedback to portfolio managers on how to serve customer needs better.

'Traditional' communications methods

Along with these overall tools and actions, CL also adopted what might be termed a 'traditional' communications programme to pull the whole thing forward.

Marcomms objectives

Long term:
To create and sustain understanding between CourseLeader.com and the various publics with which it communicates.

Short term:

1 To define and communicate the company's mission and culture to all stakeholders, internally and externally.

2 To contribute with maximum input to brand equity.

3 To create and maintain communications channels within the company.

		Success Criteria		
Service Aspect	**Measurement**	**Bad**	**OK**	**Good**
Confirmation of provisional place on course	Number of minutes to respond to automated booking request.			
Booking requests generated for courses with no spaces	Measures how up to date and accurate the site database is. Measured as a percentage of bookings in the month.			
Site availability	Measure minutes of unscheduled unavailability. Expressed as a percentage.			
Provide authorization	Measure of how quickly the client provides authorization. Hours.			
Provider cancelled courses	Number of cancelled courses (cancelled by training provider) where a suitable alternative could not be rescheduled. Measured as absolute number and percentage.	No. %	No. %	No. %
Client cancelled courses	Number of cancelled courses (cancelled by delegate) where a suitable alternative could not be rescheduled. Measured as absolute number and percentage.	No. %	No. %	No. %
Provider rescheduled courses	Number of rescheduled courses (instigated by training provider). Measured as absolute number and percentage.	No. %	No. %	No. %
Client rescheduled courses	Number of rescheduled courses (instigated by client provider). Measured as absolute number and percentage.	No. %	No. %	No. %
Response to non-catalogue training request	Average number of hours it takes to provide profile and availability for a non-catalogue course.			
Response to in-house training request	Average number of hours it takes to provide profile, availability and quote for an in-house (on-site) training request.			
Problems reported	Number of training problems reported.			
Problem resolution: Initial response	Average time (hours) to make initial response to problem.			
Problem resolution: Final response	Average time (hours) to make final response to problem.			
Courses booked	Number of courses booked in the month, expressed as an absolute number and percentage of estimated booking.	No. %	No. %	No. %
Revenue booked	Total revenue in the month, expressed as an absolute number and percentage of estimated booking.	No. %	No. %	No. %

Figure 8.5 Example SLA matrix

4 To create and maintain communication channels with all targeted external publics.

5 To support the leveraging of strategic corporate relations.

Core concerns:
Summary of its objectives:

1 Brand equity.

2 Infrastructure.

3 Info-structure.

Target audiences

The following is a list of the audiences targeted by CL.

External:

- IT professionals
  - Those responsible for their own training.
  - IT departmental senior staff responsible for sourcing training.
- HR and Training departments responsible for sourcing training.
- IT media.
- Training managers.
- General media.
- General industry.

Internal:

- Company Staff.
- Board of Directors.

Key market sectors:

- Individuals (e.g. contractors).
- IT professionals.
- Public and government organizations.
- Private companies.
- Corporate buyers.

Tools used

External audiences:

- *Traditional media relations*
  - *Ongoing*
    - Create off-line media list
    - Create on-line media list
    - Establish a contact list
  - *Press pack*
    - Company loose-leaf information
    - Product information
    - Photos
    - Press folder
  - *Corporate photo file*
    - Photos of all staff
    - Job descriptions
  - *Press releases*
    - On-line media tactics used
    - Story bank
    - Features file
      - e.g. Second generation site activities
        - Personalization system
  - *Video diaries*
  - *Leverage relationship with corporate users*
  - Work with PR departments of strategic partners
  - Coordinate activities with Customer Relationship Manager
  - Leverage press coverage of partner companies
  - Newsletter to investors
  - Monthly Company Activity Report for investor
- *Banner advertising* (keenly targeted sites)
- *Exhibitions, seminars, conferences* (face to face, stands, speakers provided)
- *Print advertising* (trade press, recruitment ads as well as directional ads).

Internal audiences:

- *Intranet site*
  - Contents:
    - Management
    - Events
    - Company news
    - Organizational charts

CourseLeader - Mar-Aug	Ims/Cir	20-Mar	27-Mar	3-Apr	10-Apr	17-Apr	24-Apr	1-May	8-May
ONLINE	Ims/Cir								
Altavista	37 000			■	■		■		
Computer Weekly	75 000			■		■		■	
IT Events Bulletin	55 000				■				
VNU Net	50 000							■	
Yahoo									
PRINT									
Computer Weekly	134 000			■		■		■	
Computing	135 000				■		■		■
Network News	60 000				■		■		
IT Training	20 000							■	
TS Exhibitor Listing									
Government IT (60 000)	10 692			■	■				
Exhibitions									
Windows 00, Olympia	40 000		■						
Exhibitor Guide	25 000		■						
Networks, NEC	22 000								
Training Solutions, NEC	5 000								
Virtual Exhibition									
PR									
Press Office		xxxxxxx	xxxxxxx	xxxxxxx	xxxxxxx	xxxxxxx	xxxxxxx	xxxxxxx	xxxxxxx
Direct Mail									
Olympia Training Mailing	3 000			■					
Windows 00 Mailing	650					■			
HR Forum Mailing	450								■
Forums									
HR Forum									■
IT Directors Forum									

Figure 8.6 Example of advertising schedule – March–August 2000

Forms centre
Social centre
Op shop
Idea classifieds (wanted – incentives)
Library
　Company style sheet
　Staff profiles
　Company profile/history
Global timesheet

● *Meetings and cascade management discussions.*

Effectiveness

As an example of the sort of research carried out by CL, Figure 8.7 shows a summary of the results of the activity carried out in the detailed communications schedule shown in Figure 8.6.

> ### The end of 2000

By this time the marketing objectives had tightened to the following:

- To drive traffic to the site and establish CourseLeader.com as the market leading IT training portal (one-stop shop) in the UK.
- To position CourseLeader as the most authoritative source for information, advice, services and product relating to the IT training sector and continue to forge links with the major content suppliers and market leaders in their own field.
- To consistently raise the bar of competitor entry and develop the brand in terms of value added offering.
- To market the brand as an e-commerce solution/a cutting edge e-commerce website.

The overview marketing communications strategy for the final quarter of 2000 was stated as follows.

To achieve these objectives, CL will launch an integrated through-the-line media campaign from late November for three months.

The primary target market will be reached through highly targeted on-line activity in the form of sponsored e-mail bulletins and the placing of banners and keywords on targeted sites. On-line activity will coincide with the initial media announcement in the IT and training media.

Joint marketing initiatives with strategic partners will kick off in January with co-branded microsites and full advantage taken of the 'partnerships', e.g. sponsored seminars with major players to provide 'feature' material without overshadowing the CL product.

Further PR initiatives will focus on the development of new value added features/partners as they are bolted on to the site and encourage users to consistently return to the site for the latest offering. There will be no supplier advertising that is not beneficial to the user on the site.

CL will launch at one major IT exhibition within this timeframe and will trial tactical promotions directly on-site, e.g. the first 20 to book a public course win a session at Daytona with the CL.com team. Proposed merchandising will be bright yellow T-shirts and stressbusters.

STATS
- Y2K Hits @ 11.7   878 523
- Registrations   1740
- June Hits   269 715   May + 41%   Mar + 338%
- June Registrations   446   May + 70%   Mar + 49%

Biggest Performers
- 29.6.2000   50 registrations (Networks)
- 11.7.2000   15 853 hits

ON-LINE
- Ranked no. 7 in 'New on-line ad campaigns in order of estimated spend', *Revolution*, **24.5.2000**
- For April and May 0.52 yield against average of 0.5–1% (one click per 500 impressions)
- IT events   £1.26 per click
- Alta Vista   £2.53 per click
- VNU   £13.04 per click

***Computer Weekly* Sponsorship**
- 6094 clicks in April and May   82p per click

OFF-LINE
Free Advertising
- Computer Reseller News Webwatch × 2
- Networks News
- Acquisitions Monthly in the company of Ann Summers

Prime Positioning
- Network News – CL.com advertising on first page of Networks Telecom Preview

Government IT
- 40 public sector leads

FORUMS
HR Forum
- 30 meetings
- 730 leads

IT Director's Forum
- Meetings (MM/RC)
- Leads

EXHIBITIONS
Networks Telecom
(still no ABC audited attendee figures. Forecast – 22k)
- Launches CourseLeader.com: Fast Forward in IT Training – road and station campaign
- Introduces the Flasher

Training Solutions
(still no ABC audited attendee figures. Forecast – 5k)
- Introduces Euphoria, the Avatar and Mr G with photo opportunity in IT Training

MAILINGS/PARTNER PROMOTION
- 10k total
- Windows (650), HR Forum (450), Networks (540), Training Solutions (600), Oracle/MSB (8000)

Figure 8.7   Top-line March–August marketing campaign results

CourseLeader.com

**Media Plan. Sep-Dec
2000**

TITLE	ITEM	IMS/CIR	2.10	9.10	16.10	23.10	30.10
ONLINE							
Computer Weekly	Sponsorship	75 000					
Altavista	Keywords/Banners (tbc)	50 000					
E-mail Bulletins							
Emedia	Bulletin Item	55 000					
Silicon.com	E-mail sponsorship	120 000					
Print							
Computer Weekly	2 x Strip ads Monthly	134 000					
Computing	2 x 1/4 Pages Monthly	135 000					
Training Magazine	1/2 Pages						
Human Resources	Website list						
IT Training	1/2 Pages	20 000					
Learning Technologies	Full page	30 000					
The Guardian	1/4 Page - RIP seminar						

Figure 8.8 Marketing communications activity, Quarter 4, 2000

An underlying factor in all marketing communication is that CL is branded as an e-commerce solution. It is important to remember that the relationship between CL and its training providers is symbiotic. Having the education arms of the major IT vendors behind CL endorses it as a credible business solution in the IT training market, but equally the major IT vendors get validation of their dotcom status and positioning as e-commerce supporters and suppliers through their association with a cutting edge e-commerce solution.

OVERVIEW

The result of the total communication effort was that CourseLeader went from obscurity to one of the top 10 most recognized brands among London training managers, according to a survey done by *IT Training* magazine.

The organization recognizes that the majority of its communication success derived from:

1 Building in quality, service and communication abilities to the core of the actual business.

2 Using guerrilla tactics and a very personalized effort when dealing with planned advertising and PR plans.

The communications programme has been handled mainly by the Corporate Communications Unit, a small dedicated team of communications specialists.

Budget

CL reserves the right to keep this undisclosed.

THE QUESTION

You have to put together a proposed marketing communications programme that will take CourseLeader the next step forward. Yes, you will have to seek investment funding to do so, so develop a full communications plan – including target audiences, objectives, creating a communications programme, costing it, projecting the effects and preparing this in a report format.

 # Launching Aerospan.com

The world of aviation is full of adventure, romance and the call of distant places. True, most of us are likely to experience a flight these days (not something that could have been said even twenty years ago!), but how many of us think about the business behind the means of transport upon which we rely to take us on that exotic, once in a lifetime trip, or to that all-important business meeting?

Aircraft are hugely expensive items, so the world of aviation is not populated by business midgets, but by business giants. Names that have a resonance throughout the history of manned flight still top the lists of companies involved in the industry. And once you have purchased or leased an aircraft, and managed to fill it with passengers or cargo and get it off the ground, it has to be maintained to keep it up there safely, because it's only when it is flying that it is bringing an income – all the rest of the time it just costs you money.

BACKGROUND

With the advent of B2B e-commerce, a new opportunity emerged within air transport to provide fast on-line parts procurement, creating significant supply-chain savings for the airlines and new market opportunities for suppliers.

SITA – a global IT solutions provider – saw the potential of the new e-business opportunities and partnered with a parts supplier called AAR to form a joint venture – which would become named Aerospan.com

According to market analysis conducted by SITA/AAR, the global aviation/aerospace engineering equipment and parts procurement marketplace is worth approximately US $80–100 billion.

Each partner brought complementary strengths to the Joint Venture (JV): AAR brought its understanding of the 'aftermarket', or the buying and selling of parts, and SITA its global telecoms and IT understanding.

Negotiations between AAR and SITA led to the announcement of the JV on 11 January 2000 (http://www.sita.int/newscentre/pressreleases/2000/000111aar.asp). This press release was then distributed to the global press and to analysts and consultants, taking advantage of existing relationships and exploiting new contacts.

While the JV management team was being brought together and various secondments being made by each company, the communications team quickly recognized the potential of the story and the need to strongly position the new company within the market. The key resources at these early stages were to make the most of SITA's expertise in international communications management and work jointly with the AAR Financial PR manager.

During the development of the integrated marketing communications plan, the driver was always to deliver a worldwide programme that focused on brand differentiation. This would utilize a wide range of tactics, picking the most suitable to achieve the objectives.

Initially, it was determined that the aviation trade press would play a significant role in formulating industry opinion towards this new market segment. At the same time, it was felt that technology analysts would not only establish the parameters of this new industry segment, but also be influential in deciding who was a leader worthy of industry attention. Consequently, media and analyst relations would form the backbone of the marketing communications campaign.

A 'virtual' team of marcomms staff worked closely with the business development team on the business and marketing plans, to ensure that all understood the model but also that they shared their own knowledge of how to position this concept across all the teams. Deciding the boundaries around what to release externally in the first instance, and spending time working on the positioning, in what was to become an extremely competitive marketplace, proved to be a wise moment of early counsel.

THE OBJECTIVES

For Aerospan.com, the key communications objectives were to position itself as one of the top three players in the new e-marketplace, and to subsequently survive the expected marketplace shakeout.

Specifically identified in the launch plan were the following:

- Build the reputation of Aerospan.com – and the parent parties – and its capabilities in its target markets.
- Build a solid image, credibility and positioning within the new e-marketplace, for Aerospan.com, across target markets.
- Build the reputation and profile of the company, profiling key executives, to increase awareness of its strategy and capabilities.
- Enhance the credibility of the parent parties as leaders in e-business and ensure the company continues to positively contribute to the overall perceptions of each company.
- Position Aerospan.com as having strong competitive advantages against other suppliers in the market.

TARGET AUDIENCES

Focus group research conducted by Cohn & Wolfe and its sister company, Impiric, in London, UK and Miami, USA, showed that the target audiences were 'neutral to positive' regarding this new industry innovation. At the same time, competitive website analysis showed that Aerospan.com's functional capability was ahead of its competition, meaning the company was ready to take a leadership position. A Forrester Research report also predicted that only a few strong players in this sector would survive an imminent shakeout expected in 2001. The aim was to ensure Aerospan was seen to lead the shakeout.

Interestingly, despite its size, the aviation industry is characterized by a small, close-knit group of individuals. Historically, this group has been conservative in nature. Therefore, decisions amongst the target audience can be driven by the recommendations of a limited number of key influencers. Recognizing this market dynamic, three key target audiences were identified. These target audiences – *market makers*, *decision makers* and *validators* – would become the focus for the integrated public relations and marketing communications campaigns.

The *market makers* were identified as the analysts, trade media, business media and conference attendees. Essentially, this group has an influence on the *decision makers*, who are defined as the CEOs, CIOs and CFOs, along with the directors in the finance, purchasing, operations, parts, and maintenance and repairs departments. The *validators* are the managers in the parts, inventory, operations and finance departments who decide to use Aerospan.com and ultimately give the exchange approval to the decision makers.

This was worked into the following:

- Primary targets – decision makers, market markers, validators.
- Airlines/Original Equipment Manufacturers (OEMs).
- Aerospace suppliers.
- Current customer base of AAR/SITA.
- Global business, trade, IT/e-business media.
- Financial community – improve contacts.
- Analysts and consultants – establish relationship and gain endorsement.
- Secondary targets
  - Employees in SITA and AAR – improve perception of the strategic importance of the JV.
  - Employees of Aerospan.com – communicate the business plan/strategy.
- Competitors – create uncertainty and expose weaknesses.

MESSAGES

Primary: 'Aerospan.com, the e-marketplace for the air transport industry'.

Support propositions:

- Founded by industry leaders.
- New independent company, own management and staff.
- Advanced functionality, leading integration and customer support focus.
- Global player – offering the global market next door.

Competitive strengths:

- Collaboration and listening to customer needs.
- Understanding of air transport industry and business processes.
- Aviation aftermarket understanding from AAR and air transport IT and IP/e-business understanding of SITA presents a unique pedigree.
- Unparalleled neutrality and long-term focus of SITA at delivering global industry IT solutions.
- Industry ownership through SITA (which is owned by the air transport industry).

ACTUAL COMMUNICATIONS PROGRAMME USED

Overview issues

The key strategy was to position Aerospan.com as the clear 'thought-leader' on all issues relating to e-marketplaces for spare part provisioning in air transport and to be proactive in establishing both the brand name and enhancing its credibility across the global marketplace.

Part of the strategy was to focus on two waves of communications, initially using a major event to launch Aerospan.com and focus on positioning, leadership, brand awareness, etc., which would be sustained until the site was operational with broad functionality, then to use another major event to launch the operational e-market to customers/potential users. Behind this, an ongoing comms programme would be developed to strengthen the profile and build credibility.

The integrated on-line and off-line marketing communications solution developed included the following core elements:

- Strong trade media relations focusing on the industry's top journalists.
- Immediate outreach to the key technology analyst firms to develop awareness and understanding.
- A significant focus on conferences for public (industry) and analyst relations activities.
- A programme to ensure the development of content for the website and regular media and analysts updates.

Once the actual business of Aerospan.com was beginning to be set up, and its key positions were filled, the challenge was to effectively provide the new company with autonomy from its parent parties, allowing it to set its own brand and identity, whilst also ensuring that SITA and AAR had a share of the voice to reinforce the stability of a 'bricks and mortar' heritage. In this way, the comms team began to use the latest terminology and dubbed Aerospan.com a 'bricks-and-clicks' organization.

From the outset, it was clear that the team needed to work tactically, and quickly, to position the new JV within the market. There was a need not only to draw attention towards the company as championing Internet development, but also to immediately consolidate that 'mindshare' and position the company as being the first to put its 'iron into the fire' of what would become a very crowded market.

Meanwhile, it was also clear that above and beyond this work it would be essential to develop a B2B communications programme to position the company as one of the top three players in the industry, and to thereby be better placed to survive the expected marketplace shakeout. Creating brand recognition, educating and promoting the

advantages of e-procurement to the key decision makers within the industry and driving traffic (and trial) to the site were to be vital to the business's success. The programme developed was PR led, but also made the most of integrating with various marcomms activities ranging from speaking opportunities at conferences and trade shows to on-line mailing.

Team and resource issues

A key role was to clearly define and create a joint communications structure and a virtual team. As a new start-up, Aerospan.com had no dedicated comms staff. A communications protocol was created to ensure all new and updated information was secured for press releases and other marketing activities.

With the virtual team spanning multiple continents – SITA corporate PR team in London, AAR in Chicago and Aerospan.com based in Chicago – internal communication may have presented some challenges. However, time zone differences began to work in the organization's favour, as the team used web-based technology to work almost 24 hours a day and share ideas, information and materials. The process relied on the Aerospan.com and SITA intranet – a web-based site that provided staff with the ability to work on documents 24 hours a day, seven days a week, regardless of geographic location.

Initial work was by led by a virtual team between SITA and AAR. Once the initial communications strategy, focus groups and marketing communications programmes had been mapped out, it was decided that SITA's retained agency, Cohn & Wolfe, would work on the Aerospan.com account on a project basis for PR elements, with them being appointed prior to launch at Farnborough Airshow. Their sister marketing communications agency, Impiric, was also brought on board, but later in the year the decision was taken to let them go, as much of the tactical execution could be undertaken by SITA's in-house communications team.

The role of integration

Key to the whole approach would be taking and creating an integrated communications programme, using the web as an integral part of everything undertaken.

- Core to the media relations programme was to agree a list of the top ten aviation journalists, who were then to be the initial focus on any news development. These journalists were targeted with news releases, regular updates and material for forward features. This coverage from the 'must read' industry media was focused on the decision maker target audience.

- A second core element of the campaign was the analyst relations programme. As part of this initiative, outreach to the top ten US- and London-based analysts was conducted. This analyst programme resulted in Goldman Sachs and Jupiter Research endorsing Aerospan.com as a top three exchange and a programme of one briefing a month being undertaken.

- The upcoming Asian Aerospace exhibition in Singapore was to be a crucial period. It was decided to pre-launch in the week prior to the show and brand name the e-marketplace to grab attention before the event. The challenge here was: how do you launch an e-marketplace at an established international airshow that attracts industry professionals, not IT managers?

The answer was the decision to mount an aggressive guerrilla marketing campaign to stir up a 'buzz' and attract audiences towards seeking out the Aerospan.com team. This focused on 'You're invited to a trip to the future. . .'. This was to ensure that traffic to the stand was high at the show, with people marking it down as a 'must visit', but also it was a decisive means of grabbing the media attention. Sales and marketing teams were mobilized to ask people attending to visit and the media and press used to drum up interest.

The pre-show release can be viewed at:
http://www.sita.int/newscentre/pressreleases/2000/000215aerospan.asp

International media were invited to the launch event using a 'teaser' campaign of an 'Airfix' aircraft model branded with the Aerospan.com logo. This proved very popular, and successful – with many press and media confirming their attendance in the week before the airshow.

The CEO of AAR, David Storch, and John Watson, Director General, SITA, were confirmed to attend the press conference, which also attracted people to the event. The extensive Q&A and positioning document prepared for launch was updated and re-issued. The press pack contained corporate profiles, key facts/figures/personnel, recent press releases and the sales collateral.

The multimedia slides, script and presentation for the event were all prepared and delivered to the executives a week before the event, with a rehearsal held in Singapore to go through the key messages and undertake media training. A short video was also commissioned (lasting approximately 3 minutes) using a college diploma student who took images with a variety of cameras.

The press conference drew a large crowd, and the video was an instrumental part of the show. The media relations work continued and two days later Aerospan.com secured coverage on CNBC Asia. Surprisingly, no new press release was issued at the show, but the media relations, the quality of the background material and having key spokespeople available and on-hand provided an excellent launch pad for Aerospan.com.

The delegates to the show could visit Aerospan.com on AAR's stand and a multimedia demo of the e-marketplace was available for people to review, with sales and

marketing people on hand to discuss the concept. This led to numerous meetings throughout the week and several sales leads. A simple two-page piece of sales collateral was produced using the presentation materials.

Further sales collateral was developed (also used on-line) clearly articulating the strategy, benefits, direction and operation aspects of the company. This was specifically directed and targeted at educating decision makers, influencers and users across the air transport industry. The collateral, folders and material were updated as the programme progressed and other elements, such as white papers, z-cards, mailers, etc., were added when required. All materials reflected a consistent brand identity. This was also true across all elements of sales promotion, including advertising, direct mail and exhibition stands. Everything used consistent messages, style and layout to reinforce the key messages. (These elements would be reviewed as the focus group work progressed and provided the team with clarity.) A strong advertising campaign was also used, with an advertising agency appointed to develop concepts and a media schedule.

While the launch event was successful, the e-marketplace was still under development and it became obvious that 'the void' needed to be filled until it was completely tested and launched. Managing the 'void' until the product was live was now the next task for the PR team to rise to.

- Access to senior management on all major issues was bolstered with the development of an issue positioning document. In this way, the PR team wanted Aerospan.com to 'own' the subject area and this was reinforced through the 'thought-leadership' programme of speeches at events and conferences, etc. (key spokespeople were media trained and provided with positioning documents, FAQs and 'soundbites'). Gaining external endorsement from analysts and consultants was also a key way to enhance credibility, and the PR team immediately started a briefing programme with all analysts to ensure understanding of the company and the offer to the market.

- In addition to the world-leading Airshow events, numerous other industry conferences provided excellent backdrops for the customer, media and analyst communications programmes. Throughout the year, speaking platforms were secured for members of the client management team.

The air transport industry has a number of exhibitions and events that attract decision makers, influencers and end-users. So, it was decided to take advantage of raising Aerospan.com's profile at events attended by the corporate parents. For example, the need for the air transport industry to prioritize investment in IT and IP technologies in order to survive and succeed was stressed by Leo Dowling, Director of Marketing and Business Development, SITA, North East and Central Europe, during his keynote address at the 'Third Computers and IT for Airline Engineering and Maintenance'

conference in Amsterdam. This also allowed SITA to bring Aerospan to the fore and educate and create understanding around the offer.

 (http://www.sita.int/newscentre/pressreleases/2000/000323ati.asp)

Similarly, SITA @ IATA Information Management, San Jose, California, 12 – 13 April 2000, San Jose. SITA called for the air transport industry to cooperate in transforming their businesses to embrace the advantages of e-business and Internet technologies. This encouragement came at the IATA Information Management 2000 Conference from Giovanni Strigari, Vice President Industry Relations, SITA. (At several events it was decided that Aerospan.com would take a sponsorship role at a luncheon or event that drew senior level executives.)

In the background, the marketing team decided to hold a workshop to test the positioning and refine the branding strategy. This was to show that, although Aerospan.com was favourably received in principle, the communications would need to address multiple issues, especially that some people were e-literate while other target customers had little interest in the e-business 'spin'. This dealt with everything from the brand identity, value propositions and the actual positioning and development of the mission statement. Much of this work was completed with Impiric as the lead agency.

- By now the e-business frenzy was showing early signs of what was to become a massive global phenomenon – the stock market was racing ahead and media were exceptionally interested in stories and the latest developments. Once again, the team decided that a proactive media campaign was essential and put forward executives to speak to a wide range of press – from *The Industry Standard* through to the *Wall St Journal*.

- Media platforms and events would exploit the creation of 'news' through the exploitation of research and understanding of the key issues that would come to dominate the marketspace. This would be attractive not only to customers and prospects, but also through the media and analyst programmes it would attract a great deal of attention.

- Meanwhile, the issue of 'neutrality' of the trading site was to become a critical agenda item. Many analysts began to discuss what SITA had long known – that neutrality would be critical when providing a trading environment shared across an industry. For this reason, Aerospan.com strengthened its offering and formed an Advisory Board or council that would ensure that air transport companies had a route to direct and guide the strategic development of the site. This was also used as an opportunity to further illustrate that additional equity was offered to early adopters and participants.

 (http://www.sita.int/newscentre/pressreleases/2000/000428aerospan.asp).

A white paper on this issue was also produced. (Later in the year, the issue of having AAR as a competitor in the aftersales marketplace and that being perceived as detrimental to the Aerospan.com offer would result in SITA buying out initial JV partner AAR to own the majority of the e-marketplace. (Announced 12 October: http://www.sita.int/newscentre/pressreleases/2000/001012aerospan.asp).)

Media relations and dealing with interest from the high levels of coverage was now to firmly establish Aerospan.com on the agenda as a key air transport leader. A matrix of forward features was continually being reviewed and the whole team proactively suggesting new angles and potential stories to media and analysts.

● Meanwhile, the team were contributing to the development of the Aerospan.com website and forming agreements with air transport news providers AviationNow .com and Speednews to provide dynamic content to the site. Also, the announcement of key executive Hal Chrisman as Head of Marketing and Business Development provided a name and a face to the company, and allowed the team to begin to profile Aerospan.com as a stand-alone entity. All the sales collateral was updated and placed on-line at the site and a demonstration provided at Aerospan.com.

● The next event on the agenda was to be in London, England with the Farnborough International Airshow. It was decided that this would be when Aerospan.com would start the roll-out of its technical procurement solution and to announce that controlled testing with a major international airline was being undertaken. Unfortunately, the airline would not let the team announce its name due to the competitive nature of the business of e-marketplaces – this was overcome through good preparation and media training.

Prior to the Farnborough Airshow, Hal Chrisman made his first speech for Aerospan.com at the e-Commerce for Aerospace Conference. This event was exceptionally well attended by industry professionals and by media and analysts alike. This opportunity allowed the team to emphasize the benefits of Aerospan.com, whilst also bringing the issue of neutrality and security of commercial data to the top of the business agenda.

The marcomms team used an on-line registration system together with direct mail and a tele-marketing campaign to invite people to the stand and to visit the Aerospan.com chalet for lunch. This proved extremely successful, with the chalet well attended by target professionals, and resulted in a number of business leads. Logo usage and corporate identity guidelines were confirmed, including business stationery and business cards, as well as a myriad of other items. The stand and chalet were designed, developed and implemented in short timescales and trade advertising agreed was placed in key industry publications.

In parallel, SITA's corporate communications team ensured that Aerospan.com was covered in each issue of its magazine and executive communications update. Materials and regular updates were provided to the Aerospan.com website to continuously update the content.

With the PR programme once again taking the lead, media relations pre-show aimed to grab attention in the preview coverage and to get people to attend the airshow press conference. A mail and e-mail campaign was also undertaken with journalists. Once again, thorough preparation was undertaken and slides, a multimedia presentation and scripts developed and provided to Hal Chrisman, who would represent Aerospan.com. It was also decided that the customer focus group work undertaken in development provided a great opportunity for differentiation. A short video was produced with 'sound bites' showing what problems were faced by customers, and what they wanted to be able to do. This was extremely focused around memorable sound bites such as 'I just want to click and buy'. Then the Aerospan.com offer was presented as delivering in each of these critical areas, followed by a Q&A. Photos from this are still available on the Aerospan website (http://www.aerospan.com/company/press_pr7.htm). A set of Q&As and a key messages document were also produced for all staff, centring on the 'bottom line' benefits that Aerospan would have for customers.

Thought leadership was also a vital piece of the jigsaw and recent research and the PR team took advantage of economic modelling conducted by Aerospan.com indicating that airline profitability will increase by approximately 26 per cent. This provided a business message and an engaging storyline across all audiences, while the messaging was extended to drill home the benefits and explain how participants would improve their profitability by increasing the efficiency of procurement operations, reducing their inventories and the prices they pay for goods and services. These elements would once again keep Aerospan.com right at the front of the minds of journalists and analysts alike.

Throughout the programme, another channel was always included in every step – internal comms. This not only briefed and updated the parent parties' employees, but also the new people joining or transferring to Aerospan.com. This programme set up 'best practices' as it aimed to ensure ownership, active participation and involvement from the employees.

RESULTS OF ACTIVITIES

From the launch at Singapore

Over a hundred press attended. Coverage in the *Wall St Journal*, *New York Times*, Reuters, Dow Jones, *PC Week Australia*, *Times of India*, *Chicago Tribune*, *Australian Financial Review*, Silicon.com and across a wide variety of trade and industry media.

Over 100 articles by the end of April, reaching 148 million (including CNBC Asia).

Forty-nine per cent of this coverage reached air transport industry professionals.

Positioning

The primary success measure for Aerospan.com was to be positioned as one of the top three aviation/aerospace e-marketplaces by analyst firms Goldman Sachs and Jupiter Research. This also was endorsed by coverage in *Revolution* magazine, *Flight International* and *Air Transport World*.

Awareness

A second measure was overall industry awareness and understanding. In the first year, to that end the team was able to secure media impressions greater than 158 million. Of the 158 million, more than 15 million impressions were specifically among the trade media.

Speaking/appearing

Thirdly, Aerospan.com's conference strategy resulted in spokespeople presenting at six major conferences over the first year.

LESSONS LEARNED

In an interview with Karl Moore, Senior Manager, Strategic Communications and Public Relations, SITA, the following insights were gleaned:

- Take the time to clarify the real aspects of differentiation, for concentrating on generic benefits will not set you apart from the crowd.
- A new business needs dedicated resources and a clear project leader, while the management team need to focus equally on the technical and marketing elements of the company.
- Plan, evaluate and review continually to understand what works best in communicating with your target audiences.
- In a dotcom world you have to constantly adapt or die – the brand, proposition, values and mission need to adapt to feedback from the sales and marketing channels. Listening to your customers constantly and taking this on board is critical to success.
- Use the web in everything you do – internally and externally.
- You have to demonstrate value for money and an 'outcome' for every dollar you spend, so evaluate the ROI of every tactic and feed this back to ensure you continually improve. Prioritize relentlessly and be critical of how resources are expended – you must target your audiences and stimulate them – work out what makes them (and your company) tick.

- The normal rules don't seem to apply in an Internet world for a start-up business that addresses a global audience; you may need to trust yourself and have the courage to decide to go with new approaches. 'Think laterally' or rather 'think in circles' should always be on your lips as overcoming challenges will be key to success.

- Never forget to communicate constantly (and effectively) with employees and staff.

- Keep a clear overview of the agency time and their 'value-add'; ensuring that proposals are quickly endorsed by the management team helps ensure that action is taken and programmes driven forward.

- Make the best use of people that understand and have experience of communicating with the decision makers/influencers and users, and know how to communicate effectively with them to ask for advice and guidance from people in the industry.

- Use your own organization's experience and also communicate openly with customers to understand their needs. They will be happy to help and provide a great deal of insight that clarifies the key messages/tactics to reach your audiences.

THE QUESTION

There is no doubt that this set of activities represents a successful launch. It has proved to be an award-winning campaign! But what about the next stage? What would your proposals be for a fully integrated, above and below the line communications programme to sustain and build the presence of this organization and its offering?

Index